Jim Evans

A LIFE IN THE DAY
OF AN EDITOR

A LIFE IN THE DAY OF AN EDITOR

CHARLES WALTERS JR.

Halcyon House, Publishers
Kansas City, Missouri

A LIFE IN THE DAY OF AN EDITOR

Copyright © 1986 by Charles Walters Jr.

Halcyon House, Publishers
Box 9547, Kansas City, Missouri 64133

Also distributed in the U.S.
and foreign markets by:
Devin-Adair Publishers, Inc.
Box A, Old Greenwich, Connecticut 06830

ISBN 0-911311-114
Library of Congress Catalog card number: 86-081256.

For Jenny, Tim, Fred, and Chris.

Also by Charles Walters Jr.
  Old Airmen Never Fly
  The Greatest Farm Story of the Decade
  Holding Action
  A Farmer's Guide to Homestead Rights
    (Senior author)
  Angry Testament
  Unforgiven
  The Case for Eco-Agriculture
  An Acres U.S.A. Primer
    (Senior author)
  The Albrecht Papers (2 volumes)
    (Editor)
  Parity, The Key to Prosperity Unlimited

CONTENTS

A NOTE FOR THE RECORD

When I first read the manuscript of *A Life in the Day of an Editor*, I thought to myself, What an unlikely pair to come together as friends and co-workers in the most important profession in the world, farming. I believe it was Ralph Waldo Emerson who said "A Friend may well be reckoned a Masterpiece of Nature." If so then myself, and all the farmers of America, have a real Mona Lisa in Charles Walters Jr.

Two of the organizations that Charles Walters has battled with—and I might add successfully, since he has knocked those self-satisfied old structures to the ground many times—are the USDA and State University Experiment Stations. Yet here I am a thirty year researcher of state and USDA organizations writing a message for his life story.

The very fact that I have this honor—and an honor it is—is proof enough of one of Chuck's strongest points. He judges people as people and not as cogs in the huge organization which many of us serve, whether state, federal or industrial. He is able to see through the hypocrisy of overmanaged monoliths and pick the good, usually accomplished at lower levels, that emerges despite the greedy political machinations that occur at the top level. The USDA still has a few researchers whose first loyalty is to the family farmers of America and not to the agribusiness organization that would swallow them up. It is a truism of life that as organizations enlarge they spout off more and more about the loyalty of their employees. It is strictly a one way road, for while they demand loyalty, the least criticism of high echelon misdirected policies will lead to instant dismissal. The whistle blowers of life are considered traitors when in truth they are usually acting as reformers of systems out of control. There are very few real whistle blowers within any organization, for survival is the first rule of life, and it takes a rare individual to subject his family to such destructive forces.

What is needed in order to keep the great monolith of government on the straight and narrow are people like the *Acres U.S.A.* editor, people with uncommon good sense (common sense is not common but uncommon), with understanding and with clarity can give a democratic people the real story, or as Dr. Harold Willis would say, "The Rest of the Story."

It is people like William Albrecht, Harold Willis, Lee Fryer and Chuck Walters of the world who tell us how to farm correctly. However, all of their elegant work would come to naught without an unbound and free press to put the good works out. This is the main function of *Acres U.S.A.* and its editor performs his task in a lucidly superb manner.

Because of my early war days among the small hill farmers of Ireland, I had a good overview of how the job should be done with the least trauma to nature. The brain child of Chuck Walters, *Acres U.S.A.*, points us in the right direction as no other publication in the entire world. *Acres U.S.A.* tells us why there is starvation in the world.

I remember reading with dismay—since I worked for the USDA—the report of the Young Executive Committee, in the June 21, 1972 Congressional record. It was stated:

• Agriculture should be viewed as an industry which consumes resources, provides employment and produces goods of value to society.

• National policy should be diverted towards maintaining agriculture as a viable industry and not a way of life.

Those words should send a chill down the backbone of every family farmer in the country, for it elucidates the quicksand destructive forces that Chuck Walters warns us about. It demonstrates the total inability of our government leaders to understand that democracy (which—like science—is nonlinear) depends ultimately on the land and the soil belonging to as many and as diverse a people as possible and on a free press to keep those people informed. Agriculture can never be an industry, rather it is a way of life lived by a free and loving people who understand the soil!

The *Acres U.S.A.* editor, by his every action makes his commitment to viable family farms and a free press absolutely clear. He writes that "psychologists say we reveal our innermost thoughts in everything we set down on paper." His warning thoughts about the state of the press is summarized in one statement: "As late as the 1920s, informed people could turn to the public prints for the type of information available in *Acres U.S.A.*" Now, as he so well demonstrates in this remarkable autobiography of an editor and a paper, news is "managed" and such management in essence means that "since 1930 a veil of censorship has blocked out freedom of the press . . . The mechanism is adroitly American, and not at all the image of a totalitarian state—and is therefore more effective."

There is a lot more to this book, however than "the editor's" philosophy of agriculture and his battles with agribusiness and government. It is the story of a loving human being who has lived one of the most exciting lives I have ever read about. It is also an agriculture literary masterpiece. Do not take my word for it, but read the book and follow the editor along a deadly trail of modern industrial agriculture that has produced chicken flocks 90% infected with leukosis. March with him through battles with groups that attempt to label him a bigot because he attacks scoundrels that belong to one race or another.

A chapter I really enjoyed is entitled, *Literature Under Pressure*. It not only gives one insight into the never-never *Catch 22* land of grain trading, but also describes with considerable gusto the political battles fought for control of the National Farm Organization (NFO). The pressure on a sincere reporter attempting to follow the idiosyncrasies of his fellow man had led the famous correspondent Quentin Reynolds to label journalism "literature under pressure."

Most journalism is not literature but "pap for the public." This book by a top flight agricultural reporter and editor is truly literature for it is one of the few nonlinear books ever written on the way of life called farming.

What is meant by nonlinear? Life, as science, does not go smoothly from point A to B to C, etc. Rather, it jumps all over the place, as does a democratic society. Nevertheless in a true nonlinear system, e.g., the laser, unity and strength emerge from chaos. A single colored beam of powerful light emerges from the thousands of frequencies generated by oscillating molecules inside the laser. There is in fact a complex discipline called chaotic math that describes such phenomena. When biologists, agriculturalists and economists finally come to understand this, they will quit perverting life by trying to fit mankind into their constricted little black holes.

What emerges from *A Life in the Day of an Editor* is a powerful beam of light generated by the force and personality of a competent agricultural and literary craftsman. The critics will of course not recognize this and will accord Chuck Walters the same treatment that befell the author of the greatest nonlinear masterpiece of all times, *Ulysses*. James Joyce's *Ulysses* is a recording of the chaotic thoughts, during one day, in the mind of a Dubliner as he walked about town.

This book records the life, loves and thoughts of a modern-day traveler and fighter in the field of agriculture. It is a modern-day *Ulysses*. It is not only a good book, it is a great book. It has been my privilege to know the author for about ten years, and so to an old friend I say thanks for being a great teacher and a real friend of the farmer.

Phil Callahan
Author of *Tuning in To Nature* and
Ancient Mysteries, Modern Visions

FOREWORD

This book deals with a *life* in the day of an editor. Its focal point is fifteen years, the single "moment" in time when the Hydra called education, economics and eco-farming came to one head as a publication called *Acres U.S.A.*

I am one of thousands, if not millions, who make their living with the written word. Little is known about our craft by the general public. Psychologists say we reveal our innermost thoughts in everything we set down on paper, and when one of our tribe achieves fame, all these words—those published and those rejected by the editorial pencil—are measured and quoted and enshrined. Many, if not most of us, have a secret hunger to say it the way it is, to run a publication with the freedom of a William Allen White or a Harry Golden. Early in life we like to believe in man's perfectibility. If people only knew, if dishonor and injustice and megablunders were only revealed, good people would set things right, mete out punishment to the guilty and care for the widows and orphans. As journalists we have only to tell the truth, to shock the conscience of the ultimate court, the people. Public opinion is everything, always ready to do the work of the Almighty.

Unfortunately, such a view is naive in the extreme. And so when I point to venal politicians, an interlocking directorate of bureaucratic people managers, newspaper owners, lenders and financiers, vague, unseen, cold men, my *ja accuse* has to carry the flip side of the record. Most people would rather swallow lies than truth, especially if the liar has authority and the *dis*-information is soothing, like a fine liqueur. Moreover, the wordsmith's trade is full of crafty liars, workmen who think of the truth as something relative and malleable. The supply of lies, much like ignorance, is infinite.

Most of my Sigma Delta Chi colleagues enjoy a collective anonymity, which is proper for a messenger. What is not appropriate for journalism in a democratic society is the near total anonymity of the news itself. In America, certain institutional arrangements literally have erased the first article of the Bill of Rights with the thoroughness of a chisel removing a graven image from polished granite.

Even as late as the 1920s, informed people could turn to the public prints for the type of information available in *Acres U.S.A.* But since the 1930s a veil of censorship has blacked out freedom of the press. The mechanism is adroitly American, and not at all in the image of a totalitarian state—and is therefore more effective.

Security analysts tell us that 45% of the stocks traded on the great exchange are held in trust by banks. The lending institutions do not own these stocks or reap the income, if any, from dividends and sales. But they vote these instruments of ownership. Trade usage has it that 5 to 10% of the voting stock in *Fortune* 500 companies constitutes control, and it is a matter of record that bank trust departments vote four times that much stock, or fully 30% of all the ownership certificates traded in the regulated market. This fine-tuned mechanism stands guard like a colossus over corporation expenditures, which easily translates into virtual control of the nation.

I have spent my life in a historical time frame that has endured managed logic, convoluted teaching, melded political parties, and the annihilation of the basis for the political freedom won by the Founding Fathers—all to bless and sanctify a concept that was anathema for centuries, namely the interest game plan of the lending agencies. Except for the atmosphere of intimidation under which classroom instruction commonly proceeds, a grammar school child could ridicule into oblivion the chain letter projections on which modern economics rest. And the average layman can understand why no major newspaper dares tell the emperor he is naked.

The corporations that account for meaningful advertising revenue are under the effective control of bank trust departments. In the newspaper game, it is axiomatic that media either please the banks, or starve for want of ad dollars. No one can run a metro daily or a TV network without the financial support that ultimately has to have bank trust department approval.

But small newspapers, newsletters and special publications such as *Acres U.S.A.*—ladies and gentlemen, hush! They survive because there is an excellent market for news that never makes the scripts read by TV actors at 6:00 and 10:00 p.m., or the wires and pages of most print media.

I deliberately defined the scope of *Acres U.S.A.* coverage as a probe into the mundane, not the sensational. Setting the record straight seemed worthwhile in itself. Honest journalism is essential, not as much because it is a guiding light, but because it represents honorable behavior involving the reporter and the reader, some newsman once said. It appeared to me that there have been only two developments of original importance in two thousand years. One—if understood—could change the economics of the world, and one—unless understood— would change the ecology of that same world. My task, I concluded, was to expound one and unravel the other.

Simple arithmetic revealed the fact that it would be easier to start a publication than buy one, and simple reality suggested that real independence depended on remaining *small* and *beautiful* and accepting the fact that what most papers report has got to be wrong or insignificant, or both.

This much determined, I threw away the rules and proceeded to publish what interested me on grounds that people who subscribed were my type of people and would also be interested. My background made it impossible to think otherwise.

When I was a youngster in western Kansas, the American farmer had been brought to ruin. The pseudo-sophisticates, that is those who dealt with abstractions and remained unspoiled by on-scene experience, believed they knew all the answers. A prime example appeared in *The American Mercury*, January 1931.

"Getting rid of farmers," wrote H.L. Mencken, "would not only reduce the cost of living by at least a half; it would also improve the politics of the country, and have a good effect upon religion. As things stand, the farmer is always on the verge of bankruptcy, and so he hates everyone who is having a better time. Prohibition is almost wholly a metaphysic of farmers; so is Methodism. Turn the hind into a wage slave, and he will respond quickly to the better security. The city proletariat, though it is made up largely of fugitives from the farms, is devoid of moral passion. It not only likes to have a good time itself; it is willing to see its betters have an even better time . . . Thus I look forward to [the farmer's] ruin with agreeable sentiments. It will make living cheaper in the United States, and very much pleasanter. The country has been run from the farms long enough; the business becomes an indecorum, verging almost upon the obscene. We'll all be better off when the men who raise wheat and hogs punch timeclocks . . ."

Obviously, the ability to verbalize did not bestow an ability to think. But the chowderheads blithely went about the business of pulling apart America at the seams during my one lifetime. Journalism, standard style, left the full story untold.

Most people go into journalism, in the words of a Texas columnist, "to smite the villains, help the underdog and have a few laughs." To hold aloft romantic illusions about the newspapering craft, great associations have been formed, and enough plaques have been passed out to denude a forest.

My purposes in founding and publishing *Acres U.S.A.* were quite different, and those differences are the subject of this book. The trail of worthy news stories has taken me all over the world, into a thousand U.S. counties, and has prompted some few departures from the standard news format. My stories have answered the likes of H.L. Mencken, the United States Department of Agriculture, the international flim-flam people, and the hell raisers who have brains with the specific gravity of lighter fluid.

Once, I ran a series of "articles" composed of nothing more than raw field notes. I had been among the few who followed the ping-pong players into China in the mid 1970s. Each night, after the others had retired, I wrote down the observations of the day. These observations made for the best reading we've ever presented, "as was." I remember my notes without even pulling them from our office morgue.

In Marco Polo's day, possibly 85% of China was heavily forested. By the end of the Koumintang regime, the naked hills of China had become legend. Starvation followed drought and war in a regular rhythm. *We sold our children,* I was told. *Our sick went without treatment. Our old people died in misery. We didn't know where the next meal was coming from, and we lived in rags.*

There was austerity . . . austerity that was shocking in the extreme. Coming into Shanghai—a city of ten million—was like coming into Sapulpa, Oklahoma at 4:00 a.m. There were three planes on the runway, and two of them looked as if they were in mothballs. As we rode in a cold bus we noted no cars on the street—for there were no privately owned cars in China—no bright lights, no nightclubs, only bicycle and pedestrian traffic. Most of the people were dressed in Mao jackets. Each intersection looked like a dull, unlit Times Square on New Year's eve. These many Chinese people now eat three meals a day. They have quarters. Contrast this against old Shanghai, where the dead were picked up off the street the first thing every morning! Some 80% of the people in China work in agriculture—as a matter of fact, everyone works. There is no unemployment. There is no narcotics problem. Health seems to be a birthright, although birth itself is not a right. Chairman Mao had decreed that each family could have two children. [This has since been reduced to one.] A third or fourth pregnancy would be terminated at a hospital as part of the population control program.

I saw health in those faces—healthy rows of teeth, clear skins, boundless energy, yet energy held in check by a political system that we admire only with the loss of our own mental acuity.

I spoke to agronomists, laboratory scientists, physicians who perform incredible surgical procedures with no more than acupuncture for anesthesia. I watched farmers take windblown loess—probably in off the Gobi desert at the end of the last ice age—and farm it with the help of organic matter, processing wastes, composted green manure, and night soil. Night soil, as the term implies, is human excrement harvested from toilet stations at night. The Chinese figure that if whole molecules of indols and scatols are taken up by plant life, then thorough cooking will eliminate the danger of contamination.

I saw hundreds of vegetables—varieties uncounted—and only a spare amount of red meat. I saw air so clean the stars seemed very near. And I came to realize all is not doomsday, though the follies of men proceed, while nature abides. The end of an era came, and nothing could stop it. A band of communists had fled for the hills some fifteen years before that. They abandoned the junk foods of civilization, the opium of the traders, the exploitation of the international lenders, and formed their society in mircocosm. They farmed with nature because that's all they could farm with. Yet there is a continuum in Chinese history: *leader worship, control of the masses, command economy!*

It was obvious from the start that I had more to do than smite the villain or have a few laughs, although laughs there were. While tripping from Acapulco to Mexico City one day, my wife, Ann, and I stopped at Taxco, a little colonial Mexican town with cobblestone streets, bargain silver, and some of the most impoverished gardens in the world. For some people it would have been enough to enjoy lunch at Ventana de Taxco, or tacos at Los Balcones, or margaritas at Paco's, and leave.

We checked in at one of the older motels on the highway and turned in about midnight. About 2:00 a.m. "all the dogs in the world," my diary said, "gathered under my window." It was a wild cacophony that reminded me of a debate at the U.N. or Earl Butz reciting dirty stories, or policy makers drawing up their version of the future in terms of solid ignorance.

Ah-ooo, ah-ooo came the canine chorus. Like their human counterparts, some bayed, some barked, some yapped, some wailed. As relief of sorts, a heehawing donkey stuck to its part and filled in the soprano section of this Taxco symphony. Mercifully, morning came, and the thought of sleep caved in like a Taxco mine shaft, for here came the quarter notes of the chanticleer heralding the new day.

A few years later, in Italy, I and my wife were introduced to *barbed wire*. Carmel Tintle, the PR executive for Villa Banfi, had asked his people to helicopter us to their lime-laced vineyards north of Rome, and when we had finished examining the soil, thirst set in. It was duly slaked at a restaurant where only Romans eat. With wild boar and Italian delicacies duly dispatched over a several hour period, the owner brought out a clear bottle. He called it barbed wire, so named because the makers in Sardinia hid it from revenuers by wrapping a turn of barbed wire around each bottle's neck and burying the product underground. He assured us no tax had been paid on the nectar. I took a slug. A blue flame followed my breath clear across the room. It reminded me of my Dad, whom you will meet later in this narrative.

Home and behind the typing machine, it all seemed to fit into place as part of a life in the day of an editor. Surely the leaders who fondled toxic chemicals and prescribed the end of the family farm H.L. Mencken style were killing off more with their jawbones than Samson slew with the jawbone of that other historic ass. They were killing a free people world wide.

Withal, there has been something both rewarding and lonely in my editorial scheme of things. For a time—some forty years—I gloried in the fact that I had never received an award. The only thing I'd ever won was a double boiler in a bingo game in 1937. In keeping with this humble posture, I have refused to allow my picture to appear in *Acres U.S.A.* even once. It was a suggestion Gene Cervi of *Cervi's Journal* in Denver, Colorado, handed me *gratis*. *"Neither of us,"* he said, *"should make mankind suffer more than has already been ordained by the braying jackasses we have to write about!"*

Someone told me my face was the color of washed out teak the night Murray Bast of Wellesley, Ontario, veterinarian John Whittaker of Springfield, Missouri, and farmer John Bleem of St. Louis disrupted an *Acres U.S.A.* conference to present me with a plaque. Suitably engraved in metal mounted on wood, the "award" said:

Acres Conference
Kansas City
1984
Presented to
CHUCK AND ANN WALTERS

In recognition of your constant efforts in organizing the thoughts, research and solutions of many gifted scientists over the past 15 years—along with your staff—your dedication and persistence has steadied the pen responsible for writing the words that fill the chapters of our bible of Eco-Agriculture.

Acres U.S.A.
A Voice for Eco-Agriculture

We thank you from the bottom of our hearts. Many of us are enjoying the benefits of a New Life because of your untiring efforts to present the truth.

WE LOVE YOU
THE READERS OF
ACRES U.S.A.

It was an unusual award, and perfect in keeping with the maverick character of the paper I had edited for a decade and a half. Obviously, it had no institutional sanction, and I doubt that very many readers really contributed toward the expense involved. Even the ceremony had been spawned on a bogus premise. Word had come to several members of the *Acres U.S.A.* family of readers that they were in imminent danger of losing their monthly roar, that I was in a hospital, a victim of an accident that was life threatening. I had, in fact, raked a running chain saw across my ankle, split the Achilles tendon lengthwise, and allowed the churning blade to march up the back of my leg, taking out the vein usually reserved for double and triple bypass surgery. It smarted, but it was fatal only to my pocketbook. Each minute in the hospital cost $4.76.

While resting in painful comfort, the thought occurred to me that I might set down the biography of the unique paper I had founded. Sometimes the personal and the profane became one in this effort, but in the main I have tried to recite the biography of a child that has grown to maturity and achieved a life of its own.

xvii

The card files and pencil records that attended the birth of *Acres U.S.A.* have given way to sophisticated computers and a subscription system so unique the local post office sends over other publishers for the free lessons I am willing to give. At *Acres U.S.A.* we beat the publishing ratios half to death, and this explains our survival quotient. I am conservative. I have never borrowed money at the bank to sustain the baby. "How do you expect to control me if I'm out of debt," I asked one banker who was pushing for out-on-the-limb expansion. His silence was his answer. I am also a liberal. I have cracked some pretty big knuckles with sledgehammer blows in *Acres U.S.A.*, and the feedback has registered every bullseye. I have given *Acres U.S.A.* news stories a life factor that makes the public prints—by way of comparison—come off like a dirge.

Go to Chapter 1. Let me tell you a story that leads to another story, and then to still another, the whole becoming less complex than the sum of the parts. It is this whole story of which I sing, because it has made up a life in the day of this editor.

1

BLACK CANDLES AND CHERRY RED

Brenny was a fine animal, sturdy of limb and not at all like the swayback windsuckers one saw now and then going through the Ness City, Kansas auction. She earned my respect and attention one afternoon when she pitched me from the stall in which she was standing to about four o'clock low. I was only five or six at the time, and I hurt down to the last outraged cell, a fact I managed to hide from my parents. I had ridden that pony many times, usually slung up behind my brother Bob.

We always rode bareback simply because we didn't own a saddle. But we were free as the western Kansas wind while shooting jackrabbits from horseback, driving in my Dad's few cows, walking the fenced steppe, or scouting for holes in the shelterbelt. To me it was the life of the gods, even though the weather was too dry and the Russian thistles—which some farmers turned into silage the few moments they seemed to stay green—tumbled across the prairie, sometimes in precision drill, like members of the Coldstream Guard. Brenny seemed to love her human packages, an observation that prompted me to get "big" too fast.

I climbed up the stall and gingerly stepped to Brenny's back, grabbing a handful of mane for security. It didn't help even a little bit. There were three hard jolts before I took off, my first and only lesson in blind flying. I still remember that hurt, not the physical one, which soon enough repaired itself after one of my sisters rubbed me down with liniment that reeked for days, but the betrayal I felt—much like an owner rejected by a faithful dog—was the hurt that lingered too long. We mended our strained relationship as time went on, and there came a time when I could ride all the way to Mount Zion, a one-room school that accommodated eight grades of the freest people God ever put on the face of the earth, colleagues all.

The dust storms came three years later, and before long a man with a piece of paper forced Dad and the family onto the road, migrants hard on the hunt for work and land in a place where children could breathe clean air without catching dust pneumonia.

Children do not know poverty, and I was many years removed from understanding what hidden force drove Dad to sell Brenny. But there it was, etched in my memory and in unpleasant dreams at night, a battered truck with wired side rails, and a rough unfeeling man taking Brenny away. Dad kept his two Percherons and ample leather harness, which he soaped and polished and repaired endlessly. The work horses helped Dad pay county taxes. Officials accepted day labor and allowed extra credits for horses and equipment as in-kind settlement of *ad valorem* levies. But the work horses didn't like small packages on their backs. I didn't understand why Dad loved them more than Brenny—then!

I found out several years later. We had moved to Iola, Kansas, a wounded community with many open scars and lots of cheap, often abandoned housing. It had been a smelter town because of abundant gas wells in the area. For a decade or two the industrial holocaust scorched the east end of town, and by the late 1930s it seemed that only rare tufts of weeds and grass would grow on the old industrial site, which was composed of acres enough to make up a large farm. Dad rented a ten acre plot east of Iola, where he kept his work horses. But the hot-dry cycle that pulverized the soil in Western Kansas also annihilated the grass a distance east. With the last of the pasture burned away, and no money for feed, the horses started exhibiting their ribs to the passing traffic. Dad could not endure his horses going hungry, and one day they too were led away. I had never seen Dad cry before. He did that day, not with whiskey under the belt, a crutch used by one hard-pressed neighbor. He simply went to a shed, sat on a split piece of wood and cried. I watched from a safe distance before I too dissolved into uncontrolled tears. Dad never mentioned those horses again, although he kept the leather harnesses until the world moved on into the space age, his artifacts of a life forever gone.

The departure of Brenny so that the family could eat demanded an explanation, and an economic recital would not have helped. On this occasion Dad made one of his rare references to how come we were in Kansas, square in the center of the dust bowl. He told about how the Volga Germans came to Ellis County in 1876, how they sought out terrain equally as flat and harsh as the Russian steppes from which they emigrated. Great Grandpa brought a trunk of spring wheat seed—and possibly a measure of Russian thistle seed—with him. It was spring wheat that came first, but the hardy Turkish Red the Mennonites inserted into the Kansas earth stayed on to create the seventh and greatest breadbasket of the world. The Volga Germans had emigrated out of Bavaria and the Rhine Valley hard on the heels of the Seven Years' War, landing on the lower Volga when it was Emelyan Pugachev country, and raids from Kirghiz tribesmen cost the Germans several colonies. One of my kinsmen hid in a thicket along a creek during one of those raids, salvaging the family's hand written history from the murdering Kirghiz.

The stories about Pugachev driving into a town in a buggy to supervise hangings made my skin crawl, but there was always the finale— Pugachev being strangled by one of Catherine the Great's executioners. Dad missed his calling. He could easily outdo Canteflas in pantomime, and when exhibitions of fear, joy, anguish, or terror were called for, he would whip off his glasses and perform. He knew a superb performance was called for the day the trucker took Brenny away.

Dummer gesprichen, Mother would say, meaning that the recital about to take place would proceed without her approval. The words translate into *dumb sayings* and *stories*, but the way Dad told them they were high art. I wish I could recite them here, first person singular, replete with the idiom of the Volga Germans. For Dad told about the devil at Yocemento, and his telling had me on the floor like a Holy Roller, holding my side with laughter. Somehow that story had something to do with my newspapering career, and with the voice for eco-agriculture, *Acres U.S.A.*

A farmer who should have known better made a very slanderous remark about the local priest, suggesting that an unsanctified relationship was going on between the father and his housekeeper. The form of the slander was a hand-printed note sent by U.S. mail to the rectory at Katherinenstadt. The Capucian who received the note properly took umbrage, fetched the black candles from storage, and in ringing Latin recited an ancient ritual that impacted on the congregation like a stunning hammer. Those who knew of the accuser, suspected the accuser or the accuser himself had better come forward and confess, otherwise God would start hurling his vengeance forthwith. And that's the way it happened.

A well sunk down with the arrival of the immigrants in 1876 suddenly went dry. A newly erected barn burned to the ground, cause unknown. Livestock vanished into thin air, and a prize mare, with colt, suddenly collapsed and died for no reason at all. A stone building, erected by the finest craftsmen, developed a dangerous fissure. All of this on one farm pointed the finger of suspicion. As the weeks wore on, calamities spread out from the hub, touching neighbors right and left. A wheat field went up in flames the night before harvest was to start. There was talk about the Prince of Darkness surveying the countryside at night, and one local—his wit honed razor sharp with a suitable intake of wheat whiskey—actually saw the devil on the edge of his porch when he arrived home very late one night.

He had been to Yocemento. The town of Yocemento was founded in 1906, and soon became a ramshackle community with buildings that looked like they wanted to walk away. A group of Hays, Kansas citizens, headed by one T.M. Yost, built a cement plant near a suitable strata of stone, and employed the best cheap labor available on the high plains, namely Hungarians. Yocemento soon became known as the Sodom of the West.

It had a shack that passed for a saloon and bawdy house. *Aus landsmann gehen sie fort, aus kater kommen sie zurick,* Dad said, causing Mother to wince with pain. One Saturday night, Hungarians and errant Germans sought the society of their fellowmen (and women) at Yocemento's wicked place. Dad was always at his best when describing various stages of inebriation. He didn't use words like *morose, jocose, bellicose* or *comatose,* but you got the message. On the night in question the Hungarians and a few visitors from the German colonies were experimenting, possibly to impress the painted lovelies on hand. They wanted to find out how much alcohol cells and protoplasm could endure in a state of consciousness. The piano player was the first to pass out cold. Then a stranger from a dark corner took his place. His talon fingers soon had the place alive and jumping. The seconds floated by in little packages of sixty, then stretched into hours.

Eyewitness reports were somewhat at variance as the Yocemento incident made the transition from legend into history. One witness claimed that the house was doctoring the whiskey. Another said the whiskey was tested with fire, and flared up with a clear blue flame, indicating proper proof. Dad, a connoisseur and distiller of fine whis-

4

key, preferred the latter report.

In fact, the fellow playing the piano started to glow a cherry red shortly after midnight. A distinct outcropping of little horns could be seen, and a tail was surely emerging, restrained only by the canvas and rivets at the back of his pants. His smile had the eager-eyed ardency of Valentino seducing a desert maiden.

As everyone looked on, a latecomer entered and cried out in German words that translate to—"Sacrament, it's the devil." Several started making the sign of the cross, their faces ashen with fright. The devil left hastily. Outside, he seized the reins of a team, jumped into a jolt-wagon, and with wood smoking under his seat, vanished into the night. The horses made an unearthly sound. Inside, the piano keys were examined. All eighty-eight exhibited scorch marks, the after-effect of intense heat.

One of the Yocemento revelers ran all the way back to Katherinen-stadt, some thirteen miles, only to suffer the ultimate terror. There, on the front porch, waited the devil, flashing teeth as big as those in the mouth of Dan Patch. With that the reveler passed out cold, his sphincter having failed. A footnote of sorts survives. Hearing a nerve-bending scream, his good frau came out to survey the scene. She marched off to the pump, fetched a bucket of cold water and hurled it at her writhing husband. Then she went back to bed, allowing him to sleep it off in the mud until dawn.

As for the poison-pen letter! Well, the farmer wasn't an entire fool. He heard about the Yocemento goings-on, and interviewed the revelers himself, many of whom oozed sincerity and fright from every pore. He figured there would be more. So he swallowed his pride and fear, marched down the tabernacle aisle to the mourner's bench, and before congregation, priest and God Almighty admitted his black journalism. Dad always claimed that the fellow was sentenced to pray a rosary until the beads wore out, but Mother called the entire story a lie and a sacrilege.

After the horses were gone, we settled down to surviving the Great Depression. During those years I saw Dad's devilish good humor turn to dross and fade away, assaulted by the hard times he could not understand, and by Mother's constant recitations of the sins of Henry VIII, a legacy of Capuchin instruction. The great war came and went, and somehow we survived the humiliation and defeat and poverty the Depression had brought. But Dad couldn't forget it. He knew that wheat had as much food value at $4.00 a bushel as it had at the seventeen cents a bushel available during the Hoover years. I had just taken off a World War II uniform when Dad told me, "I want you to go to school and find out how it works." In a way his charge led me to several colleges and to my tryst with words, and finally to the climax crop of words that has ever filled the pages of *Acres U.S.A.*

2

THE WORD WRANGLING GAME

Mazibuko was one of the most unforgettable characters I've ever met. He was a Zulu, possibly unique, because I have never heard him claim chiefdom status. I think he was too sophisticated for such trivia, and too learned to take seriously many of the august pronouncements of the world's proved failures. His credentials said R.T. Mazibuko, Africa Tree Centre, Plessislaer, Natal, South Africa, when he came to Montreal for a conference on organiculture. During a break in the tedious French and English program, the managers provided for a field trip. Most of those who attended the meeting filled a bus or two headed for MacDonald College, Ste. Anne de Bellevue. One bus—only partially loaded—drove out to the mini-farm of a Frenchman transplanted to Canada. It was on that run, and while walking the vegetable patches and row crop acres on the farm, that I got to know the soul of Mazibuko. Almost instantly, he reminded me of my Dad. Although he hid it well, I detected in him the same gentle insolence and deviltry Dad often exhibited—half without trying—and I knew that if South Africa only had the wisdom to listen to a man like Mazibuko, problems that seem so insurmountable would evaporate like a puff of smoke, or at least a dram of home-style wheat whiskey.

I had a hunch then—and I have it now—that both Dad and Mazibuko could see the connection between black natives and their poverty on one continent used by unseen men to bring American farmers to ruin on a new continent. The connection was too nebulous for most people to understand, least of all those who looked for answers to organiculture at a university. But two men half a world apart—it seemed to me—were pragmatic enough to realize that mischief was being hidden by the high priests of mendacity who seemed always to take refuge behind the complexity of their craft.

Through the years I have kept in touch with this tough, smiling, gentle Zulu, often sending him books and papers and—not least—encouragement in a task beyond understanding, teaching black natives how to farm in harsh country without harsh chemicals. Now and then I hear from him—a postcard, a letter, a rewarding "Thank you!" But on that day in Canada he introduced himself and listened patiently for an answer to his question about the relatively new paper I had founded, *Acres U.S.A.*

Acres U.S.A. was born, not without umbilical cord, in June of 1971, but its gestation period reached back at least two decades or more. During that time I enjoyed the process of having my thinking mature, not only in terms of the two eco-expressions that would one day appear on the masthead—"To be economical, agriculture has to be ecological"—but also on the nature of news itself.

The nation's press had come to fascinate me. And at Creighton University in Omaha, seated squarely in the heart of the cornbelt, I found myself in a ringside seat as the 1948 presidential campaign changed direction without the national media even being aware of it. The story itself was backgrounded by over 2,000 years of history, starting with digs that uncovered the ziggurats, or temples of ancient Babylon. Archeologists recovered clay tablets that were an integral part of an economic system developed by the priests of Baal. Their system relied on short-changing the producers of real wealth, then loaning them the wherewithal to put in a new crop. By requiring interest the priests engineered default and bankruptcy. Because there was less money in existence than the amount needed to retire the loans and pay the interest, the farmers had to forfeit their collateral. First the priests of Baal took livestock, then land, then the children of the family were sold into slavery, next the wife, and finally the farmer himself. Joseph's enslavement of the children of Israel on behalf of the Pharaoh was little different.

Through the centuries governments have been taken over by clever lenders so that money could be created out of thin air, with borrowers—in the aggregate—taking on the impossible. No one ever interviewed for the pages of *Acres U.S.A.* cast the background of this equation in clearer terms than Richard Kelly Hoskins, the publisher

8

of *Portfolio's Investment Advisory Newsletter.* "If there are only $10 in existence, and you lend it to someone under conditions that he repay $11, and if he agrees to this, he has agreed to the impossible," Hoskins said.

This business of borrowing money into circulation, then withholding more money creation to make payment and debt service impossible, haunted Persia, cursed Greece and Rome, annihilated the defense of Carthage, and presided over death and wars from the days of Deuteronomy to the eve of the 1948 presidential election, touching people like my Dad and the Zulu, Mazibuko, without mercy, and without either of them understanding it fully.

Each year between 1916 and 1946, there had been an increase in the public and private debt—this to make the payment of interest possible. In 1946 the public and private debt stood at $396.6 billion—down from $405.9 billion. The economic adviser saw these figures as the harbinger of depression, and yet there was no depression. In fact the economy had earned enough profit during the previous four years to literally pay for World War II. The mechanism was simple enough. Production times price generated income, and with prices in all sectors regulated at a profitable level, the act of growing corn and wheat and building war material brought national earned income back to a prosperous pre-1929 level. Some $200 billion in debt expansion to fight World War II really hadn't been required. This made the management of WWII the only significant economic development between the days of the Baal priests and the present, and Truman's luck was there to nail down the benefits.

There was a feeling in high government offices at the start of WWII that borrowing too much pure smoke money into existence might backfire. The U.S. might go broke in the middle of the war, and lose it. Therefore the decision was made to permit new money to be earned into existence, rather than borrowed entirely at the expense of future generations. This meant government had to override the international traders and lenders at least until the war was over.

The World War II Stabilization Act and its Steagall Amendment used a loan mechanism to support farm prices and the national income during the war with Germany and Japan. Congress could have passed a minimum wage law for basic storable commodities, or used one of several other mechanisms for maintenance of prices. But, in their wisdom, the law-makers elected to rely on parity supported by loans.

Industry got its cost-plus contracts. Primary and secondary

suppliers—and labor—got wage and price controls. The war effort required production, not bankruptcy. As a consequence, shipping dock prices were regulated high enough to deliver earnings—and a profit. To regulate the basic storable farm commodities at less than cost-of-production—at less than parity, in short—made no sense at all. In surprising quick-time, Congress inserted prosperity into the farm equation within a few months after Pearl Harbor. The law was written to expire two years after the war was over, and the war could be ended by Congress or terminated by a presidential proclamation. Harry S. Truman in fact took that step on the last day of December 1946, and for this reason full parity for agriculture was scheduled to end in 1948, the presidential election year styled *Truman* vs. *Dewey*.

The international lenders must have viewed 1948 as a perfect time to end the dangerous parity experiment. This business of parity for agriculture had about the same effect on the national economy as newly mined gold from California a century earlier. In both cases earned profit short-circuited the requirement for usury contracts. In both cases the money was earned and didn't have to be repaid together with an impossible interest lug. The matter of debt and interest found its common denominator expression in the postwar farm debate. Obviously, if price supports were maintained, then commodity values couldn't fall to world levels. And if commodity values didn't fall below parity, there was no need for expanded farm debt.

The nation's press failed to recognize the significance of all this, but the politicians did not. In fact it had become a political absolute that there had to be a new farm bill in 1948, and the key issue in all debate that year was the fate of parity. I wrote a term paper on the subject as classroom fare, relying largely on materials published in the *Congressional Record*, reprints of which still occupy space in my files. But my real insight, if any, came from the fact that 1948 wasn't all that far removed from the seventeen cent wheat my Dad so often talked about.

Normally it is a function of literacy to comprehend the meaning of a word in the context of its usage. *Parity* is an exception. The press uses the word and readers drink it in without either fully understanding it. Yet *parity* means nothing more than balance. There has to be par of exchange between microbe and food, soil and plant, farm and city, city and nation, and finally nation and nation if convulsion at any of these levels is to be avoided.

I don't think my Dad ever used the term *cash flow* in operating his Ness County, Kansas wheat farm, but he had enough sense to know that you couldn't cash flow a farm at even 1% on borrowed money when wheat was seventeen cents a bushel. "When you're paying interest on a loan, the banker sits down at the table with you three times a day, seven days a week, and takes the first helping," he used to say. Even without much of a formal education, he knew that interest at 7% doubles the amount owed in ten years if there is no reduction in principal. At 10%, doubling takes place much earlier.

My Dad had another saying. "If you want to succeed in farming and hang on, you have to capitalize on *savings* and expand on *earnings.*" And then he added, "But they won't permit this." "They" were that nebulous entity that determined markets. *They* had impoverished the Germans who grew wheat along the lower Volga near Saratov in Russia, and *they* kept farmers along the Ganges poorer than poor. As early as the days of the McNary-Haugen Bill fights in the 1920s, Dad and the German speaking farmers of Ness County knew that farm prices were a political problem, and admitted only to a political solution. There was no use talking about supply and demand or looking for mathematical answers to a political question. Some farmers spat in the dust with anger when Dad suggested that there was no point at all in blaming the middlemen, except for the thieves among them. Without commodity prices high enough to support a solvent operation, bankruptcy had to come to many, and the only answer was parity.

I have never had the difficulty understanding parity that is usually exhibited by reporters. After all, we have a standard of weights and measures. Four quarts make a gallon, sixteen ounces a pound, and so on. If you buy a gallon of gasoline and only receive three quarts, you get only 75% of parity. This means you've been cheated. Parity simply means the total amount of annual gross income that all of rural America must receive from its production to balance payments for trade with urban America. If the flow of annual earned income to rural America is not in balance with costs, then all of rural America is shortchanged.

"It all boils down to this," one of my uncles used to say. "The American farmer is entitled to one thing no other farmer is entitled to—first crack at the American market. Without that, cheap imports will have a lot of farmers on the ropes every year until they're all gone. In the final analysis, cheap food means hungry people."

This concept is not a come-lately entry in some think-tank. It rose— not phoenix-like, but raven-like—out of the ashes of the Civil War, when agricultural discontent hovered not only over the desolate South, but even over the fertile western prairies as well. This unrest subsided during the two decades following the Spanish-American War.

11

It came to life again in the 1920s. It was then that farm bloc politicos talked about the farmer's share of national income, about fair exchange value—finally about *parity.*

George Peek of the Moline Plow Company in fact got his statistical bearing for the parity concept from USDA Bulletin 999, *Prices of Farm Products in the United States.* This tract had been written by Professor George M. Warren, and published in 1921. Warren had been going around the country presenting a varicolored chart showing the separate price movements of twenty farm commodities, the weighted average price for thirty-one farm products, and the movement of the all-commodities index of the Bureau of Labor Statistics. It was an awesome presentation. Warren was invited to come to Washington with his charts to explain things to the United States Department of Agriculture, and to put those findings into printed form. He did this in 1921.

USDA started publishing a purchasing index series in March 1922 in *Weather, Crops and Markets.* One thing stood out like a sore thumb. There was a disparity between those *all commodity* figures and what farmers were actually getting. George Peek took up the battle. Now that someone had shown him the tools for measuring, namely the parity formula, he set out to reduce that disparity. He wanted, in short, a fair exchange value. The McNary-Haugen fights, the farm bloc battles, finally the farm acts of the 1930s—when parity was written into law—were simply an extension of George Warren's findings. They answered the reality that farm prices are a political problem, much like utilities.

But then something happened. Once the law was written and put into the hands of USDA, George Warren's simple and obvious system became complicated in the extreme. Figures didn't lie, but liars figured. Taking an index of farm commodities and adjusting them to an index of all commodities wasn't good enough anymore. By WWII, USDA was computing parity figures for some one hundred fifty-seven commodities. No more than sixty-one were on a really sound basis. Those sixty-one, however, did account for 82% of the farm crop values. At that time seventy-three commodities had a 1919-1929 base, twenty-one made use of various combinations drawn from the 1920s, and two used 1935-1939—a statistical absurdity.

Few economists and fewer Congressmen really understood USDA's razzle-dazzle ploy to undo what the parity concept as a law made mandatory. Then came that infamous farm act of 1948, the one that provided for 60 to 90% of parity, and a moving average for computation of parity. With a few well-chosen words hidden in that law, the parity of Peek and Warren was annihilated.

It was annihilated because the international flim-flam men wanted it that way. They required protectionism for their flow of commerce from low cost areas to high market areas of the world, and if this meant bankruptcy in the farm country, millions in poverty, expanded relief roles and countless unemployed, the price would be paid as long as the body politic did not demand a political solution. And they would not demand a political solution as long as the scribes and professors did their job, in the words of R.H. Tawney, writing in *Religion and the Rise of Capitalism*, namely by creating "imposing systems of law," and screening reality from the people with "decorous draperies of virtuous sentiment and resounding rhetoric." The accepted mechanism of conjuring up economic maxims and blessing them as laws was usually sufficient.

The political season of 1948 threatened this scenario, and I was there to record it. I still view it as the most inadequately reported news story of our times.

Before the nominating conventions of both political parties met in Philadelphia in 1948, a bare knuckle fight had developed in Congress over the matter of support levels for agriculture—the political solution. Many lawmakers had a pragmatic feeling that depressions were farm-led and farm-fed, which they are. They didn't understand why. Others simply visualized the operation of the nation's economy as nothing more than a series of business problems raised to the *nth* power. Not even the farm leaders understood parity, except that it was good while it lasted. Cattlemen—secure in their John Wayne fantasy—didn't want loan programs or supports because they didn't have the foggiest idea about how an economy operated. By June 1948 it had become the judgment of the House Agriculture Committee, Chairman Clifford Hope said, to report out a bill that continued 90% price supports through loans, purchases and methods other than direct payments to farmers. And the House voted to accept this judgment with no more than three Representatives on record against the measure.

Then came the Aiken bill out of the Senate with its provision for 60 to 90% of parity for agriculture. The measure was written so that it would not go into effect for eighteen months, or until January 1, 1950. The time table became all important. A Republican convention had been scheduled for Philadelphia, June 20. And the Republican dominated 80th Congress had promised a long-range farm program, a point that stuck like undigested bone in the throats of the weary lawmakers. But the conferees refused to agree "under any circumstances" to a long-range program. The representatives of the international traders had sunk their meat hooks into agriculture, and weren't about to let go.

The amended records of the House told some parts of the story. "Mr. Speaker," intoned Congressman John W. Flannagan, "I have served in this body for eighteen years, but I have gone through my strangest and most unusual experience since yesterday at two o'clock . . . Thursday night about eleven o'clock the other body passed what is known as the Aiken farm bill. At two o'clock on yesterday we were called into conference, and the House conferees to a man turned down the Aiken bill. They turned it down for the reason that they did not know what was in it. I doubt that some of the conferees from the other body knew a bit more about what was in the bill than the conferees from the House, who had not had an opportunity to examine the legislation.

"At 5:00 p.m. on Friday we were called into conference. The House conferees, because they did not know what was in the Aiken bill, turned it down. So the conference adjourned.

"At two o'clock yesterday, Saturday, we were called back into conference, and the House conferees again stood pat and we adjourned. Then at four o'clock yesterday, we were back into conference for the third time and the roll was called, and the house committee still stood pat . . .

"Then a strange thing happened. In order to bring the conference report back, they had to rape the House conferees. When they came back, Mr. Murray [Reid F. Murray of Wisconsin] resigned as a conferee and Dr. [George W.] Gillie was appointed in his stead; and then we met again. The Democratic members still stood pat, the Republican members went over to the Aiken bill." As a sop to get House members to go along, the bill would not take effect immediately. House members could vote for it, and in turn have full parity accepted for the next year. There would be plenty of time to amend the Aiken bill, and bring its parity formula to full strength.

It seemed barely possible that the press missed all this, and yet the common denominator of most news reports was that they contained no important information. Truman signed the measure, and later that summer he used the threat of the Aiken bill he'd approved to win an election. He did this by handing price sheets to crowds at whistle stop points during his summer and fall campaign. Two sets of figures counseled people in the heartland on how to vote. If Truman won, corn, wheat, soybeans, milo and the rest of the storable commodities would be at parity, meaning at a level that allowed farmers to avoid debt and foreclosure. If he lost, Dewey's formula of 60% of parity would likely prevail. Truman meant $1.00 corn, Dewey meant sixty cent corn. A Dewey victory would put farming in the same situation as a business-man operating under controls, with prices set so low they forced him to consume his capital. Newsmen stood in those crowds, often beside students like myself, but they didn't seem to comprehend the significance of those Truman price sheets. I remember David Lawrence's *U.S. News & World Report* the issue after the election. No explanation! No suggestion as to what really turned the tide! All he said was, "Truman won, Dewey lost."

Indeed, Truman won. The American people lost. They would have lost equally as much had Dewey won. For now earned income would not deliver enough money into the economy. The international bankers would have their way, and a thirsty need for new money would ever be answered by credit loaned into existence. Debt, not raw materials. would be monetized.

The great John Maynard Keynes had prescribed more debt when the wherewithal to pay interest faltered. Public works, war, even a tax cut might be used to create more debt, he said. And Truman dutifully set the stage for Korea, Vietnam, Johnson's war on poverty, Carter's Pan-ama Canal giveaway—and finally the farm crisis of the 1980s, all without knowing it. Newsmen are not oracles, and none could be blamed for failing to see the details mentioned above. They cannot be absolved for failing to report the case for farm parity.

Withal, it was the character of the press that frightened me in those days. The reporters I knew were subservient beyond pale to the wishes of their bosses. Once in a while someone charged them with telling the truth, but this was never taken too seriously. While I snailed my way through school, the managers of the public prints lived well by giving the nation something to be delighted or enraged about. There was a communist under every stone. Treason was almost universal. If I hadn't been going to a Jesuit school, I would not have been able to make the comparison between the Reds taking over America in the late 1940s and the Papist Plot in seventeenth century England, when to doubt that the Jesuits ordered the demise of the King was to set up the presumption that the doubter himself was a Jesuit, or a part of the plot. In England they outdid Emelyan Pugochev, as this capital crime sentence of a Jesuit readily illustrates: "That you be drawn to the place of Execution upon Hurdles, that you there be severely hanged by the Neck, that you be cut down alive, that your Privy Members be cut off, and your Bowels taken out, and burnt in your view, that your Head be severed from your Body, that your Body be divided into Quarters, and those Quarters be disposed at the King's Pleasure; and the God of infinite mercy be merciful to your soul." In such an atmosphere, skepticism remained un-uttered. It was different in the late 1940s only by degree.

The newspapermen to whom I applied for summer work were what I called coast-along editors. All they needed to keep a good newspaper going was a heady scandal or two, a murder that wasn't too neat, and the fall from grace of a near-big now and then, and the national dialogue on the price of porterhouse steak. Then as now, those lazy minds took refuge in formula. Without a newspaper job, I spent my summers working for Rocky Mountain National Park one year, and as a dynamite monkey for Estes Park Power and Light another season.

The good Jebbie who taught courses like ontology and theodicy didn't know it, but he supplied insight I treasure to this day. In philosophy the fare on the blackboards had to do with Andronious of Rhodes, who rescued for us Aristotle's abstractions, but my mind drifted away time after time to the inability of so many reporters to handle the abstract idea called par exchange. The nuances of a statistical base year, cause and effect in income creation, and new wealth from any source, involves ideas at least as complicated as simple arithmetic or freshman algebra, ideas most men of words avoid whenever possible.

I had little truck with the brand of investigative reporting that nowadays is a euphemism for muckraking. Instead I envisioned a new brand of newspapering, reporting that meant steady examination of the mundane, routine tunneling back to reveal the real foundation for things accepted without question, and endured without complaint, usury, slaughterhouse procedures and FDA edicts included. I had little education when I first set out to publish a paper, and only two college degrees. Thousands of hours spent learning the lessons of economics and ecology had to intervene before the first issue could roll off a press.

I had landed in Denver after my recall stint during the Korean festivities, and was working the night shift at International Harvester's truck repair station when Gene Lamb, the editor of *Rodeo Sports News*, handed me a plumb of a job. He wanted a column once a month, fee $5.00, and an occasional feature article—and he asked how I would spend the swag. "In six months of riotous living," I said. Soon I was hammering out the short, punchy copy that cowboys liked.

Championship bronc riding is loaded with danger, and sometimes the glory trail is marred with broken bones, pulled muscles and violated cowboy bodies. At the age of 19 the South Dakota bronc rider, Casey Tibbs, was a long way from the title when he entered a small Olathe, Kansas rodeo. The sidewinding bronc he drew took starboard jumps that brought his full weight on Casey's legs against arena posts with every jump. Each time the sidewinder connected with a fencepost, Casey's leg was broken in a new place. The horse took in eight posts before the ride was over. Yet less than ten years later the same Casey Tibbs had arrived in the saddle bronc title spot no less than four times.

All the great rodeo cowboys of the early 1950s—Casey Tibbs, Buck Rutherford, Jim Shoulders, Bill Linderman, Harry Tompkins, Dean Butler, and two dozen more—had their happenings and wounds wrapped up in a flow of words from my small Corona portable during those swing shift hours at International. A point in fact was that I really didn't have much time to spend money, not even $5.00, except for school. My classes at the University of Denver took up early in the morning, and usually, with breaks, lasted until shortly before the evening shift. By 1:30 a.m. I was back in bed for almost five hours of gorgeous sleep. By the end of the week this computed to being short 15 hours of snooze time, all of which I made up by sleeping until 2:00 p.m. on Saturday. I managed to pick up a M.A. degree in economics in record time, and ducked the commencement exercise to avoid the cost of a cap and gown.

All the while I financed myself as a writer and a humorist. While standing in line to receive an Air Force discharge a couple of years earlier, I wrote out in longhand the chapters of a farce, *Old Airmen Never Fly*. The old airman in the book was a retread, literate in the extreme, yet really quite stupid. In strident language *Old Airmen* heaped ridicule on the Korean Peace Action, Harry S. Truman, and military idiocy. In the farce, the nameless airman arrives at his base, having been recalled to active duty:

The train slowed to sixty miles an hour, and the conductor gave me a playful shove. I got up, ignoring the abrasions and cinder burns, and looked straight into the eyes of a Cro-Magnon hulk in a bus driver's uniform.

"A soldier's got to be tough," I remarked indifferently to the man in blues. "When does your bus go to the Base?"

"Did you say *soldier?*" the monster shouted with abject disbelief. "Did you say *bus?*"

"Soldier in the Air Corps Reserve," I said proudly.

"Jeez, they get crummier all the time," he said. Then he went on at the top of his lungs: "There are no soldiers in the Air Force. There are only Airmen. Furthermore, there is no such thing as an Air Corp, except in The Navy." He spat into the dust. "Here we have only an Air Force. There are no more Mess Halls; only Dining Halls. No more K.P.'s; only Mess Attendants. No more G.I.'s; only Airmen, Airmen, Airmen. And I am not a bus driver; I am a Master Sergeant. Do you have that straight?" I licked his hand.

The boys in the line awaiting their go-home papers read each page as I finished it, howling with laughter. The book was a failure when published a few years later. But it was not until 1982 that I accepted the reason why. The occasion was a convention of beverage alcohol people in Hutchinson, Kansas. Someone greeted me as I strode through the hotel, asking—"How is your new book doing." It was a question I had come to expect now and again, so I responded, "Fine." And then, for no reason at all, I added: "All my books have done well, except one, *Old Airmen Never Fly.*" I explained that it was a farce, really far-out humor. An executive with a wholesaler out of Topeka jolted the scene.

"Well, that's understandable," he said. "You're not funny!"

I must have realized as much quite early in the word wrangling game. In rapid order I ran through the exercises, learning how to set down words. Rodeo reporting was followed by a year-long stint as editor on a chain of nine beverage alcohol trade papers followed by more work in trade paper areas such as metallurgy, air-conditioning and refrigeration—and veterinary medicine.

Ann, my brand new wife, and I moved to Kansas City within a week after our marriage on February 4, 1956. I landed a job handling an editorial pencil for a scientific publication—*Veterinary Medicine.* I soon became publisher's assistant.

Almost two years later, Dr. Robert L. Anderes, the publisher, asked me to his patio for some "serious conversation." Anderes was fifty-six at the time, but he appeared tired beyond his years. He had worked incredible hours most of his life—on the farm, in veterinary school, during WWII as a veterinary officer, in private practice, and now as

18

publisher of the profession's most prestigious journal. He had never learned to type, yet for a decade or more he had written countless reams of copy on a difficult subject, developing articles of exposition and analysis with a ball-point pen or a blunt pencil. He was exhausted as I had seldom seen him, and suffering from the sugar problem debased groceries had forced on the society at large. He was a man of rare integrity.

The pharmaceutical companies had taken over animal medicine by the time I landed on the *Veterinary Medicine* staff. Broad-spectrum antibiotics in animal feed had become an article of faith, and the "scientific papers" pressured into print proved efficacy seldom available on the farm. Dr. Anderes did not like the brand of proof he saw.

With an intake of antibiotics, the beef animal simply found the organisms in its digestive system annihilated, good and bad. Scours often became an effect rather than a cause and the color ads in the vet magazine showing a cork and a headline—*"You Can't Use a Cork to Stop Scours"*—were really begging the question.

In the late 1940s, the feed industry came out with a 50 gram per ton antibiotic level. This was increased to 100 grams per ton in the early 1950s. Dr. Anderes worried aloud about all this because "research" was now indicating a 250 gram per ton level. By 1968, some farmers were feeding 500 grams per ton out of several sources without realizing it. It was something akin to taking a human patient and injecting a megadose of penicillin each day, year after year. The only saving factor was that no year-after-year existed for red meat production because slaughter came early.

The early warning system, poultry, was literally falling apart on its feet. Delayed slaughter operations would see 10,000 bird houses stacked high with dead broilers. The chickens simply couldn't make it past nine weeks, then eight weeks of age. Epizootics became so commonplace—with government picking up the tab—that the public hardly noticed, not as long as offending tumors were whacked away before incredibly inexpensive chicken meat was wrapped for display at chain grocery counters.

Dr. Anderes wanted little of what was going on, yet here was the new era stripped of science based on nature's system. Indeed, the first signs of nature's revolt were on scene. Dr. Anderes was a leading voice in bringing vesicular exanthema under control when it ran rampant across mid-America. He detected that too soon mold problems would consume the livestock industry, poultry included, because the latter

19

was the most debauched of all. In the meantime, the arsenicals enjoyed "high science" status, when in fact they were a disgrace to the art and science of veterinary medicine.

"Don't laugh," Dr. Anderes smiled as he laid his copy of J.I. Rodale's magazine on organics face down on the picnic table.

We visited a bit about our families. My younger sister, Helen, died of Hodgkins disease two or three years before, and I wondered how this could be. Dr. Anderes speculated that the self-regulatory powers of cells in the lymph nodes had been offended. It was, he said, a type of offense the new chlorinated hydrocarbons were visiting on people, and in his opinion the Public Health Service was light years away from asking the right questions, much less getting the right answers. Later I was to carry an interview with Dr. Hal Huggins on the connection between amalgam dental fillings and the things like muscular dystrophy, Guillian-Barre and Hodgkins disease, but when Dr. Anderes offered his explanation neither of us knew much about the dangers of mercury from amalgam fillings entering the blood stream and being tagged as a cause of Hodgkins disease.

In the cell, plant, animal or human, there are chromosomes which carry almost all of the information needed to direct that cell's growth, division and production of chemicals such as proteins. These chromosomes are composed of information-bearing genes. Radiomimetic chemicals (chemicals that ape the character of radiation), radiation itself, and many of the chemicals used in agriculture can injure the chromosomes either by altering the chemistry of a single gene so that the gene conveys improper information (called *point mutation*), or by actually breaking the chromosome, (called *deletion*). The cell may be killed, or it may continue to live, sometimes reproducing the induced error. Some types of cell damage cause genetic misinformation that leads to uncontrolled cellular growth—cancer.

Cellular damage because of malnutrition or the invasion of toxicity can cost a farmer part or all of his crop. The same damage in human beings can cost a nation its heritage and its future. Damage to the sperm or ova in a human being can cause malformation or mental retardation in future generations. It can also contribute to degenerative metabolic disease.

My sister had been employed at one of those aerosol can loading operations in a day and age when the public was told that DDT was harmless, and that the chlorinated hydrocarbons were governed by a tolerance level of no consequence to an average person. Also, she

20

endured quite a bit of amalgam dental work during those few months. She sickened and died slowly and painfully over a several year period, wasting away, always surrounded by the odor of death.

Late in the afternoon, after we had talked for hours, Dr. Anderes got to the point, and a sparkle returned to his eyes. He said he wanted me to run *Veterinary Medicine* so that he could cut down his work load, semi-retire and enjoy his garden and his rocking chair. He had to go to Chicago on Monday for a hog cholera hearing, but he would be back in a day or two, at which time we would pursue the matter further, the wherewithal for my future ownership to come from earnings of the publication.

I was still walking about four feet off the floor that next Monday when a phone call came from the Chicago headquarters of the American Veterinary Medical Association.

"Are you sitting down?" asked an AVMA executive on the other end of the line.

"Yes," I said, "I am."

Just as there is often a time and eternity between incident and comprehension, so it was that day. The voice said something about Dr. Robert L. Anderes walking across the lobby of the LaSalle Hotel when he suffered a heart attack.

"Where is he?" I asked.

There was a long pause. A voice I did not recognize came on the line. The voice simply recited the name and address of a Chicago mortuary. Would I inform the widow and help with details? I was stunned beyond instant comprehension.

"Oh, my God," I recall saying. "You mean he is dead?" I had visualized the doctor resting in a Chicago hospital.

I wrote an obituary for the issue then being set in type, but I said few of the things that really needed saying. Words did not come easily because of the dull and desolate pain. Certainly the wisdom, tolerance and fortitude accumulated during the lifetime of this man could not be gifted to those he left behind, myself included.

I stayed on for several months. My wife comforted me. "It wasn't meant to be," she said. "It just wasn't meant to be."

One day I tucked away my notes, unpublished manuscripts, and moved on, satisfied that a gentle veterinarian had gifted me the foundation for what would one day be the "ecological" part of the dual meaning "eco" in the logo of *Acres U.S.A., The Voice for Eco-Agriculture*.

I met Mazibuko a few years later, when *Acres U.S.A.* was young and brash, and I assured him a world of reports would flow under my editorial pencil in the next decade or more. Perhaps his people could benefit, because the principle being invoked were valid for all. He agreed, and if the messages I get from South Africa mean anything, the pages of *Acres U.S.A.* are having an impact in even a remote section of Natal.

3

THE TRUE BELIEVER

Phil Allen loved the description one of his Jewish friends hung on him. "Phil," his friend said, "you uncircumcised philosopher!" Phil Allen was that, and more. He passed for what might be called a radio and TV anchor at National Farmers Organization, located in Corning, Iowa—a town so small not even a bread truck passed through. Phil made my frequent trips to Corning tolerable, if not cherished experiences.

I tripped to Corning routinely for some six years after leaving *Veterinary Medicine*, sometimes to gather material for my *NFO Reporter* articles, sometimes to serve as a ringside witness to the farmers' struggle for parity. I first arrived upon invitation, having caught the attention of NFO President Oren Lee Staley with my articles in a farm tabloid for which I was free-lancing. The years between *Veterinary Medicine* and NFO had been lean and hungry, even though I was busy with trade paper work in the beverage alcohol field.

Staley was a big mountain of a man, a hog farmer from near Rea, Missouri, just south of the Iowa line. As a 4-H leader he had learned just enough about *Roberts Rules of Order* to run a meeting. It was this skill and the tutelage of former Iowa Governor Dan Turner that made him proprietor of NFO, soul and body, and he protected this role with utmost zeal. Oren Lee Staley could send rolling thunder through any auditorium, and in turn have the crowds stomping their feet or pelting the floor with a tropical squall, but those same words—reduced to print—had all the substance of a homeopathic soup made from the shadow of a starved canary.

This prompted Phil Allen to join me in high treason. I wanted to slip a copy of Eric Hoffer's *The True Believer* onto Staley's desk. We deliberated over the matter for days, even red-lining an edition so that pertinent passages could not be missed. Finally we decided the risk was too great. Staley might actually read the book. He might find out what really made him tick. "In that case, we'd ruin a perfectly good social revolutionary," Phil Allen said.

I first met up with NFO in an oblique way. In 1958 I asked Earl F. Crouse of Doane Agriculture Service to write a farm article for *Veterinary Medicine*. Crouse wrote in bright optimistic homilies, reflecting essentially the philosophy of Dr. John H. Davis of Harvard, who coined the word *agribusiness* to accompany such words as *vertical integration*, *contract farming* and *specification buying*. My office was in the Livestock Exchange Building in Kansas City, and in the stock aisles below wandered overalled men with talk of a new farm movement—a national farmers organization. These men had been nurtured on the folklore of the Grange, the Alliance for Progress, the Farm Holiday Movement, and they reminded me of Dad and Grandpa discussing the McNary-Haugen bills, which had been vetoed by Silent Cal. The McNary-Haugen bills were legislative measures designed to defend the internal economy of the United States from cheap import invasion.

One day, in an antechamber of the Livestock Exchange Building, I visited with a group of these farmers. Their small talk, my questions, their answers, and the business of checkpoints outside prompted me to make a speech. In essence, though not in form, I ran these few thoughts up the flagpole:

Gentlemen, you think you have a brush fire here, that you will put it out this fall. Of course, this isn't going to happen. The Congress won't let it happen. The powers that be will stand in the way. They will continue to bleed agriculture until, finally, the Mickey Mouse economy will fail. If this foolishness continues, the food supply of the nation could be endangered. Now here is what we should do. We should take twenty or forty of our youngest and smartest farm people, short-course them in economics, law and technology. We should expand these short-courses into a junior college, finally into a university. In four or five years, there would be a fair reservoir of trained people in the countryside, people who understood the raw materials equation and the institutional arrangements required to make secure parity not only for agriculture, but for every sector of the economy. In four or five years, there would be

24

trained people to run for Congress in every state of the union. In ten years there would be well-educated, raw materials trained people to draw from in every county in the U.S. Instead of running insurance peddlers and lawyers for office, a new elite could rise to save America from the cleverness of lawyers and the ignorance of the absconders. But you won't do this. You'll say it is too late. And you'll continue to tilt with windmills for the next twenty years—and twenty years from now I'll probably stand before some farm group yet unborn and make this same speech.

As a matter of fact, I did just that. I stood before an American Ag Movement audience exactly twenty years later and made the same speech. The reaction was the same. But I felt at home saying what I believed.

I have never been at home in academic circles in any case, and through the years I have cultivated an irreverence for footnotes and credentials. I distrust the texts of history the way I distrust the numbers racket, or even the legalized lottery which preys on the ignorant and the poor. I have easily half a hundred volumes on farm organizations in my library, yet I am still awaiting the real story, the story only a Steinbeck can tell, as he did in *The Grapes of Wrath*.

Those farmers in their battered pickups reminded me of the vintage cars that rolled out of western Kansas during the 1930s. I was particularly interested in the holding actions of NFO because I grew up on tales of "dollar wheat bulletins." In 1903 J.A. Everitt told farmers to hold their crops until they got at least a dollar a bushel. It worked that year, and a year later the dollar wheat bulletin asked for $1.20—and trouble set in. Farmers literally rushed to break their own holding effort in order to get a few cents more.

They simply did not understand economics, or the fact that international manipulators had their historical equations. The flagship was gold at $35 an ounce, set in concrete and sanctified by law. Harnessed to gold was silver, its home base being $1.29. These two anchors were much like unequal balls with a string between them flung into space, each orbiting the other and controlling the useful commodities they represented as a common denominator. Thus $1.29 silver meant $1.25 wheat, $1.00 corn and soybeans in the $1.45 range. Drop silver's price on the London exchange a penny an ounce, and wheat in Kansas would fall a penny a bushel also. This ability to yo-yo commodity prices was used to ruin farmers by causing them to substitute debt for earnings.

The farmers did not comprehend the complexities of the questions that confronted them, and like Harry Truman and his Department of Agriculture Secretary, Charles F. Brannon, they simply could not fathom why it took a national parity program to override the manipulators. I think my understanding of the matter was closer to reality because of an experience I had in Nebraska.

Before I accomplished graduate work at the University of Denver, even before I met the lovely person who would be my wife, I served as an auditor for a Baltimore-based insurance and bonding house. I handled audits in the East, and then I worked Chicago for a time. Finally I landed in Nebraska, where I covered everything from Omaha to the sandhills outback. Agriculture's tie to parity, and the economy's support by parity prices were self-evident in the records I examined. When agriculture was earning parity, the local liquor or hardware store often made more money than the local bank. Now, with farm parity struck down by Eisenhower and Ezra Taft Benson, the backwash had taken Iowa down to ten cent corn, militancy and NFO, and new loans and profits for the lending institutions. Here was a lesson they didn't teach in college.

NFO came on as a cloud no bigger than the palm of a hand. It was spawned as an organization of farmers who saw the middleman as the rascal who cheated them, an organization with simple answers to complex questions. The ground level reports on all this were and remain of maximum interest. I have set many of them down in two books—in *Holding Action* and in *Angry Testament.*

Then just what was so different about NFO? Was it just another organization of farmers who were unhappy because their oxen were getting gored? After all—Harry Graham of the National Grange once told me—there have been not dozens, but hundreds of farm organizations characterized as national since the Civil War that have passed from the mind and memory of man. They often struck. They hung horse thieves, wrecked trains, burned crops, bombed elevators, dumped milk and shot hogs. On the other end of the equation, there was that senseless example called the Great Depression, when Henry Wallace shot hogs and burned corn as a final offering to the goddess of economics, the law of supply and demand.

I now have to answer my own question. Without the leadership wanting it, without the Board of Directors endorsing it, without many members understanding it, NFO became the repository for the most enlightened economic thought ever to come out of a farm organization. Shortly after the holding action of 1962, a man named Butch Swaim came to Corning, Iowa, NFO headquarters. Nothing would change, he

26

said, until something changed between the ears.

Butch Swaim knew Carl Wilken, and Wilken was the surviving member of a fantastic triumvirate—the old Raw Materials National Council—which once included Dr. John Lee Coulter and Charles Ray of Sears Roebuck and Company.

While Henry Wallace was burning corn and shooting pigs, and Milo Reno was bringing militancy to Iowa, Coulter, Ray and Wilken were doing some rather remarkable probes of economic theory. They found that capitalism had a built-in self-destruct—debt pretending to be earnings and interest compounding debt until the system dissolved into a convulsion. They also found—as did the Russian Kondratieff—that capitalism was self-correcting if left alone. But there were all those institutional arrangements that pretended to serve the people. In fact they served the power interests. The Founding Fathers understood this, but somewhere along the line the lessons had been forgotten.

The U.S. Constitution was adopted in order to establish for ourselves and our posterity a par economy. Subsection 5 of Section 8 of the Constitution requires the Congress "to coin money, regulate the value thereof, and of foreign coin, and to fix standards of weights and measures." The third act of the First Congress was a tariff law to prevent cheap foreign goods and debased foreign currencies from determining the value of American money. It was the thesis of Coulter, Ray and Wilken that the value of money could not be regulated without par exchange for the raw materials of the earth.

The arrival of this new thinking split NFO, even without the leadership or the rank and file understanding what was happening. Staley said he detested Carl Wilken because Wilken enjoyed the social class. In fact he detested Wilken because he recited an uncomfortable message to a man who wanted his intellectual fare in neat prefab packages.

The story has been told that, once upon a time, Socrates interrogated a young man to determine his qualifications as a statesman. The budget of Athens, the strength of the army, the dwellings used to house the people, all passed in review. Finally Socrates asked, *And how much wheat will it require to feed Athens for a year?* The young man fell silent, and the interview was over. *Nobody*, said Socrates, *is qualified to become a statesman who is entirely ignorant of the problems of wheat.*

The interview with Staley was usually over when someone suggested that certain foundation principles were more important to the

27

exchange equation than that rascal of a middleman. Over the years I worked tirelessly at the business of structuring a defensible rationale for the raw materials exchange equation by writing books, pamphlets and articles. Arnold Paulson of Granite Falls, Minnesota took the message to the road, and Hartington, Nebraska banker Vince Rossiter created economic models that properly and adequately explained the phenomenon.

The first characteristic of an industrial economy is division of labor. The moment farming becomes proficient enough to feed more people than the farmer has in his own family, there is a spinoff of labor free to follow other pursuits. From that moment on agriculture is diminished in the number of persons involved in farm production, but it has the same economic function to perform.

The early economists realized this. Say's Law of Markets said that division of labor sets up reciprocal markets for each of the divisions automatically. Those who farmed, for instance, provided the market for those who made tools, and those who neither farmed nor manufactured were in effect supported as a service industry by the productive elements in society. The justification for the school teacher, the preacher, the policeman, the doctor was seated in the fact that service industries allowed farmers and manufacturers to be even more productive, having had service work taken off their hands. Economists in effect said that since division of labor sets up reciprocal markets, and since human wants cannot be satisfied, there can be no such thing as underconsumption or overproduction, or unemployment.

It has never been that simple, of course. In Adam Smith's day, around the time of the American Revolution, poverty was everywhere. Child labor flourished. It took two weeks of labor in a factory to earn the equivalent of a bushel of wheat. The nobles owned the land and they regulated farm prices above par exchange. The man who made tools and wove cloth didn't earn enough money to buy industrial production—clothing, furniture, goods in general. This caused industry to embark on a policy that has ever been the curse of mankind—finding cheap raw materials for production efficiency on the one hand, and selling to the high market of the world—wherever that was—on the other hand. This curse has touched the Kansas farmer and the African Zulu alike. One could not collect for his production, the other couldn't afford to pay for and consume it.

Say's Law of Markets should have carried an addendum—division of labor sets up reciprocal markets for each of the divisions only if goods are priced at par in the first place, and if international trade is not

28

allowed to rupture the price structure.

Unfortunately, institutional arrangements—trading houses, banks, government itself—have never been used to assure par exchange, but to enhance predatory business profits, or—in the case of government social programs—to keep the worst effects of predatory profits from showing. This lack of par exchange—basically for farm raw materials—has short-circuited the system, and to keep the worst effects from showing, government has institutionalized poverty with low cost housing, relief checks, food stamps, government as the employer of the last resort, and—not least—with a cheap food policy.

And yet cheap food means hungry people in the final analysis. This was a story that went unreported because it was not understood. It was easy for me to see why farm groups missed the anatomy of all this. They did not so much understand barter power being established as primary production moved into trade channels as they did the nature of man, the predatory rascal who shared them out.

Through its effective life, and through all the farm strikes, NFO suffered from something of a schizophrenia. On the one hand were the thinkers who understood the nature of the exchange equation. They knew that repair of the institutional arrangements could not be accomplished without the help of the general public. The farm problem was a political problem. On the other hand there were those with a passionate state of mind, the true believers, and those who fantasized.

It was Oren Lee Staley's fantasy that one day a holding action would be the spark that drew flame and spread it across the country. He visualized farmers *en masse* joining the general strike the way Hungarians revolted as a prelude to their own mass executions. This is not merely Monday morning quarterbacking. I stood in those hotel rooms and argued that this would not happen, that the policy makers had been too astute, that they had paced the rate of farm bankruptcy these many years, making it never too high to bring on open revolt. But Oren Lee Staley nursed that fantasy along, refurbished it, built on it, evangelized on the basis of it, and waited patiently for *that day*. All the holding actions paid homage to this fantasy.

For all practical purposes, I handled the entire *NFO Reporter*—not only journalism, but photography and production management as well—yet my name never once appeared on the masthead. The matter of public policy contesting farm welfare became my basic theme. The policy papers of the Committee for Economic Development were stripped naked, and laid on the table for all to see and read. A steady stream of reports told how empty-the-countryside in homage to international trade was implemented by one five year plan after another. And then I covered the Brannon Plan for socializing agriculture. It called for a relief check to farmers so their production could go into international trade channels at world prices—prices half high enough to operate the American economy at an American par.

Perhaps it is sufficient to note that NFO was a genuine movement, a disciplined movement. If the early leaders were less than Spartacus leading the gladiators, it is because of where they stood on the curve of history. The farmers of the NFO era—and perhaps the American Agriculture Movement—were truly colddecked in the card game of macroeconomics.

A great man once said that *the education of a child begins one-hundred years before it is born.* Well, the economics education of a student begins even further back. In all those courses of instruction I endured, there was no room for the exchange equation, or even for knowledge of who makes those decisions that keep the game called *exploitation* afloat. Vincent Vickers, former Deputy of the City of London, former Governor of the Bank of England, said it all. "Productive industry grows rich upon stable markets, a constant price level, and the absence of violent economic fluctuation." Speculators and bankers grow richer with the ups and downs of trade. How cheap raw materials the world over create poverty and wars, and how those dedicated to maintaining the game called exploitation—both at home and abroad—won their battles could only surface at long intervals in history. People went to sleep quickly, and when they woke it was usually quite late. That there were people in NFO who were awake is a tribute to the genius of the group. That these people were ultimately overwhelmed is the human epithet.

The holding action had its function. It took a group of farmers from ground zero to where they had constructed a national organization, one with capabilities to be reckoned with. No, the nation's farmers would never drop their discs and tractors and hold as a unit, but this was not necessary. Circa 1968, 1969, NFO found itself capable of writing contracts that could inch prices upward and drive them toward a parity only international flim-flam men could undo.

Only one force stood in the way—not the middlemen, not the government, not even Oren Lee Staley himself. One high NFO staffer put it to me this way: "Staley's big fear was that someone would succeed in getting parity, and that NFO might succeed—eliminating the need for Staley." That assessment was harsh. But there was more.

There was Doris Peterson, The Queen. Peterson was simply a farm wife who came to NFO when the organization was founded. She quickly saw in the big Missourian a managerial shortfall so refreshing in its potential she was literally forced to assert herself. In turn, Staley believed he needed her, could not run NFO without her, and that his personal security depended on her. All the staffers at Corning knew that ratification of any idea by The Queen was essential, or it wouldn't fly, and most of them whispered that message openly by the end of the 1960s. I confess that I did not identify this state of affairs until after the last of the holding actions, but since then most of the Staley-era NFO leaders have supplied confirmation.

I cannot say that it was a shortfall in management alone that scuttled the dream of farmers constructing their own institutional arrangements to achieve parity. The nature of the battlefield also figured. At the end of the holding action of 1967, we all ended up in a Des Moines courtroom. A temporary restraining order had been issued. It was frankly a political move designed to send shockwaves through the countryside. Even a schoolboy's foresight suggested that NFO could have done better than bargain a consent decree, one that forever banned an effective holding action. Yet this happened in time for the 1968 NFO convention, one at which Hubert H. Humphrey spoke in platitudes and unabashed humbug. When Humphrey died a few years later, "Mr. Clean" was exposed and promptly forgotten, even though the public prints reported that Humphrey's grandchildren had been favored with trust funds, courtesy of a giant grain corporation.

For a time I wondered whether Phil Allen and I did the right thing in withholding *The True Believer* from Oren Lee Staley. Surely it would have been a better text for him than the biography of Adolph Hitler he kept in his desk. For Staley was really a man of great political talent. The ability to move people emotionally is often accompanied by a breath-taking inability to manage, and so it seemed here.

When revolt within NFO surfaced in the early 1970s, Staley's enemies accused him of denying membership access to others with a political bent, and that was true. His enemies complained that dozens and hundreds of farmers, with excellent potential, were literally carried out feet first. They could do nothing about it, except take refuge in their anger, venting it in crude iambic.

Staley had a habit of calling staff meetings at 5:00 p.m.—quitting time. Those who attended usually had been on the job since 6:00 a.m., whereas Staley frequently slept until mid-morning. These meetings sometimes lasted until midnight. About 10:00 p.m. Staley would send out for a steak and the fixings, only occasionally allowing the others a

Coke or coffee. The ritual of eating in front of the half-starved staffers caused some rather savage and humorous doggerel to surface. One poem had Oren Lee making application for entry into hell. Here the farm leader spoke in the first person, explaining how he ran NFO:

> *I met them early and I met them late*
> *And watched them hunger while I ate.*
> *I licked my chops as was my manner—*
> *Belched—and farted the* Star Spangled Banner!

The old NFO is largely gone now, its hours of glory spent. I departed the scene before that grand movement descended into massive purges, mean in-fighting and internecine strife. In my time it passed from an organization contesting middlemen to the one that became a middleman itself, living off checkoffs, hardly mindful of the greater dimension that forever keeps farm parity and national solvency a seven league stride away.

It may be unabashed pragmatism speaking, but I do not think NFO will end up like Jack London's beloved Wobblies, a few regulars with a hole in the wall office, rehashing the dreams of yesteryear much like Eugene O'Neill characters in *The Ice Man Cometh*. The economics that I and my associates injected into the grand movement stuck for many, and has been passed on to American Agriculture Movement. Others, the fallen and the disenchanted, remembered most the dreams they dreamed and the things that went wrong, and they blamed a man some anonymous versifier had talking to the same devil my Dad so often joked about.

There is little evidence that the people in government understood even one syllable of what the intellectuals of NFO once said. Once, in Washington, I testified before one of those House farm subcommittees. During a recitation that filled eight or ten pages of small government print, only Congressman Richard Noland of Minnesota listened. The rest protested that this was strong meat, that it would be best to pursue established public policy, and they found reasons to leave the hearing room.

After the 1969 NFO convention, I flew home. Phil Allen drove. He came by my Missouri residence a little later on. He had in tow two Staley supporters. NFO had just purged an excellent young man, Paul Schmucker of Oregon, in a meeting that lasted until 4:30 a.m. Instead of the expected worship, Staley met and faced down irreverent revolt from California and the farm West.

During that short rest stop, we exchanged hedged comments. The late hour, coffee nerves, whatever, must have caused me to select the wrong word. I observed that Oren Lee Staley was a "slow thinker." I had in mind that he was really "too deliberate" in the way he allowed ideas to mature. It didn't matter. Those words, frozen into an ice-spike and driven into tundra of northern Alaska, could not be recalled. They were hand carried to Corning, and within a short period I was replaced as *NFO Reporter* editor, production manager and chief photographer. A Staley clone who couldn't write a line of copy was put in charge of the paper. His first words were, "You don't even know how to write a lead paragraph," and this was followed by a lecture largely cribbed from the movie, *Patton.* Like Popeye, I had my sense of humor, and also my sense of humiliation. My first word in response should not be found in a parsonage library. The next two were: "Terminate me." And then, "Better yet, I'll do it for you."

It mattered little, for my direction was quite clear. I had long wanted to edit my own paper with real substance as the standard, and my chance had arrived, on schedule. I had prepared myself both intellectually and financially. Simple arithmetic told me it was cheaper to start a paper than buy one. During the several months before that classic termination, I traveled a lot. Each night I stayed up late writing out the chapters of *Unforgiven,* chiefly in longhand. My old friend, Ed Wimmer of National Federation of Independent Business, wrote a fine foreword, one that detailed the contents of the book and gave special meaning to the Tomasso Campanella poem, *The People,* from which I had drawn the title. "The people is a beast of muddy brain," wrote Campanella.

Most wonderful: with its own hands it ties
And gags itself—gives itself death and war
For pence doled out by kings from its own store.
Its own are all things between earth and heaven;
But this it knows not; and if one arise
To tell this truth, it kills him unforgiven.

A Cassandra himself, Ed Wimmer summed up as follows:

"Anyone who reads or listens is smart enough to know that America's so-called progress and prosperity has been kept alive with deficits, war spending, debt expansion, fear of communist aggression, and both domestic and foreign giveaways on the broadest scale in history.

"Millions of family farmers have been driven from the land in this process. The smaller businesses of the nation have been taken over or driven from the Main Streets of both rural and urban communities, closing one door after another to the ambitions of our youth, and leaving millions of men, women and children either directly or indirectly dependent on the city, county, state or federal treasury for existence.

"*Unforgiven* is no double-talking treatment of the rural crisis that has made the urban crisis explode in our faces. It is instead a compilation of facts, figures and philosophic realities that puts into proper focus the policies and plans that have left rural United States a prostrate victim of its own government, and urban United States a cesspool of social, economic and political unrest often verging on revolt."

Unforgiven rolled off the presses a few weeks after I left the Corning, Iowa scene, and the needed cash flow arrived. Ultimately 50,000 copies would be sold. Less than six weeks after my NFO termination, the first issue of *Acres U.S.A.* went into the mails.

4

BORGIA'S GUESTS

The stories that needed telling, when *Acres U.S.A.* gingerly brought itself to the attention of a few hundred people in my address book, literally cried out for equal time. An entire stage had been set for thirty years by blundering ignorance, or thoroughly informed self-interest. It had all started with shelf life in the grocery stores, then marched back to the farms. My first headline in June 1971 was,

CHICKEN CANCER HITS 90%

Even the Surgeon General's office had been forced to reveal that "90% of the chickens from most flocks in this country and abroad are infected with leukosis viruses, even though a much smaller percentage develop overt neoplasms." There was concern that avian tumor viruses would replicate or induce disease in man. Here, it seemed, was a report worth publishing, yet the industrially owned farm press and the metro dailies rejected it the way Fido rejects a mock hamburger.

That first issue rattled the cages in a few other areas, including the conventional wisdom on soil fertilization, the Wholesome Meat Act, and monoculture. *Is Modern Agriculture Worth Having?* asked one arresting streamer, and *Dilution, Not Solution* exclaimed another. A superb report on *Feed the Soil* by exiled agronomist F. Lyle Wynd and a snappy report on organic food by ex-USDA official Lee Fryer backboned that first issue and brought it to the attention of just enough biological farmers to uncork new adrenalin at both ends of the exchange.

Charles F. Denton—then sales manager with the Wonder Life people in Des Moines—was on the phone within days after the first issue was dropped into the mails. Someone had walked into his meeting waving *Acres U.S.A.* He had literally read it aloud to the audience that night, and his associate, Herb Brown, ordered his own copy so that he could cut out nearly every article for a scrapbook, certain that the brash young monthly might have a devil of a time surviving either the gendarmes or the economic buzz saw.

I had left undated that first issue in June 1971, a wise decision, because by the time a second number rolled off the presses I was referring to the first number as a June-July 1971. The delay was needed to assemble the subscription dollars required to pay the first printing bill, $400. Within a day or two the subscriptions arrived, the first being $4.00 from Harry Rash, a Thayer, Kansas banker I had met when Harry S. Truman's economic advisor, Leon Keyserling, came to Corning, Iowa. It may not seem like much now, but that day the first subscription became a vote of confidence as big as the Pulitzer Prize. Someone was actually paying for articles that hadn't been filtered through a system of censorship.

After a few issues had snailed their way through the mails, Fletcher Sims came by. Sims, a brilliant microbiologist, had taken the art of composting out of the backyard and turned it into a business. Near Canyon, Texas his windrows were sometimes as long as a small airport runway. Using bacteria from Pfeiffer Laboratories, Sims had made a business of turning used cow feed into valuable fertilizer for wheat fields, milo acres and submerged rice paddies. He coined the term, *Dr. Expert*, and used it routinely for the brand of scientists who could not comprehend the idea that manure was really a valuable resource, rather than a disposal problem.

To the well-funded Dr. Experts, Sims looked like a puny David hurling a cow chip at a chemical Goliath, and they laughed singly and in unison at the short, fisty Missourian turned Texan who vowed to take apart things like Black Mountain single-handed. Black Mountain was a pile of manure in Randall County, Texas that covered some forty acres, and was at least fifty to sixty feet high. Its rising odor molecules gifted Amarillo a miasma of overripe urine and dung. When Fletcher first talked to the feedlots about composting away their problem, the Dr. Experts had beat him to the sprawling offices of these bovine concentration camps. One had developed a Paul Bunyan plow capable of layering 90 tons of manure per acre at coffin depth. And there were scientific studies to prove that wasting forty acres per feedlot was a cheap disposal solution to the manure problem. Fletcher Sims had other answers, and sure enough some feedlots were happy to gift him the manure. As area farmers turned to Sims for fertilizers with billions of microbial workers tagging along, manure took on a new value. The feedlots started charging—first a dollar a ton, then more.

Withal, Fletcher Sims was and remained a card carrying doubting Thomas. There was something wrong about this *Acres U.S.A.* It was too slick, too well written. It reeked of professionalism, and this meant the publication was probably a straw operation for some devious assault on organic agriculture in general, composting in particular. From the Fletcher Sims point of view, which has been little revised to this day, it was no accident that Oklahoma has a law against "manipulated manure" moving into trade channels.

Fletcher Sims was visibly humbled when he saw *Acres U.S.A.* as a few months old publication. Headquarters, sequestered from a washing machine and clothes dryer by thin panels of layered wood, occupied one corner of a home basement. Two used filing cabinets, a big, badly abused desk, and a Smith-Corona typewriter manufactured in 1939, represented the complete equipment inventory. Art type and a T-square that wiggled all over a stained drawing board indicated that from time to time someone made a pass at setting up offset copy. On the office wall today is a small sign neatly lettered by my son Fred: "10-5-83, 2:09 p.m. Dad's typewriter died." It did. It gave up the ghost that day, fully twelve years after Fletcher Sims figured it was absolutely done for.

My son, Tim, then age nine, was stuffing papers, and Chris, then age fifteen, was handling mail when the used cow feed salesman came by. "OK," he said, "I'm convinced. You're not some point man for the Fertilizer Institute." He was convinced that I was doing the paper alone, and convinced that I had about as much prospect for succeeding as I had of being assumed bodily into heaven like the Virgin Mary.

I laid it out for Fletcher, exactly what I had in mind. As I saw it, homo sapiens were facing three interrelated crises because they had violated the laws of economics, ecology and energy, I said, in those words, or in words to that effect. "We have violated the principle that all systems must recycle resources. I mean raw materials, capital, even energy not fully used. We have violated the general principle that the several systems we use must not poison other parts of the environment. And we daily violate the principle that energy must be used efficiently, and not wasted."

Sims had no difficulty with any of these propositions. He had firsthand knowledge of how the air stank, how water furnished cancer to the population, how the industrial and agricultural successes of the hour threatened to cancel out the health profile and the life span of citizens, and even the natural blueprints for unborn children.

It was a prophetic conversation. Within two years, the international manipulators would compute the existence of an oil supply, faltering some decades down the road, and translate it into an instant shortage. Harry Lobel, a researcher from Omaha, Nebraska, followed this startling event with a series of articles in *Acres U.S.A.* His reports used Oil Institute figures to prove that there really was no oil shortage, and wouldn't be for several hundred years based on doubling and redoubling of consumption. *Acres U.S.A.* did not anticipate the full effect of the OPEC cartel arrangement, but the anatomy of hydrocarbons figured in the very first issue.

The archeologists had already revealed that some three hundred million years ago, spaceship earth was without oxygen. Anaerobic bacteria—that is, organisms that live without air—started the long task of manufacturing the air we use today. In time green plants produced more oxygen by splitting the hydrogen atoms of water from oxygen atoms. More and more organisms obeyed the divine injunction to increase and multiply. Then, as now, plants tied up carbon from carbon dioxide, using hydrogen atoms, and new compounds were built into plant tissues. Oxygen was released to the air.

Nature operates in cycles. Thus when plants die, the process reverses itself. Dead plants decay. Bacteria make a meal of them, which is part of their cleanup chore activity. In the process, oxygen is tied up with carbon as carbon dioxide. And so the cycle completes itself.

Millions of years ago, we are told, there were lots of shallow seas. Plants must have tumbled into them, or been bulldozed into quagmires by the earth's shifting surface. Since there wasn't enough oxygen to permit bacteria to function, these materials became buried by sediment, and pressured by millions of tons of dead weight. In time they became coal and oil—trapped sunshine, if you will—that now was spewed into the atmosphere.

An uncomfortable conclusion presented itself. As fossil fuels were mined and burned, the earth returned nearer to a primitive state of having less free oxygen. Ecological reasoning had it that all the oxygen there is will be needed to burn these accumulated plant materials. The earth is a closed eco-system. Only man's failure to find all the oil and coal could save him from self-destruction. Long before the 1970s, we were borrowing oxygen from microscopic marine plants in the Pacific and Gulf of Mexico, and even from over-populated and low-fuel-consuming southeast Asia.

There was a form of chemical reincarnation afloat in all this. The carbon, oxygen and nitrogen atoms that make up the body of Fletcher Sims may have been used before—by soaring redwoods, stupid dinosaurs, graceful antelopes, or lowly sea slimes—even by prehistoric politicians. Reincarnation in this sense was a fact of life and death.

Moreover, I told Sims—and then our readers—modern American agriculture short-circuits the cycle. It takes nitrogen from the air with the help of electricity (generated by fossil fuel), and pooh-poohs bacteria power. This has enabled the farmer to fan the microbial fires, burn up his humus supply, pollute the water, and cause greater floods than ever before. To live beyond their biological income, our chemical farmers were accelerating the water cycle and the cycle of erosion.

In May of 1963, Dr. Jerome Wiesner, science counselor to President John F. Kennedy, reported to a commission assembled to examine the premises of *Silent Spring*. He said, "Use of pesticides is more dangerous than atomic fallout." This statement had always puzzled me, just as had Rachel Carson's statement to the same effect—"We are rightly appalled by the genetic effects of radiation," she wrote, ". . . how, then, could we be indifferent to the same effect from farm chemicals used freely in the environment." Tunneling back to see whether this was merely hyperbole, or something to be taken literally consumed quite a bit of my time. Then, one day, an answer fell in over the transom, so to speak. It came styled as a term—*toxic genetic chemicals*—to designate the phenoxy herbicides, the organophosphates, the chlorinated hydrocarbons. I picked up the term from Dr. Americo Mosca, an Italian scientist and winner of the chemistry prize at the Brussel's World's Fair. I had structured several articles around his work, and passed on to our readers the intelligence that farm chemicals were generally radiomimetic, meaning that they aped the character of radiation. This was exactly what Dr. Anderes and I had discussed so often. Somewhere in the flow of correspondence and scientific papers that passed between Dr. Mosca and *Acres U.S.A.*, I heard of calculations equating the ion exchange in man-made chemistry to the same fallout effect in atomic explosions. I asked Dr. Mosca for his calculations. They arrived soon enough, pages and pages, all of them complex in the extreme. None were more devastating than a short summary he added as a codicil.

Atomic fallout is formed by alpha, beta and gamma rays and neutrons. In the human, animal or vegetable body, a radioactive particle is dangerous only when it disintegrates and discharges its energy. These reactions are determined by the electrons. Atomic fallout and chemicals having free valences in contact with men, animals and plants spontaneously subtract electrons from the hydrogen atoms of amino acids, alter the natural frequency of genetic mutations and afterward form the respective proteinates.

"The damage resulting from nuclear radiation is the same as the damage resulting from the use of toxic genetic chemicals," Mosca wrote. "The use of fungicides of organic synthesis [Zineb, Captan, Phaltan, etc.] annually causes the same damage to present and future generations as atomic fallout from 29 H-bombs of 14 megatons—or damage equal to fallout of 14,500 atomic bombs, type Hiroshima."

Mosca computed that in the U.S. the yearly use of toxic genetic chemicals was about 453,000 tons, which caused damage equal to atomic fallout from 145 H-bombs of 14 megatons, or 72,500 atomic bombs, type Hiroshima. And in charts, graphs and statistics—all of which appeared as part of this running story—the great Italian scientist revealed that mentally retarded babies had reached 15% of live births. He concluded that damage to plants, crops and soil fertility—and water pollution—was practically incalculable. Continuation of the scenario would see the destruction of the American people in a few generations.

The story behind those calculations saw print only in rare histories of science. It was during the middle of the 19th century that Friederick Kekule of Ghent conceptualized methane (CH_4) as a basis for organic compounds. Here was a hypothesis that explained the structural formulas for chain compounds common to petroleum. However, benzene remained unexplained. It belonged to a class known as hydrocarbons, compounds made up entirely of hydrogen and carbon, and characterized by a deficiency in hydrogen per carbon atom— C_6H_6. The story has been told that this great scientist watched the curling smoke in his fireplace and visualized a gamboling carbon compound grabbing its own tail—the hexagon. And so the riddle of benzene came clear. When he realized that a fourth valence could be absorbed intramolecularly, the door flew open. And the aromatic hydrocarbons (they call them that because they smell) filled the compendiums.

There are rings and chains and branches in this world of man-made molecules, and there is no instant natural counterpart. It is true that bacteria can take chlorinated hydrocarbons apart. Bacteria can even take atomic waste apart, or demolish the bed of a truck, but not in a time span useful to man in terms of his life cycle and in terms of his generations.

Rachel Carson summarized: "For the first time in the history of the world . . . every human creature comes in contact with poisonous chemical substances from the moment of conception till death." And she correctly accused the chemical industry of poisoning humanity with the consent of scientists whose knowledge and concept of toxicity dated back to the Stone Age. On the scale of Stone Age toxicology, table salt is more toxic than Captan, a mild fungicide used in apple orchards, but Captan is a member of the thalidomide family. One atom can so offend the protein of the chromosomes that a mentally retarded child results, or a cancer is started, or a death is made more painful. Rachel Carson charged that we have become victims of cancer, nerve paralysis and genetic mutations—and that we are in no better situation than Borgia's guests.

Before World War I, German scientists concluded that the chlorinated hydrocarbons were so dangerous they ought not be made available for release into the environment. However, Germany lost that war, and sealed patents were made available to the victors. By the time of WWII, probing scientists discovered in DDT certain insecticidal properties. The age of toxic genetic chemicals was off and running.

In issue after issue, *Acres U.S.A.* slammed home the point that toxic genetic chemicals *do* offend the genesis of life, they do alter the very blueprint of a life pattern, and for this reason they have no safe level or no tolerance level in the human environment. And to suggest differently, we often chided, was to admit that scientists had been on white bread a little too long. A lack of mental acuity had come to underscore public policy.

The Stone Age science of which Rachel Carson wrote is the lethal dose, LD_{50} system for measuring toxicity. Sometimes LC_{50} is used, meaning lethal concentration in water. LD_{50} means that the cited milligrams of poison per kilogram of test animal bodyweight will kill 50% of the test animals. In *Acres U.S.A.* terminology, it came to be known as the make-it-to-the-door system. LD_{50} gives no consideration to damage that may surface later—in human beings, many years later.

In 1958 and 1959, the government set up Poison Control Centers, and published Stone Age type regulations, all of which were duly reported in professional magazines such as *Veterinary Medicine*. The Centers were to rescue farmers and industrial users from sudden death, and not much more. In the process, the hard chemistry industry gained a free sales arm, including the entire classroom-to-the-field apparatus of USDA and the land grant colleges.

Because so few understood either the premises for the government blessing of safety, I developed the following definition for toxic genetic chemistry, and caused it to be published in both *Acres U.S.A.* and in *An Acres U.S.A. Primer*:

Toxic genetic chemistry. A term used by *Acres U.S.A.* to designate man-made molecules of poisons used by some farmers to rescue crops from insect, fungal and bacterial crop destroyers. The word *genetic* is inserted here because the most commonly used molecules offend the genesis of life at the cellular level in plant, animal and man. Properly managed soil systems produce crops that do not require rescue with toxic genetic chemicals. The term also includes herbicides, which presume to rescue crops from weed takeover in the wake of management mistakes. Under U.S. regulations, materials with an acute oral LD_{50} value of 0 to 50 milligrams per kilogram bodyweight must carry signal words "DANGER" and "POISON" as well as skull and crossbones. There must be an antidote statement, and "Call Physician Immediately" and "Keep Out of Reach of Children" language must appear on the label. A poison with a LD_{50} value of 50 to 500 milligrams per kilogram is considered moderately toxic by the government. It has to have the signal word "WARNING," but no antidote statement is required. The federal people figure a victim will live long enough to call a Poison Control Center as listed in the yellow pages of a telephone directory. A moderately toxic substance must nevertheless carry "Keep Out of Reach of Children" language. If it takes 500 to 5,000 milligrams per kilogram of bodyweight to bowl over 50% of the test animals, a poison is considered of low order toxicity. The next word in the signal word pecking order is "CAUTION." No antidote statement is required. The usual "children" language is mandatory. A 5,000 plus LD_{50} rating is considered comparatively free from instant danger. It may deliver a cancer or a scrambled child—but that won't be this week or this year. No warnings, no cautions are required. The government frowns on unqualified claims of safety, and it requires the "Keep Out of Reach of Children" mandatory line. Toxic genetic chemical poisoning can mimic brain hemorrhage, heat stroke, heat exhaustion, hypoglycemia, gastroenteritis, pneumonia and other severe respiratory infections, and asthma.

What Dr. Mosca said has become transparently obvious ever since Rachel Carson released *Silent Spring*. Cellular damage because of malnutrition or the invasion of toxicity was costing many a farmer his crop. The same damage in human beings was costing the nation its heritage. Damage to the sperm or ova in human beings routinely was causing malformation or mental retardation in future generations. It was also contributing to degenerative metabolic disease.

As one who drove the country roads quite frequently, I could not escape noticing the early cancer funerals among farmers, formerly a healthy profession. The scrambled children I saw in the countryside—the mental retardations, the teratogenic births, the deformed bodies—all were paying homage to a technology that simply did not belong. The stick-figure wheelchair parking sign has become as much a symbol for fossil fuel technology as a sign of compassion for the unfortunate.

This was a big story, possibly too big. It was something akin to reporting on parity—or even carrying first hand information on the assassination of President Kennedy. From the Warren Commission, naming names and citing conspirators might have been accepted, but not from a lesser source. Few have listened to Dr. Mosca or to any of the international scientists who agree with him.

In each of the *Acres U.S.A.* issues that passed by the board during fifteen years of operation, I have interviewed an interesting person—not necessarily a famous individual, but always someone who had something to say. The first interview was with the late Bill Graves, then proprietor of Hy-Brid Sales, a firm that has since passed from the scene. In one exchange, Graves pointed to the inescapable link between economics and ecology, the twin components of eco-agriculture.

"I don't know how that will be resolved, I mean the ultimate ownership of the land. We know what is happening to the farmer. Dr. William A. Albrecht of the University of Missouri made one of the finest statements I've ever seen on this business of chemicals and farm prices.

"Under present and prevailing marketing arrangements, the farmer's operations require his liquidation of his creative assets every time he makes a sale. He literally sells the fertility elements and organic matter

of his soil. The economists call this good economics and taking a profit.

"The fact is that our acres are undergoing a declining productivity. We see this in increased plant diseases and the numbers and kinds of pests. So we have decreased productivity and we're calling it efficiency. And we have another element that is now being discussed openly for the first time—lowered quality of farm production for food and feed values," Graves said.

Dr. William A. Albrecht had been head of the Department of Soils at the University of Missouri. He had been retired early because the school believed it needed an administrator capable of getting grants, rather than a microbiologist and scientist in charge of that department. I called the university and was told that Dr. Albrecht could not be interviewed because of his poor hearing. With that, I pointed my car east on I-70, and headed for Columbia, Missouri.

5

ENTER WITHOUT KNOCKING

"Enter without knocking, and leave the same way."

It was a greeting I would hear at frequent intervals until May 21, 1974, the day Dr. William A. Albrecht passed from the scene. Between the founding of *Acres U.S.A.* and Dr. Albrecht's death, I taped over a hundred hours of conversation during one-on-one study sessions that literally recapped the life and career of this great scientist. During one of our last meetings he provided me with almost eight hundred published papers, over one hundred of which have since been recycled in *Acres U.S.A.*, another seventy—appearing in two volumes called *The Albrecht Papers*,—were published by *Acres U.S.A.*

I had encountered Dr. Albrecht on paper in my *Veterinary Medicine* days because of his connection with the discovery of aureomycin. In the mid-1940s, aureomycin literally leaped into the nation's headlines as an antibiotic similar to penicillin. It held great promise as a blunting instrument against death dealing viruses, and as an answer to gram-positive bacteria.

Fletcher Sims, the Canyon, Texas composter mentioned earlier, knew Bill Albrecht as "the little professor," a gentleman with a quick gait and an even quicker mind. Both were in high gear, Sims said, when he made those trips from Waters and Mumford Halls to Sanborn Field, the eight acre experimental plot that has since become a national historic landmark at the University of Missouri. Sanborn Field was established in 1888, and remains the oldest agricultural experiment field west of the Mississippi. Starting with Dr. J.W. Sanborn, then dean of the Missouri College of Agriculture at Columbia, these thirty-nine tenth acre plots have given up more of nature's secrets than any similarly sized piece of soil on the face of the earth. At the time of Albrecht's retirement, nineteen of the plots had been operated for the full eighty-six years, most of the time under his tutelage.

During that period of continuous planting and reaping. Bill Albrecht wrote down nature's lessons and requirements. His eight hundred-plus papers ended up as a record that would tell all who wished to know the values and some of the fallacies and shortcomings of rotations in soil improvement, the beneficial effects and some limitations of undigested farm manure, and the benefits and some misconceptions of legumes in soil improvement. In Albrecht's papers one can find the bedrock rationale for limestone in crop production. Through the years Sanborn Field told Bill Albrecht and his associates more than a little about acidic effect of some nitrogen fertilizers and the influence of seventy-five years of chemical fertilizers on soil properties and crop production. During his forty-three years on the job Albrecht asked nature about the possibilities of rejuvenating soil with non-legumes and plant nutrients, and nature gave her answers largely because Albrecht knew the right questions. The influence of cropping systems and nutritional inputs on soil organisms and organic matter composition commanded a big share of his attention, and the little professor duly made a record of everything he learned.

"If you really stop to think about it," Dr. Albrecht pointed out during our first meeting, "all I have done here is write down what we've learned through the years about how everything connects."

Dr. Albrecht was not oblivious to how the world had turned over, and how the coming of the atomic bomb altered the planet for all time to come. In fact the influence of radioactive fallout on the composition of plant tissue was given the Sanborn Field treatment. The university had soil samples collected prior to the initial nuclear detonation, samples reaching back for decades.

Plot 23 had been established as a rotation field by the old stormy, crotchety Dean Sanborn, and had remained unfertilized for fifty-seven years—and cropped to timothy all that time. One day a botanist named Benjamin M. Duggar, then with Lederle Laboratories, asked his former colleague, Bill Albrecht, to send a sample. There were things undreamt of by philosophers in the soil of Sanborn, and he figured Albrecht would supply the question to which the laboratory had the answer.

46

It was hot enough to fry catfish on a pavement when Albrecht ran that probe into the soil of Plot 23. The mere selection of Plot 23 took on the form of a question.

Take the matter of crop rotation. Over the years Albrecht had gathered in evidence that had face-reddening implications. Rotations under certain conditions were far from beneficial, and even became outright harmful. Folklore had it that legumes always improved the soil, but Albrecht determined that instead of becoming the catchpen for stored nitrogen, legumes—overdone—could impoverish the land as much as the monocrop sharecropper's approach. When oil company shills came to Albrecht with their appeals for testimonial and endorsement, he was forced to demolish their folklore with the fact that salt fertilizers without rhyme or reason were worse than no fertilizers at all.

Albrecht knew that there was dynamite in Plot 23. Sure enough, when the results were returned, the fungus *Streptomyces aureofaciens*, Strain A-377, was isolated from the soil sample. It became the parent of all the aureomycin to enter worldwide distribution.

Bill Albrecht had added "Emeritus" to his title when I first met him. The word was out that he had been retired because he wouldn't "go along," and there was some truth in this. He had been a scientific gadfly since 1916, when he came to the University of Missouri as a microbiologist on the staff of the Soils Department. He was the seventh of eight children reared on a farm in Livingston County, Illinois.

"As a boy—before I left country school—I told my mother I'd learned something. There are no hoop snakes. And I said, *Mother, I'm going to study snakes.* I got myself an Osage orange cane with a little fork at the bottom. And a cane is longer than most snakes. That snake has to keep at least half of its body down to get the leverage for the other half to strike. It has to have an anchor. When I finished my graduate school work, I had over two hundred specimens of various things of that nature preserved and put away on the stockboard nailed on the joists in the basement, all cured. Alcohol only cost fifty cents a quart. And I knew the saloonkeeper. The thing that disgusts me is that your scientists go into technology instead of teaching. They patent everything and make it secret. I don't like that. So I decided that I was going to study and learn."

In agriculture, in soil microbiology, and in medicine, Albrecht discovered what the country boy said when he came home to his dad from the college of agriculture. He said, "Dad, they teach so much that ain't so." So he spent most of his life finding what is so. As he learned, he

47

wrote everything out and studied it out, and put it into manuscript form.

Speaking into my small tape recorder, Albrecht wrote his autobiography. "In prep school I heard a physician give a lecture on health and hygiene and for a while I threatened to go into medicine myself. My entire four years of undergraduate work at the University of Illinois were devoted to a preparation for medical school. But I finally realized that my real interest was in life and biology.

"After my four years at the university I taught for a year at Bluffton College Academy, my prep school. Then I returned to the University of Illinois to study agriculture. By this time, my background and education had produced a distinct attitude. I went into agricultural college not as one seeking to be trained for a particular, narrow job, but as a scientist."

Albrecht was never content with superficial answers to superficial questions. He never rested until he had pushed his way back to the fundamentals. "I have always felt that it is my duty and the duty of all who call themselves agricultural scientists to go much further than the farmer goes with his questions. The banker and the income tax collector help the farmer ask the superficial question. If we don't do more than that we really can't justify the appropriations that are given us."

Telling the Albrecht story—rather, the story Albrecht told—became workaday stuff at *Acres U.S.A.* For here was first-rate scholarship explaining soil fertility, microbes, organics and life in the soil in understandable terms, starting with the Creator's plan, and ending with minds capable of thought and reason. Some of Albrecht's earlier papers had to do with legume inoculation. This was not a simple task. For one thing, farmers had a belief "that all you had to do was introduce the bacteria into the soil, and the bacteria would compel the plant to fix nitrogen with their help," Albrecht said. "As a young man I had learned on the farm that you could not just get a fancy bull and he would make the cow have a calf, because the cow had something to do with her part."

Albrecht was more than a background scientist. He was an active publicist, a forceful spokesman for scientific sense, and a voice for reason. By the early 1930s, soil mining techniques in the United States had reached a climax point. In the West this meant a hot-dry cycle and a dust bowl. In the East it meant faltering production in terms of protein. The first government lime program surfaced under the Agriculture Adjustment Act. Possibly half the soils in the U.S.

were helped by liming. *Lime and lime some more* became a catch-phrase. *You can't overdo it.* As with most programs, this one was continued to comply with political strategy, not science, and Albrecht came up fighting from his chair.

There was more to reclaiming the soil than fighting acidity. Speaking into an *Acres U.S.A.* tape recorder, Albrecht put it this way. "Professor M.F. Miller [then head of the Department] thought I should grow bacteria that would make the cow have a calf whether she wanted to or not. And I had to politely show the points I wanted to make." As usual, Albrecht had his "vision" to lean on—that is, his informed conceptualization. He liked to tap foreign scholars, and so he knew about Russia's Serge N. Winogradsky and Holland's M. W. Beijerinck, who had proved that nitrogen fixation took place in the soil without any legumes whatsoever. The essentials of rapid fixation were found to be absence of readily available nitrogen and the presence of carbohydrates, phosphate and lime. He pondered the findings of Thomas Way of England. It was Way who in 1852 discovered that when soil absorbed ammonia, a corresponding amount of calcium was released to the drainage water. The exchange mechanism, he found, was seated in the clay. Continued study revealed that such an exchange did exist, and that it involved all cation (positively charged) elements. Moreover, it had been developed that the total exchange capacity of soil depended on both the colloidal clay and the organic matter. With these few points in mind, Albrecht continued observing as nature revealed herself. The titles of early papers suggest the usual method of approach. "We took things one leg at a time," Albrecht said, "and wrote down the results." Often as not, significant findings went out under the imprimatur of the Department, students being the authors, special credit being given to "Dr. William A. Albrecht, under whom the author worked."

Albrecht described his own role in these studies as follows: "I separated the finest part of the clay out of Putnam silt loam by churning in a centrifuge running at 32,000 r.p.m. after the clay had been suspended and settled for three weeks. At the bottom, that clay finally plugged up the machinery. But we had thinner and thinner, smaller and smaller clay until about halfway up in that centrifuge, there we had it as clear as vaseline. We took the upper half of that clay. We made pounds and pounds of it. We put it into an electrical field and made it acidic. We took off all the cations so it was acid clay. That was how we studied plant nutrition. We put on different elements in different orders. We mixed them, balanced them." Standing on the shoulders of giants, Albrecht knew he had to begin with calcium.

"Your acid clay is nothing more than one that doesn't have the positive ions on it—hydrogen, calcium, potassium, magnesium, sodium and the trace elements. I've got to have 65% of that clay's capacity loaded with calcium, 15% with magnesium. I've got to have four times as much calcium as magnesium. You see why we ought to lime the soil? We ought to lime it to get it up to where it feeds the plant calcium, not to fight acidity." The formal paper giving expression to these findings was given at the International Society of Soil Science the day Hitler moved into Poland, 1939. There were formal papers presented in Russia and Australia as well, but in a manner of speaking Albrecht did his best work at home. He stood alone against the Fertilizer Institute, for instance, even when speaking to them.

"Fertilizers are made soluble, but it's a damn fool idea. They should be insoluble but available. Most of our botany is solution botany. When we farm as solution botany, the first rain takes out the nutrients."

Albrecht met often and long with Friends of the Land, and became a regular guest at Louis Bromfield's Malabar Farm. He liked Bromfield, served as his counsel, and watched with keen interest progress on the farm where Bromfield had set out to prove that natural farming would work, although he admitted, "Louie drank too much."

Bromfield had seen most of the world's abused acres. Indeed, for some twenty-five years he was known as a "citizen of the world." He lived in India and Europe, and he wrote novels—*The Green Bay Tree, The Rains Came, Mrs. Parkington, Early Autumn.* The latter won for him a Pulitzer prize.

During the 1930s the world came unglued at the seams. Bromfield's harsh, critical tone seemed to be offset by the fact that he could do nothing about it. And so, in 1939, he came "home," to a place called Pleasant Valley. Here he found a situation he could do something about. Land had been abused. Bad practices and poor cultivation filled the territory with erosion gullies and poverty. Bromfield picked up one farm after another. Using what we now call eco-farming principles, he produced abundant crops.

He did more. He studied the works of Dr. William A. Albrecht, and in a practical arena started to prove that insect damage and disease could be controlled with humus, plant nutrition, and sound soil management.

In *From My Experience*, published in 1955, he cited his finding that "insects showed an aversion to all plants grown in good, balanced, living, productive soil."

At the time public policy was trying to cast agriculture into the role of an industrial procedure, Bromfield spoke out. He spoke for preservation of the nation's topsoil, and he proved out the role of the individual farmer on the Muskingum River watershed, where small dams and soil management practices showed their worth as opposed to big dams and naked hills.

At one time the big soup companies sent their agents to Bromfield's Malabar Farms, and for years the farmer's intellectual advisers saw the road agriculture ought to travel. Then something happened. Farm parity prices fell into their 60-90% cadence. And high pressure technology picked up speed. Before many years had gone by, the nation's schools and Extension agents—acting as one—touted toxic technology. The Malabar experience was eclipsed.

Also eclipsed at approximately the same time was E. R. Kuck, the founder of Brookside Dairy Farms, another of Albrecht's friends.

In fact, it was a case of animals telling Kuck about vanished nutrition that launched Brookside Laboratories. After plastering the walls of a new calf barn, Kuck noticed that the animals literally ate the plaster off the walls of their stalls. Calves had been scouring at the time. Almost immediately, scouring stopped, and Kuck—consulting with Albrecht—determined that the hungry animals were in fact after the calcium carbonate and the magnesium carbonate in the plaster material. These nutrients had been mined out of the soil of the dairy operation and never replaced.

Other observations came to the fore at Brookside. Soil and leaf tests revealed a wide variance in crops produced on *treated* vs. *untreated* acres. In December 1946, Kuck issued a report, *Better Crops with Plant Food*, published by the American Potash Institute. The article was picked up by the farm press and given wide distribution. Feedback arrived almost immediately—some one thousand letters from farmers telling of their own problems and asking for help. There were also sixteen letters from academic folk condemning Kuck in vitriolic terms, and denouncing the significance of magnesium in animal nutrition. Moreover, the college people seemed to think that no farmer had the right to make such observations and tell it the way it was without the imprimatur of a credentialed institution.

The sheer desperation of those animals emerged time and time again in Albrecht's writings. "Our dietary essential minerals are taken as organo-inorganic compounds. We are not mineral eaters. Neither are the animals. When any of them take to the mineral box, isn't

51

it an act of desperation?" On another occasion, Albrecht came right to the point. "Cows eat soil or chew bones when ill with acetonemia, pregnancy troubles, or deficiency ailments. Hogs root only in the immediate post-winter period after confinement to our provision for them and their behavior suggests past deficiencies to be quickly remedied in desperate digging of the earth."

Even in retirement, Albrecht worked overtime at schooling people. He corresponded tirelessly. People with minimum training could count on this quiet gentleman to explain complicated chemistry in terms that could be understood. C. Haynes Thompson, the proprietor of a phosphate firm, couldn't understand the *Insoluble Yet Available* paper. "Calcium and magnesium are divalent elements, hence offset two hydrogens or two equivalent weights of it. Potassium is monovalent, hence offsets only one equivalent weight of hydrogen per atomic weight (not per atomic number)."

Albrecht's visitors were farmers, consultants, and students in the main, but well known people of vision also came to pay homage. One day, quite unannounced, I drove down to Columbia with Eddie Albert, the movie and TV personality. Albrecht gently excused himself from a recording session with the university archivist and gave Eddie Albert both barrels: an hour-long lecture on the Pottenger cat studies, and another on the miracle of the Ozarks. I can remember Albrecht's lesson as if I heard it last night, and I spent the trip back to Kansas City visiting with Eddie Albert about what Albrecht had said.

For about twenty-five years Albrecht worked on his Epsom salts theory. Frequently, after a hernia is repaired, bowels wouldn't move past that hernia. So the procedure was to give Epsom salts. "If they check," Albrecht told Eddie Albert, "they'll see that urine is throwing the protein out of the blood. Protein is wasted because the Epsom salts ruin the membranes in the kidneys and keep them from doing their normal work. When you take Epsom salts, that salt replaces the calcium in the wall of the intestines and it throws everything it can because that membrane is no longer normal. It just throws everything from the bloodstream till it flushes it and can go back to your bones to get some calcium to rebuild intestine walls." When Albrecht gave that suggestion to Dr. F. M. Pottenger, he replied, *"You've got a good theory because if we've got a highly rheumatic person and give him Epsom salts, he's so low in calcium he throws the calcium out so badly that it kills him."*

"Now the medical profession knows that they shouldn't give Epsom salts," Albrecht said, "but they do. But you see with this hernia, the kidney wasn't functioning when the magnesium went through. The magnesium that the bloodstream had to throw out through the kidney was knocking the kidney. Now here's my theory. If I didn't have my soil loaded high enough with calcium, the nutrients were going from the plant back to the soil exactly the way they go from an intestine. If I don't have this calcium saturated soil high enough, the plants throw their fertility back to the clay, instead of from the clay to the plant.

"The plants will build the fertility up in the soil and starve to death themselves. If you put chemicals into that soil you've ruined that root. These laws of physiology hold. It doesn't make much difference whether it is a person or a plant. I'm convinced that the Creator knew his business, and man still hasn't learned."

Lady Eve Balfour of England found a lot of news when she heard Albrecht intone, "Enter without knocking, and leave the same way." She was making a tour of the United States to learn about the state of agriculture in what the British once called "the colonies," and what she learned both alarmed and delighted her. The highlight of her trip was a study session with Bill Albrecht. You didn't just visit the professor, you studied. For Lady Balfour, Albrecht was in the Weston Price-Sir Robert McCarrison class. The literature, of course was available to Lady Eve Balfour, and in her report she assembled some memorable statements. But it was Albrecht's critique of the ash mentality that captured her imagination, and she returned to England the best of the best from the U.S.A.

"When the effects from fertilizers on soils are measured only by yield variations in vegetative bulk, recorded in tons and bushels, there is little chance that we shall recognize crop differences demonstrating the varying effects between the use of inorganic and organic fertilizers. Our animals, however, tell us that the crop's nutritional quality reflects the different organic and inorganic compounds feeding the plants. When we learn to measure the crop's responses to soil fertility by more than bulk values and ash differences, then the contributions of the soil, both organic and inorganic, to plant nutrition will be more correctly realized," Albrecht said.

After the first few issues of *Acres U.S.A.* had landed in rural mailboxes, some of my NFO buddies figured the larder would soon be exhausted. To the untrained eye it appeared that way. I had started publication with a stack of notes, reprints, Xerox copies of reports, facts, figures, vignettes, and so on, about three inches high. In the first fifteen years, I have removed material measuring at least twenty feet high, and the remaining stack is still over a foot high. Not used, but available, are the background materials—the Albrecht papers included—that fill a dozen filing cabinets.

One day when I came to Columbia to see Dr. Albrecht, he was moving out of his office in Mumford Hall. His library was for sale. I filled my trunk with books and enjoyed a fine lunch with the professor and his wife, Gertrude. Dr. Albrecht could no longer drive, but his mind was still as sharp as a glass bell. He apologized for warming slowly, and he admitted he just couldn't trust economists, not even Thorstein Veblen, who used to teach at the University of Missouri, Columbia. In fact he had always voted to keep that discipline out of the professional societies to which he belonged. "Cheating and distortion, that's all economics has to offer. It isn't science." I had handed him my book, *Unforgiven*, both to defend myself, and to prove that economics could be a science, hinting slightly that true science was being distorted by the makers of salt fertilizers and toxic genetic chemicals. Albrecht responded, "I read your book. You do good work. And you're on track." Those last four words meant more to me than a medal etched in gold.

There was no reason why this gentle old man could not have lived longer. His health was fair to good, and he knew how to take care of himself. "I know how they'll get me," he confided. "One day they'll get me out to one of those restaurants with all that synthetic food and preservatives, and I'll suffer an attack. I won't be able to get to my bathroom. They'll take me to a hospital, and they won't know what to do. I'll be a goner."

It happened that way. A group of colleagues ordered Bill Albrecht to a restaurant to honor him. In the convivial atmosphere of the hour, he made an error. He ate chemical-laced fare that triggered a metabolic problem he had been living with for years. They took him to a hospital. In a few days he belonged to the ages.

One day, not long before he passed away, Dr. Albrecht told me where I could find still more news for *Acres U.S.A.* "You go see Gene Poirot down at Golden City, Missouri. He is one smart old cookie," Albrecht said.

I did that—and when the time came to publish a fair selection of Albrecht's papers in book form, I asked Eugene M. Poirot to join Dr. Granville Knight in writing a foreword. Poirot had first met Dr. Albrecht in 1926.

"We began research for making artificial manure out of straw in order to have a bit of organic fertilizer. This, we hoped, would encourage the growth of nitrogen-fixing bacteria on sweet clover in soil where the organic level was too low to support the bacterial life in then available laboratory cultures of inoculation materials. Later I was granted two patents on the process which was made available to farmers by the Capper Foundation of Kansas," wrote Poirot.

It was on Poirot's acres that Albrecht proved the contention that calcium was the prince of nutrients. The year was 1928. Later observations of cows chewing bones, grazing where the soil was high in magnesium and where extra phosphate and lime had been applied, and still later—when cows walked through what appeared to be good grass to eat seventeen different kinds of weeds where calcium limestone, magnesium and phosphate had been applied—caused Albrecht to think in terms of fertilizing crops so they would be more nutritious to animals eating them.

The Albrecht Papers told this story. They told more, but not all. For it is a fact that Albrecht's findings enabled the nutrient-deficient Ozarks to produce good calf crops so that now Missouri is second only to Texas in calf production. Dr. Albrecht lived his life as a scientist, a writer and a speaker, always serving tirelessly as an interpreter of scientific truth so that inquiring minds could use this knowledge in service to mankind. His papers and continuing reports in *Acres U.S.A.* provide a glimpse of that story. And Gene Poirot, his best practical student, remained as a living testament.

6

THE SOUL OF A POET

The craft of printing has changed since I first reported football for the Chanute, Kansas *Tribune*, or worked on a college paper. Hot lead has been eclipsed by cold type. And the computer has come of age.

The cumbersome old linotype, with its curious "e-t-a-o-i-n s-c-h-r-d-l-u" arrangement for keys, has vanished, except from museum displays and some few die-hard shops. Sleek typesetters that push out cold type are now seen in newspaper composing rooms. Copy often marches straight from the journalist to galley type with hardly an intervening technician. More important, technology has put the publishing enterprise within reach of low budget operators, and has contributed mightily to the flow of information. Technology enabled me to beat the odds and survive. Things were different at the end of what I usually refer to as "the unpleasantness with Germany and Japan."

The colleges were full to the gunwales when I finally said goodbye to Air Corp discipline, gunnery wings, and Special Orders. Special Orders involved lots of mimeograph work and a signature. We had a contest in Special Order Section at Lowry Air Field, Denver. The grounded pilot who ran the place had the task of discharging people from the service, and I was ordered to forget the B-29 tail turret and help muster people out. This called for a signature on each stencil, an on-scene chore the young lieutenant did not want to perform because of the staggering offense to his golf time.

We had a contest, and I won. It turned out that my rendition of his signature looked more like the lieutenant's than his own. All I had to do was maintain a presence, and sign on the stencil giving thousands of GIs their cherished walking papers. In the army they called this rocking chair duty. To me it meant lots of time to read. In some few months I consumed the modest library on the air base the way fire consumed Richmond. In the process I ran into a wonderful little story called *Leiningen Versus the Ants*, by C. Stephenson. If anything, it renewed my interest in nature's curious ways. There is no connection whatsoever, but somehow Gene Poirot has always reminded me of Leiningen. When the marabunda ants marched on Leiningen's Amazon bottoms, they took everything in sight—leaf, blade of grass, animal and human being. In the time it took to smoke a cigar, the ants could consume a pullet. The soldier ants were the epitome of destruction, but after a march they rested for perhaps seventy years before they marched again.

Gene Poirot's enemies were the twin engines of erosion, wind and water, and they never rested unless the farmer solved his problem with singular intelligence.

Somewhere in Albrecht's papers were items co-authored by Eugene M. Poirot. Much of the research thus accounted for during Gene Poirot's career has been forgotten—that is to say, it has not been communicated into the mainstream of American agriculture. Other voices from other rooms took over at the end of WWII. Bad philosophy and bad technology resulted in diminished returns agriculture. This type of agriculture is now ruining both farm acres and the nation's posterity.

In 1964 Poirot published a little book called *Our Margin of Life*. One passage has haunted me ever since I encountered it. Poirot told of failure in farming and of recapitalization on free land out west. But, he warned, the government did not make this land new and fertile. Only nature could do that. Relief money as such could not solve the farmer's problem because the margins in his land were lost. The penalty of death was prevented by the mercy of others, but the violation remained. "Perhaps the thought becomes more understandable if we think of the tenant as the captain of a ship and his eighty people, its passengers," wrote Poirot. "The captain makes a mistake, strikes an iceberg, and his ship goes down. If any of them are to survive, it will be through the mercy and charity of a more skillful captain of another ship who makes the rescue and shares his space with them."

There is futility in building industrial greatness, warned Poirot, "without also building a soil potential to feed the people it represents." Now the choices divide, said Poirot. One leads to the ruin of land, the other to restoration. The first road is marked with signs such as "unrestricted agriculture," "unregimented production," and the selfish interest of hungry people urge one on. "I am tempted to follow such a road. It would serve me well. I could take from the soil all it has to offer and then—like the strip miner—abandon it and pass the problems I have created on to another generation. All this I could do, but as a farmer, I must point out two failures, theirs and mine. Noble words, power and national greatness cannot turn them into success."

When Gene Poirot arrived at his family's prairie home in northeastern Lawrence County, Missouri in 1922, he planted a corn crop with high expectations only to reap a bitter harvest. Eighty acres failed to produce even one ear of corn. It was not until after he harvested his "non-harvest" that he understood why tenants refused to stay on that farm. It was worn out. Sedge choked many acres because they were poverty acres. Gene Poirot was crushed, but not defeated. He was fresh out of the University of Illinois, where he had majored in agriculture, and he had ten hours toward a master's degree. Soil tests revealed a need for calcium, three tons to the acre. At $7.00 a ton, this represented an impossible fortune in those days. The soil also needed phosphate. He purchased a railcar full of phosphate and put it on his acres. But what he really wanted was cow manure. There wasn't enough of that because the land was so poor it wouldn't carry ten or twelve cows an acre. The used cow feed he managed to lay his hands on was hardly enough to dress a test plot. This he planted with alsike, red and sweet clover. Everything went well with the manured plot, but the red and sweet clover inoculation did not take elsewhere due to a lack of organic matter.

Poirot went to see Dr. William A. Albrecht, an act that opened Pandora's box of wonders in the form of lessons harvested off Sanborn Field. Albrecht knew all about erosion, naked clay, and vanished carbon from the soil. A classic experiment had been conducted to measure soil and water run-off. The plot used was no bigger than a pool table. A senior student designed the plot so that every drop of water could be caught in a barrel set just below the plot. A little later another student added two more plots under different tillage systems to measure erosion.

The results were staggering in their implications. This prompted Dean Merritt F. Miller to authorize another experiment involving seven crops and tillage systems. Every drop of water and every speck of soil was measured. After years of replication the results remained generally the same.

The plot in corn continuously would lose its top seven inches of soil in fifty-six years. But . . . it would require 3,547 years for erosion to remove seven inches of topsoil in a plot kept in bluegrass sod. A three year rotation of corn, wheat and clover was eight times more effective than continuous corn in keeping the soil in place.

Here was news for Poirot, just as it was news for *Acres U.S.A.* readers a few decades later, even though those experiments were conducted shortly after Albrecht joined the Missouri University staff. Gene Poirot worked with Albrecht in a program for making artificial manure.

The systems that Poirot introduced to his farm through the years would have rated *Acres U.S.A.* attention in any case, because the readership was always hungry for reports on growers who made eco-farming a reality at a profit. Poirot did that. Having lived through several depressions, he in effect told the big machinery makers he would not participate in their run-the-farmer-out-on-a-limb, then-saw-it-off game. He changed his system. Animals could distribute their own manure. Great round bales could solve his feed transportation problem. Land that could not sustain a dozen cows three decades earlier was harnessed to nature's requirements so that it could produce beef measured in tons.

Poirot's story brought more than better technology to our readers. It reached the soul of the chemical farmer and eco-grower alike, for as Frank Farmer of the Springfield daily newspaper put it—Poirot "has the hands of a laborer, the mind of a philosopher, and the soul of a poet."

Some years after I met Gene Poirot we re-published his little book, *Our Margin of Life.* It had been printed by a vanity house once before, but too few readers had picked up on it, and we believed it ought never go out of print. Read these opening lines aloud!

"Come walk with me in my virgin bluestem prairie on this night in early May. Listen while it reveals its past. Learn, since it teaches the lessons of survival. Take hope from the beauty of its flowers and renew your faith from the murmur of its creatures." Who can read those lines without a tingle of emotion crawling over every cell? The Environmental Protection Agency turned Poirot's story into a film of quality, and film producer Tom Putnam did the same with the same book.

As one of the top stories ever to appear in *Acres U.S.A.* on a continuing basis, this one had a special dimension. It proved that a farmer could do more than banish hunger with bacon and beans. He could also nurture the soul of man. Some twenty years after most people retire, Gene Poirot was still trying to teach other humans what he had learned about survival of any species, man included.

Without that indispensable instrument for *Acres U.S.A.* journalism, the tape recorder, it would hardly be possible to interview a man like Gene Poirot. The few words a pencil could capture would be an obscene distortion, an insult to the purity of his ideas.

"Long before man could make a plow or a test tube, nature was creating life, including man, and providing an environment in which all life could live.

"She used the resources of air, water, sunshine and soil plant food minerals to make life. If she had created life only, these resources would have been tied up in all living things. So she also had to create death so that the resources could be recycled and used again and again.

"There is a basic law which says, *All life forms must return at death what they took from the resources of the earth during their lifetimes.* For example, when any creature dies, the water it took returns to the environment. The air it used in terms of the elements of oxygen, nitrogen and carbon dioxide are returned. The minerals which make up the human body return at death to the earth. And because death occurs, either on the soil or in the water, these resources are held within reach of new life forms, which also come from the soil surface and from close to the water's surface.

"In release of these elements of life, energy goes out, but energy cannot be recycled. Where, then, does energy come from?

"Nature stores energy," Poirot said. "She begins with plants. The plants are eaten and the stored energy goes to animals and finally to the human body that lives on plant and animal life. So to live with this philosophy we must follow this basic law of nature that says, *Return to the environment all of that which is taken from it and made in growth and hold these additions within reach of life.* That is the guts of it, right there."

Gene Poirot would be worth the space it takes to write a book, and his thoughts and technologies have been extended at least that much space in the pages of *Acres U.S.A.* through the years.

When DDT first arrived on the scene, a Texas farmer named Chester Jordan informed Dr. Albrecht that "I can make that stuff, and it works." Albrecht answered, "Yes, it works, and it will work ten years from now. But ten years from now you won't know where it is." He never made it again.

Acres U.S.A. became heavily involved in the great DDT debate in

1971 and 1972, and it may be that our articles of exposition and analysis figures in having the substance "banned." *Banned* is used loosely. Firms that make it are still making it in foreign countries, and the presence of DDT must be considered ubiquitous. Dr. Richard Penny, one of the scientists who served at the South Pole Ice Station, has written several articles for *Acres U.S.A.* While he was in that deep freeze territory he performed biopsies on penguins. He failed to find even one that did not have DDT in its fatty tissues. We joked about it at one time. "Do you realize," I said, "that under FDA guidelines, you have so many chlorinated hydrocarbons in your system you would be unfit for human consumption in a cannibalistic society."

Gene Poirot knew all of this, and over the years he helped me frame an overview of the technological drift, one that has served the readers of *Acres U.S.A.* very well. *Synthetic economics wasn't all that gushed from the colleges following WWII,* became a lead line in a short book I wrote and published—*The Case for Eco-Agriculture.* There was synthetic technology as well. First to be purged from the texts was the knowledge that the good soil is alive with bacteria, fungi, yeast, protozoa, worms, insects, microorganisms. Little mention was made of the fact that good soil contains trace elements, copper, iron, boron, manganese, magnesium, to mention a few. Forgotten was the fact that people need these trace elements to be healthy, that the people in New York need tons of iron in their food supply each year, as an example. Downgraded was the requirement for organic matter in the soil, and the fact that without organic matter it takes bigger tractors to turn the soil and more dams to hold runoff water from dying acres.

DDT was invented by a German chemist in 1874—indeed, almost all of the miracle poisons of today can be found in some form in the old German compendiums Dr. Albrecht kept on his shelves. At the end of WWI, many of these patents were handed to the world, and—at the end of WWII—Dr. Paul Mueller of Switzerland was awarded the Nobel Prize for discovering the insecticidal properties of DDT. DDT became hailed as a means of stamping out insect-borne disease and as a tool for the farmer's war against crop destroyers. The chlorinated hydrocarbons became household words—and the profitable base for a fantastic business.

Like my friend Chester Jordan, Gene Poirot remembered sadly that he knew where the DDT was. It was everywhere. This troubled him. "I am a farmer," he said. "My final product is human bodies with minds capable of thought and reason. My profession requires me to bargain with my fellow man to get dollars according to his economic laws. I

61

must also bargain with nature to get human foods according to her laws of life and death."

Poirot farmed so there were byproducts—wildlife, beauty and life in general, all values he could not sell. He rejected steel posts in favor of multiflora roses for a fence, biological control instead of insecticides, ponds and gravity flow instead of irrigation pumps and plastic pipes.

This was his philosophy. A half century after his complete corn failure, Gene Poirot could point to results. First, he had increased his crop production sevenfold using scientific principles that work with nature. The health and quality of his products increased even more. His animal herd, once a walking disaster and a debilitating drain on his bank account, became disease free for thirty-four years at the point of his fiftieth year in farming. This improvement was enough to earn him a good living, give college educations to his family, and ride out depressions that annihilated so many of his friends.

And what about the products he could not sell, but which were of value? From fifteen prairie chickens in 1922, the population had increased to one hundred fifty birds. The quail population had proliferated, and the sixty-four pounds of fish, seined from Coon Creek in 1922 had increased to more fish available in a single Coon Creek hole to support a similar catch by hook and line in one afternoon. There were no ducks when there was no corn. Now some 30,000 survive the winter by feeding on gleanings. There were no geese the year Poirot started farming. Fifty years later over 8,000 stayed for two months in late winter. There were no coons in 1922. Yet some sixty-five were taken in one eighty acre field at the half century mark; no deer, and now deer have returned; no song birds at the bottom, yet forty-two kinds were counted when the half century inventory was taken. Biological insect control has worked well for fifty years on that farm. Wildlife proliferates. The ponds are full of fish. Three colleges bring their students to the Poirot farm to study biology according to the parity of nature.

Poirot's eco-territory is not marked by great flood control dams which impound the acres of water so a few can play within a half mile of poverty. The soil controls flood waters because it soaks it up.

Poirot thinks hard and long about the values his farm delivered, other than those for which he collected a short price at the market. He told all who would listen about the 6.6 tons of oxygen each acre of corn sends into the air, and about the nine tons of carbon dioxide each acre takes from the polluted atmosphere. Most important, he is proud of his organic bank account in the soil—the real wealth of the nation.

He knows it is tough business being an eco-farmer. The world applauds those who go the other way and violate the laws of nature. The big companies licked their chops, and the professors who shared in the grant money sanctified the procedure with scientific mumbo-jumbo.

In *Acres U.S.A.* I reported these things a thousand times in a thousand ways. Sometimes I used the intemperate language of a frontier editor. It was difficult to keep a civil tongue when one heard science politicians, company shills and government agents say—as did a few at Iowa State University—that for $100,000 they'd prove anything.

Poirot felt strongly about supporting farm legislation that would account for soil and water restoration. His idea was based on the fact that the production of farm products is, in most cases, destructive. Symptoms of that destruction could be seen at every hand—loss of wildlife, poor plant and animal nutrition, muddy streams, floods, a sewage system that carried nutrients to the sea instead of looping it back to the land! On the way to the rivers, he said, these plant foods destroy rivers and lakes. Springfield, Missouri, for instance, discharged 1,750 pounds of phosphoric acid equivalent into the James River each day.

Poirot described soil and restoration in *Our Margin of Life*, and he expounded on its merits in *Acres U.S.A.* When he presented his legislative idea to farmers in four states, and to all those on a tour to Spain, all approved of it without exception. Over the years Congressman Durward G. Hall introduced three bills regarding the Poirot Plan. The last go-round it came within a twenty-two vote shift of passing in the House. It had come that far without a single letter supporting it from a farm organization, a Chamber of Commerce, a college of agriculture, a conservation group or assembly of bird watchers or friends of the earth. It failed, in the words of one Congressman, because "it is not yet time for this kind of legislation."

Maybe not! More farmland must first go to the sea. More air must stink, more water must become thick with sewage. More people must understand that the creeping, crippling illnesses of body and mind that come with polluted air and water, with malnutrition, is nature's way of destroying the creatures that cannot obey her laws—be that creature a man or a bug.

One day, standing at the edge of a pond on Poirot's farm, the gentle old farmer philosopher pointed to the landscape that unfolded below. He noted that between where we were standing and Kansas City—some ninety miles distant—water could have a gravity flow. Instead of Corps of Engineer dams, wild water could be held ready for farmer use on millions of acres via natural flow aquaducts. Water that seemed below where we were standing was actually on elevated ground, and could be used to fill his biggest pond.

This is not done, of course. Instead, millions of tons of topsoil are sent swimming off to the sea, and city folk complain that groceries are too high. "We in the United States are becoming a have-not nation because we are too silly to understand the resources that provide our food and fiber," said Poirot. "We do not understand our margin of life."

Poirot should not have included himself in "we!" He understood, and he caused others to understand. Read his matchless prose and marvel at the man, just as he marvels at the sharp-skin hawk.

"The full meaning of the margin of life was forcefully brought to my attention by a sharp-skin hawk who lives in one of the great elms along Coon Creek. The great horned owl, another killer of wildlife, lives in the same tree.

"I hear you, great horned owl, resting in that century-old elm down there by the narrow place in the creek. I know the sharp-skin hawk is in that tree with you, but he never says a word. It is you who tells of his evil deeds during the day and then, under the cover of night, you do worse ones.

"I don't know why I let you live. Perhaps it is because I don't know all the evil things you do. Or could it be that I like to hear your terrible hooting cry tear apart the peace and quiet of the night? Or even, perhaps, could it be that I feel the same Mother Nature who made room for me on this land also thinks there is room enough for you, old owl?

"I give sanctuary to that sharp-skin hawk for an altogether different reason. I know you are there, Mr. Sharp-skin, even though you don't say a word. I know you are guarding your nest with a fury which, in proportion to your weight, would make a dog appear as ferocious as a tiger. I hate your cruelty, but I admire the fury with which you guard your young. That, however, is not the reason you have sanctuary in that tree.

"You are unlike the marsh hawk who makes his kill with feminine grace and, therefore, is destined to a diet of snakes and mice and cripples. Your charge is like the speeding arrow, timed with the precision of a marksman. Though I hate your cruelty, I love the perfection with which you perform. But even that is not the reason I give you sanctuary in that tree.

"Once during the hunting season I winged one of your cousins while he was in hot pursuit of a quail. I saw the blood-stained feathers on his dying body and, in sympathy, I came too close.

"In one burst of fury he left a scratch which later became infected and from which I still carry a scar. In not more than three seconds a faraway look replaced the anger in his golden eye. He dropped his head on his shoulder and a white eyelid closed forever.

"Let me confess that, in that moment, I hoped to have the courage to fight to the end for that which I believed to be right, and to leave a scar by which to be remembered for so long a time!"

Poirot taught me to trade in skepticism for logic any day of the week. Let me explain.

Between 1400 and 1865, scurvy was the scourge of the high seas. Natives in Canada and in the South Seas knew that vitamin C was a certain cure. They didn't call it that, but they knew. Skippers and owners found it expedient to be skeptical. A sailor's life was cheaper than lime juice. Dr. James Lind made his findings in 1747. It was not until 1795 that the British Admiralty gave sanction to the now famous lime ration—hence the term Limey—but the merchant fleet didn't abandon its skepticism for still another seventy years.

This posed a dilemma, one *Acres U.S.A.* identified as its own. As a sailor or skipper, what would we have done during those seventy years, assuming we had the knowledge? Or the forty-eight years before that? This, indeed, was our editorial dilemma as we sought parity of health—and economic parity. Are we to starve ourselves economically while we stink ourselves to death with cancer? Are we to waste our acres into the streams and the sea while the slow thinkers in white coats resolve their skepticism? At press time each month I was reminded that the experts were skeptical about eco-farming. They said fifty million would starve, and they ignored evidence to the contrary. Earl Butz said God put the worm in the apple, and that man took it out. That, of course, was a Hitler-sized lie. Man put the worm in the apple with inept farming, and he put cancer into that apple as well when he sought to hide his mistake. The predators were what they were, a cleanup crew assigned the task of disposing of production that doesn't measure up to nature's laws of life.

It was a mark of Gene Poirot's genius that he understood the answers long before mainline agriculture even dared ask the right questions.

7

LITERATURE UNDER PRESSURE

"Literature under pressure." That is what Quentin Reynolds, the great WWII news correspondent, once called journalism. It is probably the only really appropriate definition of the newsman's craft ever developed, yet I have never considered the manufacture of paragraphs under the gun real pressure. I used to joke with my wife that if all I had to do was fill the pages of *Acres U.S.A.*, I'd have time to take up aardvark watching. For two years my wife and I ran the paper from the underground bunker at the far end of our basement, and then we moved to another underground office, one that flooded three times before my son Fred and I remodeled a small house for a business headquarters. Subscription money and some few ads kept the operation afloat while I sorted out the direction and thrust of this brand new baby. When revenue faltered a bit, I joined the Ken Stofferahn for Senator camp in South Dakota. Senator Karl Mundt had announced his retirement, hence a five way scramble for the Republican nomination.

Stofferahn had no chance at all, the odds had it. He was an ex-NFO official, short on funds, and almost entirely unknown outside that organization's circle. Former NFO Vice President Erhard Pfingsten was on hand in a Vermillion, South Dakota motel room in late January 1972 when I set down my terms—air fare to and from Kansas City each week, and a small fee I never managed to collect. Late in the evening Pfink held forth on problems in NFO, a discourse that became so vicious and personal in its attack on the NFO leader, I figured the break with Oren Lee Staley was permanent. My small tape recorder was setting on the window sill, but I didn't dare move toward it as Pfingsten unloaded. Nevertheless, I wrote out a memo on what was said before I turned in that night! Ralph Kittleson, Ken Stofferahn and Steve Blomeke—all NFO staffers at one time—were there, and would later confirm the conversation.

Pfingsten said NFO emerged from the ordeal of the 1968 all commodity holding action with financial problems. The action accomplished nothing that straight organization and bargaining could not have delivered. NFO had written some contracts in South Dakota, and organization was moving ahead at a good pace. Several felt the holding action wasn't necessary. But Staley had promised a holding action, and he threw the full weight of his office behind calling a holding action as promised.

"Immediately after the holding action," Pfingsten said, "squads of NFO members went out to raise money. At the time, they gave promissory notes. Money that was collected was dissipated immediately."

As of January-end 1972, Pfingsten figured "not one of the escrow or custodial accounts is in balance." He computed that there was a great shortage. The grain account in particular was out of balance because contracts were written when there was an inability to fill the same. Careless and irresponsible management prevailed everywhere. "God knows what the situation is in dairy," Pfingsten said.

Pfingsten said that there were hundreds of these custodial accounts. Pfingsten, Ken Stofferahn and Jim Horne, among others, wanted to put the many accounts on a computer in a central location so that accounts could be balanced, shortages made up, and the bargaining program pursued with attention to sound accounting principles. "This Staley refused," Pfingsten said. He had no real reasons. He did not seem concerned over the fact that people were being slow-paid, and big sums were lost on bad deals. In 1971 there was another drive for funds. The eyewash reason for the 1971 fund drive, which was accompanied by the issuance of notes payable, was to "war chest" the legal battle with AMPI, the dairy co-op. In meetings throughout the country, members were told that the target figure was $500,000. Actually NFO gathered in something in excess of $1 million, according to Pfingsten, much of it for The Iowa Trust Fund.

In turn, The Iowa Trust Fund was diverted to cover regular NFO expenses. The Securities Exchange Commission ultimately checked on this in a rather oblique way. At a meeting with bank officials, SEC asked three times whether NFO was solvent. The answer each time was, *Well, they're still operating.* Had a question been asked whether funds were being diverted, the bankers would have had to answer. Some aging NFO leaders believe to this day that the government had made the judgment to leave NFO alone. It wasn't going anywhere under Staley.

Pfingsten swore he would never go back to Corning. So Staley agreed to meet with him at Omaha. A ten hour meeting took place in a motel room. Both men argued their points, and finally Pfingsten gained 100% capitulation except for one thing. Pfingsten called for reduction of salaries of high level officials pending a straightening out of the organization's financial mess. This Staley absolutely refused. "It was the only point on which I could not get agreement," Pfingsten said. "It was understood, of course, that the corrective measures would take some time to accomplish." And it was at this point that Pfingsten told Staley he would refuse to run for vice president in December if Staley did not keep his word.

The NFO office got back to normal after that, but Staley took no action. By late summer the funds gathered earlier had been used up. The parting of the ways came a little later on, and the refusal of Pfingsten to run for vice president was the closing chapter. At least that is what Pfingsten thought at the time. Pfingsten said he told Staley, "The time for being friends is over—but we do not have to be enemies."

At the time of our late January meeting in Vermillion, Pfingsten said the "cause" of NFO was being turned into a "greed club" for a few officers. Pfingsten bowed out, making a clean break with Staley. He even nominated Staley's candidate, DeVon Woodland, for vice president. "I did this so I could not be maneuvered into having to nominate Staley," Pfingsten said.

Now he had come to South Dakota to help Stofferahn talk me into helping with the campaign.

It was not my first venture into politics. Two years earlier I helped hammer out press releases and campaign materials for no less than four House candidates in Iowa and Nebraska, two Democrats and two Republicans, using the same stuff for both camps. In Stofferahn's case, the first order of business was getting a little name identification.

STOFFERAHN: Hello, my name is Ken Stofferahn, and I'm running for the U.S. Senate.
LITTLE OLD LADY: What did you say your name was?
STOFFERAHN: Stofferahn. S-T-O-F-F-E-R-A-H-N.

68

LITTLE OLD LADY (laughing): Young man, how do you expect to get elected with a name like that.

It sounded like a good radio spot, but the little old lady selected to handle those twenty-one words blew her line no less than thirteen times before another actress was sought.

I wrote position papers, talks, scripts and the miscellany needed for a campaign until I wore my typing fingers down to the first knuckle, casting things in understandable terms so that they could roll out and provide the candidate with image. Ken Stofferahn was quick, smart, and possessed of good judgment, but he needed orientation.

Yankton, South Dakota is a gem of a town, the kind that might prompt a journalist to settle down. It was something like twenty degrees below zero when Stofferahn and I set up a press conference. I remembered that Ray Dykeman, an old associate, lived there. I greeted him over the phone—"You have a nice town, but gawd it's beastly cold here!" Ray responded, "It certainly is, but it keeps the riff-raff out." Dykeman quit his job at the bank and joined the campaign. By comparing notes we felt we had a handle on what was going on. The great Russian grain trading deal of the early 1970s was in the wind at the time. You could smell it coming, and back home, in *Acres U.S.A.*, I flatly announced the parameters of the game.

The discerning knew something was afoot when the Baltic Exchange started leasing a large number of lake-fitted vessels. The Exchange had been operative since the Industrial Revolution first lured farmers into the cities, even before Adam Smith wrote *The Wealth of Nations,* and called for free trade to break the stranglehold of the landholding nobles on the population. The five great companies in control of global grain all had their origin in the era when the expanding cities of Europe needed "more wheat," wheat from the Crimea, wheat from the lower Volga where my great-grandfather ran an *ambar*, wheat from Canada and the Ganges, wheat from California. Seven families were and are all powerful. They are the Fribourgs at Continental, the Hirsches and Borns at Bunge, the Cargills and MacMillans at Cargill, the Louis Dreyfuses and Andres at the companies with those names. Cargill headquartered in Minneapolis, Continental Grain in New York, Andre in Switzerland, Louis Dreyfus in Paris and Bunge in Buenos Aires. All have meandered over the continents of the world, surviving wars, famines, economic crashes, revolutions, always moving, always changing countries, trading nationalities and religions as well as grain, forming alliances with kings and communists, with any-one and everyone when it suited them. Biographers of the grain trade say these five companies have the greatest newsmen in the world, the finest gatherers of information—all craftsmen who never write a line for publication. Those companies own a resource that runs beyond comprehension—millions of farmer serfs all over the world, among them the farmers of South Dakota.

Stofferahn had his work cut out for him. He had to convince South Dakota that he was one of their own when at the same time his intel-lectual life had parted company with his hoped-for constituents. For one thing, South Dakota's farmers believed themselves independent when in fact they were indentured servants on their own farms. They believed surpluses were killing farm prices when in fact downward manipulated farm prices were creating surpluses. They believed in free international trade, and yet free trade was their nemesis.

In Joseph Heller's famous novel, *Catch 22*, Milo Minderbinder had the job of supplying fresh eggs to the Air Corps mess in Italy. Milo was a very enterprising fellow. He bought the eggs in Malta at seven cents, sold them to the mess in Italy for five cents to impress the Air Corps with his greatheartedness—and he still made a profit. He was a grain trader in spirit, and here's how he operated. Actually Milo bought the eggs in Sicily for one cent "at the hen." He transferred them secretly to Malta, sold them for four and one-half cents, then bought them back for seven cents, then resold them to the Air Corps for five cents. When one of his friends wanted to know how he could do this, Milo ex-plained, "I'm the people I buy them from."

Quite possibly Heller knew a lot about commodity trading. Milo Minderbinder, in fact, operated much like a modern grain company. He functioned in several countries at the same time. He made money on outlandish price fluctuations. He could do this because he alone knew what was going on. He was to Air Corps eggs what Cargill and the rest are to the grain trade—both buyer and seller. Not Milo Min-derbinder, not Cargill, Continental, Bunge, Dreyfus or Andres dedi-cated one atom of their international apparatus to seeing justice done "at the hen."

In any campaign, hardly 20% of the voters develop a defensible ra-tionale for how they vote. The Democrat and Republican labels ab-solve most people from thinking, and few of the rest manage to tune in to what is going on "now." In a state like South Dakota, most people view government and its functionaries with awe and reverence. And the government went to great lengths to develop statistics proving surpluses, supply and demand pressure, on and on. The fact is prices are made where grain is sold in actual physical quantities—in Geneva, Winnipeg, Ottawa, Paris, London, Moscow. Those markets called exchanges simply tell the government about supply and demand balance *after the fact.*

Nor can the governments verify the overview facts. Once, when Tradax was being investigated, the Congressmen were told that under Swiss law Tradax and its employees would be subject to criminal prosecution if they supplied certain items of information to the U.S. government. The government agencies, in turn, like the arrangement because—as one CIA official once testified—"they keep us informed as to what's going on."

The playwright Bertolt Brecht said it all. *Famines do not occur. They are organized by the grain trade.* Hungry people do not make markets in Chicago. The poor do not affect spot prices in Rotterdam. The people who deal "at the hen" affect those prices, and they can profit by fluctuation because they alone have the information. The government knows all this, and it also knows what it should do to protect the egg. But the government has something else in mind. It thinks in terms of a cheap food policy and protectionism for the traders and international financial houses, and the wonderful people who so willingly supply CIA with up-to-date information. The rules are simple enough. Statistical data are changed to keep the prices down. If the wheat inventory falls to six hundred million bushels, the serfs get an embargo. If the feed grain situation looks like it might deliver benefits to the farmer, whammo, there are price freezes. The price freeze of the early 1970s came on not because of a shortage of beef, but because of a shortage of feed grain. The price freeze went into effect as soon as USDA was able to project the corn crop. The projection gave indication of what supplies would be available to be fed the following year. Each of the great storable commodities has a sunset level. When inventories fall to that level, exports stop.

All this was too heady for the political hustings. A good joke probably earned more votes, and Stofferahn simply didn't deliver jokes very well. The absconders seemed to know how to invent myths and make them stick. This put all five candidates at a disadvantage, and stripped the campaign of any real issues.

Some years before that South Dakota campaign, Dr. John Forbes of the college at Carlinville, Illinois badgered me endlessly to wrap up the exchange equation—this business of rural and city parity—in one line that could be told between the tenth and seventh floor on a fast elevator. For months I strained at the chore. It was impossible I told myself. And yet we had this whiplash line under our noses all the time. Lincoln told his administration that if we made the rails for the transcontinental railroad in the U.S., we would have both the rails and the money. If we bought the rails from England, they would have our money and we would have the rails.

The assumptions behind all this are basic. No one in his right mind would so administer an economy that one sector had to become bankrupt to benefit the others. Yet this is what became public policy. The U.S. chased foreign markets and neglected its own, all to administer a cheap food policy and a world order for the traders.

Stofferahn could comprehend this inventory of information, but those he hoped to sell on voting could not.

If only 20% of the voters had a clear rationale for how they voted, then the business of talking issues was only about 20% effective in any case.

I have always taken the position that news belongs to the one who has it, and it is up to this individual to gift it to others. It had long become my habit to find a story almost everywhere, and the South Dakota political scene was no exception. *Acres U.S.A.* carried an interview with Stofferahn, and I unloaded some 10,000 copies of the paper, at my expense, into the South Dakota outback. I don't know whether they helped or hurt. On those plane rides back and forth I could reflect on where we were and where we—meaning *Acres U.S.A.*—were going.

After only a dozen issues, it had become obvious to me eco-agriculture was no plaything for amateurs. In spite of this I detected the movement taking form, gathering speed, and moving ahead. Some people were trying to make the transition to eco-agriculture, and they were failing. Some were proceeding with unrealistic expectations and unreal counsel. In some cases farmers simply walked away. They had been weaned on label reading, toxic rescue chemistry and the killer advantages of sloppy fertilizers, and they could not change. But there were a sizable number who had gone into a holding pattern pending the arrival of better tools with which to make the transition.

Several thousand readers hung on every word as we told the story of the empire building, soil destroying machine called the moldboard plow. They followed our analysis when we explained how faltering farm production caused farmers to seek virgin lands out West. That, in effect, was the agronomist's advice before the founding of the U.S. Department of Agriculture—go West, young man, go West. New land would replace worn out land in a big country. Our blend was strictly

Albrecht and Poirot—and it was expanding.

Then came the day when land was gone, and the crops faltered again. USDA advanced the idea that low yields were due to the poisoning effects of excreta left by previous crops. Science said that if corn followed corn, and more corn followed that corn, this poisoning effect would take hold. Research plots indeed revealed that rotation would sustain and improve crop production. And after a while the crops began to falter again.

In the meantime, those who read nature pointed out that the bluestem prairie had followed bluestem for thousands of years without poisoning the soil, and in some countries of Europe specific crops had followed specific crops for centuries.

At the University of Illinois, Dr. Cyrus Hopkins and other chemists proved that inorganic elements such as calcium or phosphate were necessary for abundant growth. They found that symbiotic bacteria lived on the roots of legumes such as clover, beans and alfalfa, and that these could take nitrogen from the air. And when this was discovered, the scientific era guided by chemical analysis was off and running.

But a great cloud had settled over the land. There was a hot-dry cycle afloat, a depression, and there were dust storms in the West. The Soil Erosion Service came into being, later to be called the Soil Conservation Service. Almost overnight restoration of nutrients became public policy. Lime to the neutral point became the advice—you can't overdo it. As a consequence half the country was overlimed because it needed no lime at all. But a dangerous fiction became established—that pH 7 was ideal. pH designates the degree of acidity or alkalinity, less than seven being acid, higher than seven being alkaline, pH 7 being neutral.

Yet pH 7 was little more than an insurance policy for selling farmers on the "damn fool idea"—Dr. William A. Albrecht would say—of water soluble factory acidulated salt fertilizers, since a non-acid soil could not tap its own nutrients from the rock, even if they were there.

That the salt fertilizers constitute imbalanced nutrition became an *Acres U.S.A.* contention from the start, and imbalanced nutrition—we submitted—brought on nature's disposal crew. Thus the NPK fertilizers in untrained hands became an insurance policy for the sale of chemicals of organic synthesis. Nevertheless the research plots proved that more bins and bushels could be grown with N, P and K. Because of this, two false concepts swept the republics of learning—partial or imbalanced fertilization, and toxic rescue chemistry.

And now if production didn't falter, the land did. Muddy water ran

73

from the fields. A hundred sixty-acre farm's top soil is deposited into the Gulf of Mexico each and every day of the three hundred sixty-five day year. The soil has lost its tilth, and after forty years of the most feverish dam building in the history of man, we still experience the worst Mississippi floods in history.

Then a new menace surfaced to endanger mankind, *Acres U.S.A.* reported. The science that picked up agriculture by its bootstraps had turned to hucksterism, and no longer cared about the biochemistry of immunity seated in fertility management. A mistake was no longer a mistake if ever more powerful chemistry could intervene. As a consequence degenerative metabolic disease became the legacy of a nation. Substances that were teratogenic, mutogenic and carcinogenic became commonplace in, around and on the food supply.

Eco-agriculture stepped forward from the underworld known as the organic movement with the birth of *Acres U.S.A.* Initially it leaned on folklore, common sense—and a measure of science. It appreciated the fact that farming depended on the welfare of a soil system, and its chemical, biological and physical balance. The tools that emerged from the literature of science and the extension that human ingenuity accounted for seemed dazzling in their purity. They serviced the needs of biotic life. They made available nutrients that imbalance had locked up. They were non-toxic and ecologically sound, but!

And there was a big *but.*

Acres U.S.A. had still to develop a definitive rationale for farming that was both economically and ecologically sound. The South Dakota interlude, and all those free hours on airplanes helped.

I lost track of Stofferahn and his NFO friends for a time after that campaign. Once, Ben Stong, the former assistant to Congressman Melcher of Montana, later an adviser with NFO, came to Kansas City as an emissary for Oren Lee Staley. He would like to have me rejoin the effort—like old times—and of course he hinted that *Acres U.S.A.* couldn't survive in any case. My answer was simple and to the point. "Help me and I'll help you," I said. We left it that way. Once only, Staley asked me to go to Washington to meet with Paul McCracken, then head of the Council of Economic Advisers to the President. I prepared a forty-eight page paper for the occasion, and was not surprised when I got less minutes than I had pages. The young economists in the outer office couldn't seem to comprehend the lessons in *Unforgiven,* and were chomping at the bit to abandon the Mecca of their profession and go back to university teaching. McCracken was a different article.

It may be that I was being given the right nods and the proper "I see" responses in order to speed up the presentation, but I had a feeling that McCracken understood this business of monetizing raw materials rather than debt, and mandating parity prices as they moved into trade channels. Otherwise it was always a case of pouring pure smoke money into an economy to achieve inflation, then returning the purchasing power of the government's bond to the people via depression, with the cycles of war and peace geared to the ups and downs of debt money creation. I pointed out that nothing had been learned in two hundred years of American history except that monetizing raw materials at parity meant stability, low unemployment, and both vanished poverty and poverty programs. McCracken responded, "Yes, but how do you do this politically?"

In the summer of 1972 some of the old gang from NFO invited me to a meeting at a small Holiday Inn near the downtown airport in Kansas City. I had no knowledge of an organizational purge then underway, and the cloistered renegades seemed slow to tell me anything. I drank coffee until my kidneys became outraged. I announced that I was leaving. With that I was invited into the inner sanctum. There I was told about a pending trial during which several NFO leaders were to be expelled from the organization.

I had plenty of firsthand information on how Staley used his political clout, how he forced resignations or drummed from the corps those who objected to dictatorial methods, inept programs and a general lack of results. So what else was new?

Early in 1972 it came to the attention of several NFO directors—usually as a result of testimony from former NFO Vice President Erhard Pfingsten—that custodial accounts were not in balance, and that the NFO bank account was being operated without attention to sound accounting principles. Careless and irresponsible management had caused the organization to mount drives for funds, either as stepped-up dues collections, or on a loan basis.

"You'd think the Marx Brothers were running the place," one office regular told me.

Such rumbles were bound to reach even the rank and file. This didn't bother Staley. Since he employed two-thirds of the Board members, their votes were in his pocket. But there were a few who were not on the payroll, and they stood up to be counted. They were Ken Spitzer and Greg Dahners of North Dakota; Robert Speer and Walt Farrar of Kansas; Don Kimball and Don Moskal of Texas; John Oster of South Dakota; and Jack Grimmer of California. Spitzer and Dahners fell

75

into the Staley trap and resigned when pressured by the remaining fifty-one man, Staley-dominated Board of Directors. The six surviving members demanded a fair hearing, not a routine purge.

They employed Van Ballew, a Texas attorney, who promptly informed Staley that the charges were vague and that "a cursory appraisal of the rules of procedure which have been forwarded to said members relative to the hearing . . . in Corning, Iowa, contravene all notions of justice and fair play for the accused members—and offends the conscience of even the average lay person and, in fact, smacks of star chamber proceedings or kangaroo court, if you please."

Mature reflection told me to stand aside, that the coming battle was not my affair, but I became a victim of my own words, not among the rebels, but at home. I had been telling my family about the drift of national economics. I had compared those who stand aside to the Germans at Nuremberg who pleaded innocent because they were doing their duty. The law was not involved here, but a tinge of ethics was. Should I, a former worker with NFO, align myself with the rebels? What about the ethics of journalism? My son Chris responded, "But what about the Nuremberg principle."

He had me there. I understood Oren Lee Staley, his strong points and his weaknesses. I really could not duck the issue with appeal to professional rules when Chris put my feet to the fire, so I decided to help. After all, it would only cost me a few days time producing a paper for the '72 Convention Committee. Willis Rowell, writing in *Mad as Hell*, called our *'72 Convention Report* "a hate paper aimed at destroying Staley." He charged that it "impugned his character, his integrity, his morals and his motives. It tried to stay close to the truth by using innuendos, half truths, and vague accusations." Rowell was an expected stalwart in the Staley camp, and so his evaluation is not surprising. From my chair, the three papers I produced were corking good political pieces, hard hitting and well documented, chiefly with materials that had surfaced in court as part of the big AMPI milk case. They possessed a lethal charm.

I cannot quote the contents here—for want of room—save one item. I still regretted not serving up Eric Hoffer's matchless work to Staley when Phil Allen and I discussed it. Here was a second chance. So I used Hoffer quotes in italics and provided commentary in a Roman typeface to—as Willis Rowell put it—"impugn" the character, integrity, morals and motives of the opposition—thus:

The greatest mass movement expert of them all is Eric Hoffer, the self-educated longshoreman who made it his business to know what made movements tick, what made them succeed, and what made them fail. Let's listen to Hoffer.

No matter how vital we think the role of leadership in the rise of a mass movement, there is no doubt that the leader cannot create the conditions which made the rise of a movement possible.—Eric Hoffer
True enough. The rank and file in NFO know what brought on the organization. They know how government decided to make farming unprofitable. They know how Secretary Ezra Taft Benson pulled the rug too fast, how ten cent hogs arrived. They know that the conditions creating NFO were deep seated. There is hardly a man alive who wouldn't agree with Hoffer, who wrote that the leader "cannot conjure a movement out of the void. When conditions are not ripe, the potential leader, no matter how gifted, and his holy cause, no matter how potent, remain without a following."

Once the stage is set, the presence of an outstanding leader is indispensable. Without him there will be no movement.—Eric Hoffer
True. There was such a leader. First it was a feed salesman, then a cornbelt governor, finally a Missouri farmer with a gift for speaking. Their services during those lonely hours were incredible. They had the credentials required. They didn't know it couldn't be done.

For men to plunge headlong into an undertaking of vast change, they must be intensely discontented yet not destitute. . .they must be wholly ignorant of the difficulties involved in their vast undertaking.—Eric Hoffer
Not one of the farmers who launched NFO understood the tangled web called international finance, or chain store monopoly. Not one realized what they were attempting was rather impossible. Ignorance is bliss when a mass movement starts. It is a curse when a mass movement matures.

There were about eight such exchanges, each more biting than the last.
As the '72 battle reached its climax, Erhard Pfingsten and Butch Swaim remained the mystery men. Pfingsten had exploded against Staley on more than one occasion. Swaim had been more discreet. I

knew he was an intellectual ally, but would he stand up to be counted under pressure? I doubted it.

In any case the '72 Convention Committee made no effort to loop in such powerful help. The other NFO headquarters regulars—men like Meat Commodity Director Bill Lashmett and Negotiator Gordon Shafer, stayed on their own side.

Pfingsten had gone home to his farm at Sergeant Bluffs, Iowa. He had been promised a few speaking engagements, but these soon dried up. When county organizations called into Corning asking for Pfingsten, they were told he was booked up, which was not true. After being in the limelight for so many years, the solitude and abandonment must have proved hard to take. Very few people called him. But as the months wore on, Staley found it more difficult to control the Board of Directors.

Staley became the one who placed long distance phone calls to Erhard Pfingsten. The conversations must have been friendly. Over a period of time, Staley charmed Pfingsten into coming back so he could have help in driving out the traitors. And eventually Pfingsten came back. He assumed a speaking role, and he helped Staley hammer down opposition that might stand up at a national convention. This after all, had been Pfink's role for years—to speak on the circuit, and then to "gift" to Staley the personal popularity his excellent talks had earned for him. On the '72 Convention floor he did just that. I know of no effort to enlist Butch Swaim.

'72 Convention Committee foundered. Staley took the first round when the Convention voted to uphold the Board's expulsion of the six accused directors. This removed Don Kimball as a candidate for president of the NFO. Only at the last moment was a new candidate, Bill Struckmeyer of California, selected to oppose Staley. I drafted an address, and he used most of it—warning the body politic that it would not be good enough to discover a month from then that "this was the last chance." The decision had to be made within the hour.

By the time the battle was joined, Pfingsten and Swaim were well in tow. They stood with Staley, solid as a slab of granite.

Within weeks after that failed effort, the mails brought home the consequences. I was forced to answer a long deposition under oath.

Apparently Staley wanted to know how come we scrapped an entire edition of '72 *Convention Report,* and the lawyers spent all day and a two hundred forty-four page deposition finding out. When the key question came, I handed over both versions of the paper. In an interview, Stofferahn had answered a question about The Queen, Doris Peterson. On tape he responded to my question, "Did Doris Peterson really resign at one time?" "Yes, she did," was Stofferahn's answer. "She arrived at her conclusion—that the situation was almost hopeless—on her own. She knew that the things leveled against me and others were absolutely false. This disgusted her so much that she wrote a letter of resignation and presented it to Staley around the [time of the] Kansas City convention. He finally lured her back by working at it twenty-four hours a day."

At the latest hour Stofferahn insisted on that paragraph being deleted. He did not want to embarrass Peterson, and accordingly 20,000 fresh copies were trundled into a paper drive, and the edition reprinted too late to be of value.

And there was the matter of my subscribers. "Send my money back," wrote one after the other amid a sulfurous hailstorm of criticism. More frequently the messages were simply refusals to renew subscriptions because I "was no friend of the farmer." Most of those who cancelled out not only thought the same way, they expressed themselves in exactly the same language. I recognized the modus operandi. Butch Swaim was handling the coordinated "get Chuck Walters" effort.

Arnold Paulson was probably the best friend NFO ever had. His economic messages cracked more impenetrable territories than all the other voices for NFO put together. But for some reason Paulson came under suspicion, Eric Hoffer style. After that NFO set up meetings across the country, time and location to coincide with Paulson's seminars. Butch Swaim coordinated them all. I had a hard time forgiving Butch for that, and I had a hard time accepting his opposition in late '72 and all of '73. But time intervened, and when the word came down that Butch was dying, I made a special trip to Corning to see him.

His hair had fallen out in homage to chemotherapy, and he eliminated through a tube in his side. He was now a shadow of a man. We talked of the good times, and before we parted he blessed the new effort, *Acres U.S.A.* He didn't scold me for Convention '72, and I didn't scold him. He said he understood, and he hoped I understood.

I tried to cheer up the hour. I told Butch about a French battalion, men and officers, that broke and ran in battle. Word came down from General Headquarters to execute four soldiers for this cowardice. The commandant pondered the order and decided to draw lots. In due time four French soldiers were stood before a stone wall to be shot. One objected with tears in his eyes. His honor was at stake. He had been in sick bay the day of the battle. Why should he be included? The commandant answered. "But you would have run had you been there.

79

Don't you understand, my good man, *there's nothing personal in this.*"

Butch smiled. I think he understood, certainly he knew that time had run out for him. Within a few weeks he was gone. The NFO survived—but barely! For the great movement had spent itself, leaving the old way of doing things in charge of the field. As for myself, I returned to the business of soils, human nutrition and ecological farming.

Stofferahn remained in politics, and finally became the Commissioner of Utilities for South Dakota and a candidate for governor.

Most of the personalities in this news story dropped out of sight after 1972, some to farm, others to venture beyond agriculture. Bill Lashmett left NFO when a successful organizational effort in red meat was scuttled by Staley because the NFO president felt that "if it isn't stopped, they'll take over at the next convention," Lashmett said. He later became interested in eco-agriculture, established a field testing operation, and in the mid-'80s materialized at an *Acres U.S.A.* conference.

Jack Grimmer continued to operate his grain, rice and mosquito farm near Arbuckle, California. I last saw him on a quick trip to Sacramento. He was doing his best to plug *Acres U.S.A.* Other "tried and convicted" NFOers did the same.

Bill Struckmeyer, the last-minute challenger to Oren Lee Staley in 1972, retired from farming, then died in a tragic small plane crash, probably the victim of downdraft.

Doris Peterson retired, leaving Staley undefended.

Oren Lee Staley's demise came when the bank "ordered" the NFO Board of Directors to dismiss him or be foreclosed. Staley uncorked the charm that had worked so well on Erhard Pfingsten and Doris Peterson. The bank stood fast. After he was removed, and DeVon Woodland became president, Staley remained in his office as though the unreal wasn't true. He left about a week later.

Erhard Pfingsten returned to his farm and retired, remembered for his speeches and for the fact that he shunned greatness.

8

PERMISSION FOR LIFE

Acres U.S.A. achieved a definite style quite early. Its front page almost always featured a big story that was not being told.

BUTZ VS. ORGANIC FARMING

read one banner headline in those early issues. Others . . .

THE ROMAN ROAD TO RUIN
LOCKER CLOSINGS SWEEP NATION
CROPS WITHOUT POISONS
MORE DANGEROUS THAN ATOMIC BOMBS
BIOLOGICAL PRINCIPLES IN FARMING

Letters to the editor were answered, sometimes at great lengths. *Acres U.S.A.* has seldom printed run of the mill letters. Almost all have contained substance, and in each case the challenge or commentary has led to my in-depth response. There were letters commenting on *Roe* vs. *Wade*, the Supreme Court's ruling on abortion. One by Lilly Belle Baima of Nevada City, California rattled the cages, speaking out against "the horrible abortion laws which were destroying children in mothers' wombs, and making wombs unfit and impotent." The *Acres U.S.A.* response was several times longer than the original letter, and represented the only instance in which I handled a major issue in a letter-to-the-editor response.

"We have been told by high court judges that the Supreme Court decision was a blow for women's freedom," my response read. "If *Acres U.S.A.* recalls correctly, the first major case came out of Texas. Since the slow pace of court action could not force a decision in time, the woman in question carried her child to term, and a healthy baby girl was born. *Acres U.S.A.* would like to see that young lady—now a grown woman—before the judges. We would like to hear explained to that young lady how a more speedy decision in her case, denying her permission for life, would have been such a great blow for freedom." And as icing for the cake, *Acres U.S.A.* ran an instant replay, comparing slavery to abortion. It had appeared as an ad in *The New York Times.*

This was my Jesuit training speaking together with its heavy emphasis on natural law. Under natural law the end never justifies the means, and there are certain absolutes, things that are absolutely right or wrong. I have long been a fan of Arthur Koestler, the author of *Darkness at Noon,* and I can identify with a statement he first made in a BBC broadcast series in 1947. "I am not sure whether what the philosophers call ethical absolutes exist," he said, "but I am sure that we have to act as if they existed." Koestler explained the dilemma in terms of Captain Scott's march to the South Pole.

Captain Robert Falcon Scott and four companion explorers reached the South Pole on January 18, 1912 after marching for sixty-nine days. While returning to base camp, Petty Officer Evans took a fall and was disabled. Scott was forced to make a decision that was at least as moral as logistic. He either carried Evans and slowed the march at risk to all, or he left the sick explorer to die in the trackless snows. Scott decided to carry Evans on one of the sleds until he died. Then blizzards caught up with them. Six months later the frozen bodies of Scott's party were found a mere eleven miles from their supply depot.

Scott could have followed the path of expediency—that the end justifies the means—and denied Evans permission for life. Would not sacrifice of one be justified by saving four? The problem is that this road, soon enough, meanders into politics. Evans becomes Czechoslovakia, and Neville Chamberlain sacrifices one small nation to purchase the safety of bigger ones. As we march on along this end-justifies-the-means road, the first Munich leads to the second—the Ribbentrop-Molotov Pact, and the Polish people go the way of the Czechs. Now the Evanses number in the millions. Next, the German government invokes the same logic in order to annihilate the infirm and mentally retarded. Are they not a drag on the national sled, and rations are low? After the incurable and mentally retarded come those with unac-

INSTANT REPLAY

A B O R T I O N 1972	S L A V E R Y 1857
Although he may have a heart and a brain, and he may be a human life biologically, an unborn baby is not a **legal** person. Our courts will soon make that clear.	Although he may have a heart and a brain, and he may be a human life biologically a slave is not a **legal** person. The Dred Scott decision by the U.S. Supreme Court has made that clear.
A baby only becomes a **legal** person when he is born. Before that time, we should not concern ourselves about him because he has no legal rights.	A black man only becomes a **legal** person when he is set free. Before that time, we should not concern ourselves about him because he has no legal rights.
If you think abortion is wrong, then nobody is forcing you to have one. But don't impose your morality on somebody else!	If you think that slavery is wrong, then nobody is forcing you to be a slave-owner. But don't impose your morality on somebody else!
A woman has a right to do what she wants with her own body.	A man has a right to do what he wants with his own property.
Isn't abortion really something merciful? After all, every baby has a right to be wanted. Isn't it better never to be born than to be sent alone and unloved into a cruel world? (Spoken by someone already born)	Isn't slavery really something merciful? After all, every black man has a right to be protected. Isn't it better never to be set free than to be sent unprepared, and ill-equipped, into a cruel world? (Spoken by someone already free)

83

ceptable genes—the Gypsies and Jews, six million of them from all over Europe, if we are to believe Adolf Eichman. Then the ethical ball is passed to the U.S. and Harry S. Truman orders the first atomic bombs dropped on the crowded cities of Hiroshima and Nagasaki, thereby accepting something all Americans had previously condemned—indiscriminate warfare on civilian populations, children and women included. Next, the Supreme Court, using convoluted logic, conjures up new laws to permit the slaughter of new human life, eighteen million of them, or three times the number annihilated by Eichmann since *Roe* vs. *Wade*. Surely abortion will absolve us from having a crowded planet!

We know of course what happened to Scott and his associates because they sought to have the means determine the end. And we can guess the results if Mohandas K. Gandhi's concept of non-resistance had been invoked to deal with the Japanese invaders of WWII.

I was not prepared to argue that this dilemma had a solution when *permission for life* joined *toxic genetic chemicals* and *parity* as prime issues for the pages of *Acres U.S.A.* Hard decisions seem inseparable from the human condition: without a revolution, no America; without the revolt of the Barons, no Magna Carta! It may be suggested that the end justifies the means only within narrow limits. A surgeon might use the knife on a single patient because the outcome is somewhat certain. But the knife on the entire body politic involves too many unknowns. Too soon the scalpel becomes a butcher's hatchet, and the surgeon an Eichmann.

Abortion and its blood brothers—infanticide and euthanasia—have gained the same respectability in Western society they had in pagan Rome. The Christian revolution, apart from its religious character, was really a social revolution against the frightful excesses of Rome.

The populations that were despoiled, enslaved, tortured—and the relics of barbarism—abortion, infanticide and euthanasia—conspired to make Christianity leap from the depths of the abyss. There was no prospect of Christianity leaping from the abyss when the Supreme Court made its *Roe* vs. *Wade* decision. There was some lip service on the permission for life issue, but little more.

The most sensitive and most personal area of morality is sex, and for this reason it was chosen for attack by the people who believe that the end justifies the means. With the help of liberal Christians, they also chose the same area for an assault on Christian values. Demythologizing the Scriptures became the new nomenclature, and it was applied to everything from doctrine to history.

I do not think many people understand how far this agenda for demythologizing extends. Apparently it seeks to leave no religious stone standing. It hopes to vanquish all moral absolutes. That is why there is really no basis for compromise between the orthodox and the liberals. The latter simply have to call into question everything heretofore believed, including the right-to-life. I didn't think I could deal with this in a monthly newspaper—hence a snappy response to an *Acres U.S.A.* Zip letter. Yet the matter of permission to life was never out of mind.

In any case, there was a terrible airlessness, a feeling of suffocation, that attended bringing the *Acres U.S.A.* message to the surface. Once, I addressed members of the Jackson County, Missouri Fruit Growers Association. Hostility fairly crackled in the air. My opening lines, read a decade or more later, suggest the tone of the times.

"Gentlemen, I would further amplify the introduction that I have received. I am not a farmer or a fruit grower. I am not a professor or an expert in pomology. I am simply a reporter. It is axiomatic in my profession that you can't stay in the newspaper game by ignoring the news."

The news I had to offer came couched in suitable terms. I told about a new art, foliar nutrition, established for over a decade on the West Coast with hardly a land grant college being aware of it. I reported on seed treatment and anchored everything to the findings on Sanborn Field, and in due time I summarized that the anatomy of insect and weed control was seated in fertility management, and not in more powerful goodies from Monsanto or Dow Chemical. The term *organic* did not pass my lips for a valid reason. Farmers simply rejected the idea sight unseen. They viewed organic farming as folklore and the babblement one finds among little old ladies in garden shoes. Thousands of Extension people on the federal payroll had sold that proposition. The United States Department of Agriculture—vastly concerned with its client corporations in the international grain trade—had turned its "sneer" technicians loose on organics. They were polished experts in administering the down-turned glance and the wry smile. It made less sophisticated farmers on the receiving end feel like peasants up to their armpits in mud.

When spring arrived each year, it awoke first in the voices of birds, the buds of trees, the glands of men—and in the metro dailies with attacks on organiculture. Metro farm editors, and even those serving the industrially owned farm magazines, do not report on technology not approved by that nebulous entity known as "the university," just as writers in the National Association of Science Writers do not presume to comprehend the subject they cover, and suffer having everything they report cleared with their betters.

The betters, in the 1970s, issued their clumsy attacks each spring, and each spring *Acres U.S.A.* became locked in deadly combat with Extension agents, Departments of Agriculture and universities across the country. This was not as difficult as it seems. Usually someone would initiate a broadside. It would be passed from one state or agency to another, and reissued over a different signature state by state. The great leaders of American agriculture not only thought alike, they sent their individually signed messages to the farmers in exactly the same words.

Farm Bureau and young farmers' groups indulged themselves in single factor analysis in those days. Usually they took two worn out plots, planted both, and waited to discover that nature, alone, did a poor job. The managed plot was fertilized, irrigated and weeded. The other was left alone. In due time the curse of the amateur emerged in papers like *Omaha World-Herald*, with a proclamation that nature, alone, did a poor job. *Crops and Soils* magazine, and North Dakota State Extension were particularly vicious in their published distortions, which prompted paragraph by paragraph refutations.

I had met C.J. Fenzau almost a year before he wrote *Exploding the Chemical Myths*, an article he offered to *Crops and Soils*, where it was rejected. In due time it appeared on the front page of *Acres U.S.A.*

"There are few, if any, truly trained soil nutritionists who are able to understand or present any comprehensive judgment, other than mere lip-service, to the standard viewpoints that are important to soil bacteria, earthworms, soil drainage, tilth, structure, and particularly, the true function of organic materials in the soil system. After all, organic matter converts, regulates and releases nutrients to the biological systems of the soil from which man has originally evolved. His creation and permission to life is profoundly linked to this biotic beginning," wrote Fenzau. And he added, "Nature's way is biological. It is a combination both chemical and organic."

What C.J. Fenzau was saying had become obvious during the first year or so of *Acres U.S.A.* reporting. We often talked about that dichotomy, and now C.J. Fenzau expressed it in matchless sentences.

"The chemical industry has accumulated a body of knowledge and financial capacity to sustain the chemical system. On the other hand, the amateurs of organic systems have accumulated amateur knowledge to teach others to be good amateurs. We have few professional producers of food and fiber because, in the absence of adequate compensation and/or profit, they have not been able to support or develop a responsible body of knowledge that could define the ultimate biological system of life."

Obviously, the chemical and organic systems were both essential. Both had an important role in nourishing plant life. Yet neither was capable of doing a proper, sustained job without an ecologically balanced soil system. It infuriated C.J. when authorities and farm leaders expounded the merits of one system or another. "Neither group is willing to comprehend the full meaning of nature's way of providing biological products for the biological sustenance of all forms of life." Fenzau went on to note that this concept was detoured by "von Liebig's Law of the Minimum in 1848, and has been fully perpetuated by science, by institutions, by laws, and by commercialization, none of which have to account to nature or give credentials to life."

Clarence J. Fenzau and I were the same age approximately. He was working with Doane Agricultural Services while I was doing graduate work at the University of Denver. His agricultural career dated back to 1949, and touched almost every aspect of scientific management and planning from that day forward. His career figured in the development of dairy and livestock systems, trace minerals research, machinery design, silage and hay storage programs, crop fertility management and maintenance of improved farming concepts. His original developments included loose housing dairy and bulk milk handling systems, bunker silo and self-feeding systems, rotation pasture systems, management of soils to better utilize water, and numerous original tillage tool designs—such as big discs, Rip-'n-Ridger, twin row planters, mulching tools, flotation tires and pull type fertilizer spreaders.

He was the most responsive man I've ever interviewed. His answers were always to the point and framed in well structured sentences. He was a regular Clarence Darrow with words, with this exception. Darrow could compose well only on his feet. His writing took on the labored rhythm of a workhorse used beyond conscience. C.J. Fenzau wrote and spoke equally well.

C.J. Fenzau's partner for many years was Don Schriefer, a vocational agriculture teacher turned agronomist and consultant. Neither Schriefer nor Fenzau were what one might call "folklore organic." They worked in tandem translating the lessons that had emerged from over three decades of practice into understandable terms. Both opted toward the eco-farming concept *Acres U.S.A.* was reporting and developing because farm production had become an entanglement of unrelated, single-shot inputs, and there was no systematic approach to production. Few if any farmers had come to know the interrelationship of sands, silts and clays, and how they interacted and affected water-holding capacity, fertility management and fertility placement—the do's and don't's of fertilization, in short. Moreover, the farmer had to understand the soil chemistry, how to read a soil audit. Seat of the pants knowledge was fine, but it was obsolete.

Schriefer and Fenzau walked hand in hand with Dr. William A. Albrecht in counseling against liming for the sake of pH. They walked farmers through the heady exercise called knowing when certain phosphate fertilizers could not be used because the soils locked them up. Schriefer had done his graduate work on tillage, and it was to tillage that he turned first in bringing a farm to peak performance. Compaction was the farmer's first problem. In dozens of issues and several *Acres U.S.A.* conferences, Don Schriefer helped tell the story. His taped interviews became verbatim fare for our readers.

"There are two things that counteract gravity," he said. "Number one is the product in the soil we call humus. Humus, as you well know, is the end result of complete decomposition of residue. Humus coats soil particles. It expands and contracts, and acts as a shock absorber between soil particles to prevent them from locking horns and touching each other the way they do in the subsoil. The second thing that counteracts the force of gravity is the agent for making humus, namely biological activity in the soil. When bacteria go to work they cause a coating of soil particles around the colony that is developing. They pull soil particles into a granular structure. They build a ventilation system into the soil. They protect the soil from going anaerobic and losing its oxygen supply, which bacteria in turn totally depend on. So they protect themselves. And their ventilation systems benefit crops."

Schriefer's thinking became so important to our view of permission to life that dozens of articles, conversations and extracts from his book, *From the Soil Up*, came to fill our pages. For what Schriefer was saying was transparently obvious. Management of air, water, and decay figured first and foremost before a definitive tillage system could be designed. Management of fertilization was way down the line. At conferences, with tapes, and in interviews, Schriefer told our readers just about everything there was to know about the role of temperature, barometric pressure, rainfall and gas diffusion in the management of soil air. His workshops and text dealt with subjects rarely found in books on agronomy—carbon, soil oxygen, compaction, surface insoak, water penetration into subsoil, and the rule of fence post.

The fence post rots near the surface of the soil, and that is the zone in which decay must be managed. The trip of the plant from the soil up is governed by how well the farmer handles those few inches and its billions of residents, the soil bacteria.

Since the advent of herbicides [counseled Don Schriefer], farmers have been conditioned to believe that cultivation is an unnecessary operation. This seemed to be a logical conclusion since cultivation was used primarily as a weed control operation. In many soil types and conditions, proper cultivation can contribute substantially to greater yields. Improper cultivation under similar conditions can also reduce yields. Soil types and conditions vary greatly. Limitation of time and size of operations all enter into the decision making process. Here are some guidelines for study and consideration.

1. The roots of row crops like natural soil firmness. Roots will not enter a wheel track or any other compaction area. These areas lack sufficient oxygen to permit root extension.

2. Deep cultivation destroys roots. You cannot afford to disturb the roots on any annual plant. Deep cultivation smears the soil colloids, causes excessive drying and creates large air pockets. Roots will not enter these areas until the soil firms up after considerable rainfall. For this reason a rolling cultivator or flat shallow sweeps must be recommended. A rolling cultivator puts finer soil around the base of the plant.

3. Soils must breathe. Changes in barometric pressures and the alternating heating and cooling of soil and air causes air to enter or exit the soil. This process is essential to getting carbon dioxide out of the soil and oxygen in for root growth, uptake of nutrients and biological activity. When the soil is short of oxygen, yields suffer.

4. The surface layer, one to two inches deep, is the area that limits soil breathing. Even though a tight soil has adequate moisture, a rainfall can stimulate plant growth because rain absorbs oxygen and carries it into the soil. This fresh load of oxygen permits roots to immediately increase the uptake of nutrients. Corn standing in flood waters will start to wilt as soon as the oxygen supply in the water runs out. The water or nutrients can't be taken in if the roots can't get oxygen.

5. A tight surface permits the capillary water column to reach the surface and evaporate thus creating excessive loss of soil moisture. A

loose mulch decreases evaporation and reduces weed seed germination.

6. Hilling corn or soybeans will stimulate the covered nodes to shoot out two or more sets of roots thus increasing the total root volume. This also permits new roots to bypass any plugged basal nodes.

7. Herbicides have side effects. It has been shown that herbicides retard the soil bacterial systems. They will also reduce yields and may add toxins to the food chain.

8. It is up to the farmer to minimize and make unnecessary the use of all toxic chemicals.

9. Nitrogen can be applied at time of cultivation whenever necessary. This is the most efficient nitrogen application system when the natural nitrogen cycle is not working at optimum level.

The last line in almost every *Acres U.S.A.* issue was that there is nothing occult about science. And we added, there was nothing occult about the rationales constructed by the grant receivers to protect the commerce of their patrons. As our lessons unfolded, certain principles emerged, each dazzling in the purity of its challenge. These principles took on the air of a credo, one I recited, proved out and refurbished month after month as a reason for being, and a goal to be followed fearlessly and without vascillation.

1. Simplistic nitrogen, phosphorus and potassium (N, P and K) fertilization means malnutrition for plants, animals and men because either a shortage or marked imbalance of plant nutrients prevent balanced plant health and therefore animal and human health.

2. Plants in touch with exchangeable soil nutrients needed to develop proper fertility loads, structure, and stabilized internal hormone and enzyme potentials, provide their own protection against insect, bacterial and fungal attack.

3. Insects and nature's predators are a disposal crew. They are summoned when they are needed, and they are repelled when they are not needed.

4. Weeds are an index of the character of the soil. It is therefore a mistake to rely on herbicides to eradicate them, since these things deal with effect, not cause.

5. Crop losses in dry weather, or during mild cold snaps, are not so much the result of drought and cold as nutrient deficiency.

6. Toxic rescue chemistry hopes to salvage crop production that is not fit to live so that animals and men might eat it, always with

consequences for present and future generations of plants, animals and men.

7. Man-made molecules of toxic rescue chemistry do not exist in nature's blueprints for living organisms. Since they have no counterpart in nature, they will not likely break down biologically in a time frame suitable to the head of the biotic pyramid, namely man. Carcinogenic, mutagenic and teratogenic molecules of toxic rescue chemistry have no safe level and no tolerance level.

This summary, I believe, stacked up like any college syllogism. NPK formulas as legislated (and enforced by State Departments of Agriculture) mean malnutrition, insect, bacterial and fungal attack, toxic rescue chemistry, weed takeover, crop loss in dry weather, and general loss of mental acuity—plus degenerative metabolic disease—among the population, all when people use thus fertilized and protected food crops. Therefore the answer to pest crop destroyers is sound fertility management in terms of exchange capacity, pH modification, and scientific farming principles that USDA, Extension and Land Grant colleges have refused to teach ever since the great discovery was made that fossil fuel companies have grant money.

In the one hundred forty plus issues of *Acres U.S.A.* that went to press between our first meeting and C.J. Fenzau's last appearance at a St. Joseph, Missouri meeting—the one at which John Anderson announced his non-candidacy for President of the U.S. for 1984—readers became the beneficiaries of Fenzau's amazing insight and knowledge. Because of his in-depth criticism, help with certain passages and because he stood as a technical guardian over *An Acres U.S.A. Primer*, I asked him to by-line the book with me. In one of the last chapters, we quoted from his *Exploding the Chemical Myths*.

"When living life emerges into an ultimate objective of our nation," wrote Fenzau, "only then can we begin to construct the understanding of the ecology of the soil and be able to benefit from its minuteness and wondrous patience. Nature has no limit on time. She is patient and forgiving. She is able to repair herself from the ignoble treatment of man in spite of his tremendous physical capacity for destruction. As we continue to replace nature, we assuredly prevent the development of our mental capacity to learn and fully complement nature—a requirement expected from us—in permission for life. Apparently the growing interest of many farmers in searching for answers reflects the beginning of an intellectual attitude in conflict with agronomic science and industry. This virgin knowledge is finally emerging as a test and challenge to the introverted and integrated industrial exploiters, and absconders of our most precious resource."

I could not help marveling at Fenzau's grasp of natural law. He never tired of pointing out that nature opts for new life. She lets the fittest survive. She does not use her resources saving worn-out life. Only man opts to spend his resources installing new kidneys, hearts and blood vessels in those suffering from degenerative metabolic disease, at the same time visiting death when birth cries threaten. Such an evaluation made C.J. conscious of his own predicament.

"Our population cannot survive on pre-1930s organics alone, but neither is it healthfully surviving through chemicals either. Witness the millions of livestock that are carcassed to rendering factories across our land. Then witness the overflowing hospitals treating the symptoms and diseases which could be averted by wholesome and nutritionally ripe foods. Witness the billions spent on fuels and dryers to take water from physiologically immature grain crops, the nutrients of which were not able to fully mature into nature's intended ripeness. Animals and people cannot experience health and ripeness in life from this type of food. Through chemistry, we can too hopefully keep trying, but it is futile.

"Witness the cost of keeping sick plants alive in the sick, sick soils of our nation, and yet we have the audacity to simply treat this problem with NPK aspirin tablets while we close our eyes to the actual causes of these diseases and problems. No, the aspirin treatment is not the answer either, because with ineffective life in these sick soils, nature is not able to supply adequate calcium, humus or water to all regions. Neither can the proper decay of organic materials be accomplished. Organic composting illustrates this weakness of nature also— and out of sheer economic impracticality, we cannot compost all of our land either. We must learn how to make every acre a compost acre— and this is not done by chemicals or by organics. We must create a unity of both to permit the biological system to work. Herein must lie our fundamental objective."

He came to the St. Joseph, Missouri *Acres U.S.A.* Conference in 1983 to say goodbye. His fire was now a fading glow. His health had worsened suddenly, and his charm and wit had turned into a whisper. He recited anew the principles we had assembled and set down in short staccato lines. Rapid adoption of these principles was something devoutly to be wished, he said.

C.J. Fenzau was so dedicated to these objectives that he fell for what I call the "Arab money scam." Hard on the heels of the oil crisis, a new breed of hustlers crossed and recrossed America. They were Arabs or represented Arabs. They had lots of money. Sometimes they drew hapless farmers, businessmen, even Congressmen into deals. The end product was frequently a prison term, the key Arab vanishing. I have long suspected that these forays were nothing more than promotion devices for government gumshoes. Once a sentence is handed out, the proper papers go into the proper dossier, and a promotion follows. I have known several farmer-promoters caught up in one of these backfiring schemes and visited with them after they served their time.

C.J. Fenzau was tormented during the last years of his life by the dangling carrot called Arab money. They would set up the educational facility he wanted. They would earmark farms for research on biological principles. They would arrange parity markets for parity crops. They were so strong they could pick up the national debt. The problem was, C.J. was honest and never tumbled for anything that wasn't signed, sealed and delivered properly. So the papers were always to be closed next month, next week, tomorrow, this afternoon, whatever. The target hours never arrived. There was always an excuse: a political problem in the Sudan, a change in ministry in Saudi Arabia, trouble with exchange transfers. This went on for four years. I tried to tell C.J. to walk away, but he couldn't, not from a Never-Never Land that held so much promise.

He passed from the scene in the sixtieth year of his life—and *Acres U.S.A.* missed his reliable counsel after that. Agriculture will never again miss his wisdom. It has become part of a new agriculture that can no longer be delayed or stopped. This is his legacy.

9

FED TO LIVE PEACEFULLY

It did not bother Albert Carter Savage that the university people disparaged him. "The university people," he said with a tolerant smile, "can't do anything to me. They don't know enough." Indeed, most of them merely read books. Albert Carter Savage wrote them. In the twilight of his life, he was willing for them to read his *Mankind's Folly*, and his *Mineralization, a New Basis for Proper Nutrition*, and learn from each.

Dr. Albert Carter Savage talked about these things one day when I came by. That was his way. He talked as he and I walked from his mineralized garden across his mineralized fields and came to his Kentucky terraces that caught the rainfall and drained it to settling ponds so that not a drop would flow away. The banks of the ponds were piled high with hundreds of tons of mineralized settlings that had been scraped by a bulldozer from the pond bottoms in the dry season—enough, he said, to mineralize 10,000 acres.

Albert Carter Savage passed from the scene in late 1974, hardly three years after *Acres U.S.A.* was founded. He had become an international figure in soil management, but he was well ahead of his time. His basic work on mineralization received the full treatment—removal from libraries, threats from agribusiness, and finally obscurity. His formulas were rather general, but he nevertheless hit a balanced concoction with the simplest of rocks, all of which were available near Lexington, Kentucky in such quantity that it was difficult to exploit that resource. The rocks were Kentucky Devonian oil shale, potash marle, secondary fossiliferous limestone (famous for making race horses fast and strong) and raw rock phosphate. These, in combination with manure or compost provided a powerful fix for the soil and those who ate the food from it.

Savage was more than a soil scientist. He understood geology, anthropology, history, geography, the whole gamut. When he spoke, the soil, animals and wise men listened, but not the university people. Albert Carter Savage said there was healing in the plants, and he was rewarded with laughter and an academic smirk from the university folk. He often stood in his mineralized acres where the lambsquarter was head-high and the hog weeds thrived, weeds that men of little wisdom mowed and cast into furnaces with thorns and thistles. Savage argued that with fit soil to feed upon, certain weeds were food containing strength for the weak, and relief for the afflicted.

Savage grew three crops each year, but then his plots were furbished and refurbished with minerals that the soil had to have to fulfill its mission. Lesser men robbed the soil, not so much because they were rascals, but because they were ignorant. Always, Albert Carter Savage hoped to teach men something about building it back. This was his reason for being, and he came by it quite naturally.

It was a long drive across Kentucky to the small Lexington holdings of Albert Carter Savage, but C.J. Fenzau had referred me there for a story that wasn't being reported. The old gentleman started talking the minute I arrived, and my ever-present tape recorder captured his words. Edited and condensed, what he said came out approximately as follows in *Acres U.S.A.*

When Savage was a young boy, he wanted to know *why*? What makes things grow? The answer he got didn't satisfy him. Grown older, he saw around him imperfect plants and animals and people. He looked at the sky to find the fault and discovered no flaw. There was perfection at the top of the world. There must be, it seemed to him something wrong at the bottom. Industrial pollution hadn't fogged the whole country yet.

If plants did not thrive it was not because of the air that they breathed, surely. So it must be because their roots were not nourished. He was just a lad when he realized that, for he was precocious. His great uncle, Dr. Charles Savage, had recognized his precocity and had stimulated it by giving him test-tubes containing colored chemicals, instead of toys, to play with. His parents provided him with laboratory equipment of a sort before he was eight. As a high school pupil, in a better laboratory that he had fitted up in the barn loft, he brooded over the mysteries of chemistry, seeking answers to his questions.

He came to know that the rock in the soil had something to do with the growth of plants. In the beginning there had been abundance of rock and the soil had been rich. But it had been robbed of its richness and more weathered rock was needed to replenish it. His father gave him a little piece of land. He crushed rock and spread it out. The vegetables that he grew were better than his father's. He had something there but it was not enough.

He saw animals languish and waste away and human beings sicken and die before their time. His father died and his great uncle died. He asked the doctors why this was so, and they couldn't tell him except that disease had fastened upon them and they had gone the way of all flesh. It was the law of life that found its fulfillment only in death.

Their answers didn't satisfy him. There must be a better reason. There must be a fault somewhere that the doctors hadn't found. It wasn't in the sky. It might be in the ground. Plant life, he knew, was the product of soil, air, sunshine and water. The air elements were constant and shiftable. The sunshine was changeless. The soil elements were inert and stayed where they were except as they were displaced or washed away. The soil was subject to deterioration by natural agencies and unnatural uses, necessitating restoration of its elements. Restoration had been neglected, then there had been deterioration of the plants because of the deficiencies of the soil upon which they fed.

Animals fed upon the plants and human beings fed upon the animals and the plants. Could not the basic deficiencies be in that manner communicated to animals and human beings? Savage was satisfied that they could be and that they were, but he knew that he had to prove it. For years the man applied himself with consuming fervor to the proving of what he knew to be true. There were countless experiments and tests that, by their progressive revelations, strengthened his faith.

Not until 1942 did he write the testament of his faith, though many knew of his work and numbers had claimed benefits in health and well-being from the mineralized foods that he offered without money and without price. The pamphlet that he privately printed he called *Mineralization.*

On the title page he anxiously asked. "Will It Reach You In Time?" The booklet told of the mineral garden that had been planted in Jessamin County, Kentucky, "where the vitally important but rarer minerals and metals, as well as the common ones, are supplied to the soil, balanced and proportioned to the needs of the soil, the plant, and thus, in turn, to the needs of the animals and humans consuming the vegetables." The book set forth solemnly the inescapable conclusion from extensive tests that "all life can be and is now completely controlled by the amounts, kinds, proportions, combines and preponderances and arrangements of the chemical elements in the soil."

The human body, it was pointed out, was in vital need of the "trace" mineral elements, as well as the better known common ones. These elements are noticeably lacking or insufficiently present in the plant and animal food of the nation, with the result that there is slow starvation, gradual weakening of the body cells and susceptibility to infectious diseases or organic weaknesses, and accordingly national deterioration. Appealing to the proofs of science that 90% of all diseases come from nutritional or chemical deficiencies, due to a preponderance or lack of some of the ninety-three elements or their ill-combination or ill-balance, Savage blamed it on the stripping of mineral elements from the soil. He offered his proofs that health can be restored by the restoration of these elements to the soil at the source, including importantly the iodine, manganese, copper, zinc, nickel, boron, cobalt and others, heretofore considered negligible if considered at all, as vital necessities in plant and animal nourishment.

The scientist of the soil looked into the future as he stood there in his garden, or visited in his living room, visioning a better world: "A program of countrywide mineralization could and would create, within a generation, a new type of human being . . . The nation can be changed practically and easily 50% by a reasonable control of mineralization in fruit and vegetable sources. People can be fed to live peaceably or fight, to think or dream, to work or sleep, to be virile or pathologic, physically, mentally and spiritually developed or retarded, and for any possible degree of advance or variation, within the mechanical limits of the organism."

It was the scientist and also the prophet prophesying.

"A scientist should be like a prophet," he said. "He should give the people the truth. I want to be free to give. I believe I was born for this. I never was satisfied with what anybody told me or with what I knew myself."

The man of science spoke of creation's climax when God, having formed man of the dust of the soil, breathed into his nostrils the breath of life. Daringly he said: "Man couldn't be created from the dust of the soil today because the dust doesn't contain the twenty-nine elements recognized as required before the breath of life, the air elements, can be breathed into him. Money has never meant much to me," he explained. "I have enough sense to get out of the soil all that I need. I don't have to use money to make a living. I want to be free to give away what I know. If I took money for it I wouldn't be free."

Unfortunately, money is the blood of commerce, and for a lack of it Albert Carter Savage, an old man, was dying in a hostile environment. It was the fate of many who dared to suggest ecologically sound agriculture in those days.

John Hamaker, in our index of materials covered in fifteen years of publication, takes up almost a column of eight point type, starting in 1973 and going up to the present. Hamaker was a blood brother of Albert Carter Savage without knowing it. A student of geology, history and half a dozen other disciplines, Hamaker discerned that where the glaciers marched across the landscape, glacial gravel remained to provide the proper mix of essential nutrients. Unfortunately killer agriculture had been imposed on the nation's acres to accommodate the needs of the fossil fuel people for a dumping ground. The hard nitrogens and salt fertilizer in turn had locked up and complexed the soils, and otherwise deprived them of the nutritional mix required by soil's life. In 1969 Hamaker took his concepts to Dr. Lynn S. Robertson, a Michigan State University soil scientist. He told him about his early results with powdered gravel dust, and even took him out to see several plots where gravel dust had worked its specialty. John complained to *Acres U.S.A.* that he'd run his findings up the flagpole with Dr. Sylvan W. Wittwer, the agronomist who first proved foliar nutrition with atomic tracer studies. He said he got the brushoff. "So then I got mad and decided to figure out what happens in the soil without help from the great scientists."

In the opening issue of *Acres U.S.A.*, I had announced that we would operate more or less as an open forum, that those with something to say would be extended space to say it just as they might be handed the microphone at professional assemblies. John Hamaker seized the opportunity, and in time several dozen of his in-depth reports told *Acres U.S.A.* readers about the same kind of mineralization Albert Carter Savage envisioned. Both men had vision. They didn't much concern themselves with the brushfire affairs that bring farmers thundering into mass meetings. Instead, they looked down the road, outlining in understandable terms the shape of the future if technology did not mend its ways.

During those early years as proprietor, editor, production manager—and with my wife Ann as the circulation arm—of *Acres U.S.A.*, the underpriced subscription fee of $5.00 kept the checkbook on the edge of its seat, as if it had intelligence all its own. I picked up the balance of solvency doing trade paper work. This meant frequent trips to New York for interviews with captains of industry, droll work, since most of the executives hadn't had an original idea since they first leered at some young pretty in high school. On one such trip I rented a car and drove up to Spring Valley, New York, the headquarters of Pfeiffer Laboratories.

Dr. Ehrenfried Pfeiffer had passed away some years earlier, but Erica Sabarth and Margrit Selke were there, Sabarth making Pfeiffer's strange chromatograms, Selke propagating the bacterial cultures used in Pfeiffer's compost starter and field spray preparations. It was here that the many facets of biological farming began to merge, not only for myself, but for the readers of the paper as well. Drs. Albrecht and Pfeiffer seemed to stand at different poles, and yet they were brothers in science who respected each other. Albrecht was always the orthodox scientist. Pfeiffer's approach was strictly organic.

Long before industrial waste became a national problem, Pfeiffer busied himself solving it. In California, farmers complained that rice straw was not biodegradable, and in New York Pfeiffer answered with field sprays that literally breathed life into the dead soils that killer agriculture had accounted for.

As Pfeiffer and Albrecht worked, they exchanged their findings and views, and they were drawn closer together. When Lady Eve Balfour came to visit both of the great men, she found they talked a different language, but they were both reaching for the new common denominator that would one day find full expression on the new uplands of eco-agriculture. Finally they settled for an answer. Both Albrecht and Pfeiffer accepted the verdict of the animal.

Pfeiffer's biodynamic farming systems have never proved too popular in the United States. J. Carsten Pank, a German-born farmer who settled in New York, told an *Acres U.S.A.* Conference that he had not been able to interest even one neighbor in biodynamics after nearly thirty years. Yet Pfeiffer's inventory of knowledge proved so rich and timeless that for almost three years his papers became regular entries in the pages of *Acres U.S.A.* The exposure, Margrit Selke told me, literally saved the laboratory.

It did more. It led me to a little bit of heaven called the Lubke farm near Peuerbach, Oberosterreich (Austria). I had been invited to address the Grunes Forum, *Stirbt der Boden*, at Alpbach, about an hour from Innsbruck, where German speaking agronomists and farmers from Switzerland, Germany, northern Italy, Austria and a corner of France had assembled to examine the claims of biological farming. The remarks I made were consistent with the message in this book, including the biting one—*"Ein College-Professor der Iowa State University hat gesagt: Um 100,000 dollar konnen wir alles beweisen."* The audience thundered applause, perhaps indicating that Europe's "intellectual honesty" and "academic freedom" people also have this thing about being able to prove anything for $100,000. With the forum ended, my wife and I proceeded to see Austria, Budapest in communist Hungary, and that slice of heaven called the Lubke farm.

Sigfried and Uta Lubke had been to the U.S. and to Pfeiffer Laboratores for lessons that schools do not teach and the Grunes Forum people did not even like to discuss. On their farm the most important tool was the microscope, and then the spadenmachine, a unique tillage tool that demanded low power. The most important livestock were the microorganisms, most of which arrived via Pfeiffer's Field Spray and compost innoculants. Using the microscope as a window into the soil, and chromatograms (blotterpaper tests devised by Pfeiffer that trace out food factors) for laboratory answers, the Lubkes learned how to turn soil as hard as macadam into mellow *boden*, and they grew produce that literally jumped with life. Later that same year, 1985, I had Uta Lubke and her daughter Angelika come to Kansas City to tell American farmers how they could return life to dead soil via the mechanism of Pfeiffer Field Spray, and freshly innoculated green manure crops such as rye, giving the good earth a fix of both new life and food for that life.

One would be rash and perhaps several times a fool to select a representative passage from the "Pfeiffer news" that *Acres U.S.A.* was able to bring to its subscribers. Still, in one of the last papers we ran, there was a statement that jolted me back to an earlier premise, that to be economical, agriculture had to be ecological. Please read aloud this abstract in depth of what Dr. Ehrenfried Pfeiffer, medical expert, biologist, scientist, wrote in one of those papers.

"Comparing the economic body with a real living being and its laws with the laws of life, we find only two functions which involve something constantly produced in order to be consumed: the functions supported by food and red blood. Food comes from the outside, yet stimulates and supports the body's life just as productive ideas nourish an economic process. Blood, on the other hand, is entirely from within, always circulating, being constantly produced and consumed in order to maintain life, supporting the organic functions necessary to growth and reproduction. It is important to realize that blood is produced by the same organism by which it is consumed: that it is rarely stored and then only in small amounts—in the spleen, for instance—that it is in constant circulation and is properly, not evenly, distributed wherever it is needed.

"Money fulfills a similar function—that is, it is or should be in constant circulation. It supports and maintains economic life and growth. It is produced by the same body economic that consumes it. It should not be stored for long or in large quantities. Think of a depression as an economic hematoma, or think of a boom as a hemorrhage."

The proper distribution of blood is what gives us an understanding of an organism or biological unit and its functions, because there is a higher constructive idea behind it, a higher wisdom of life forces—higher than our intellectual, analytical thought can grasp.

The proper distribution of money—which alone can maintain a healthy economic body—has to be governed by a body of wisdom—that is, the concentrated economic and cultural wisdom of a nation directed by a mutually acceptable idea. Such wisdom is not to be found among people who have been stripped of their mental acuity with highly refined carbohydrates—sugar and whiskey—and who have lost their vision.

Ehrenfried Pfeiffer was not alone in comparing the circulation of money in the economy to the circulation of blood. During the great depression, William Aberhard, a Canadian minister, turned the government of Alberta out on its ear by visiting lessons from the *Bible* on his constituency, and by comparing money in the economy to blood in the human body. His government lasted for forty years. He said the nation was hungry and there were farm surpluses. Citizens wore shabby clothes and there were too many factories. Children and old people starved and there was too much food. Aberhard said this was idiocy, that something was wrong between the ears when the great minds of economics could come up with no better answer than to freeze and stink and annihilate the population. The answer, he said, was simple. There was no broad-spectrum distribution of money because agriculture languished. Banks no longer wanted to risk loans. Borrowers never had enough collateral. Capitalists were sitting on the money at 2%. Obviously a mechanism was needed to deliver purchasing media to the people. And great minds literally shouted: Where will all the money come from? Remember John Law? Remember The Directory in France? Remember the Great German inflation. And now, they would shout, remember China.

And here was Aberhard's answer. The human heart, he said, beats seventy-five times a minute. In one minute it sends a gallon of blood through the body. In one hour it pumps sixty gallons of blood. It does this day in and day out. In a single day the human heart pumps 1,440 gallons of blood. That's enough to fill thirty-two oil drums containing forty-five gallons each, enough—in terms of gasoline—to operate a fair sized farm for a month. Yet the human body has only ten pints of the vital fluid.

Editorially, and in feature articles, I used such analogies to illustrate what circulation of money was all about. My tag line often referred to the public policy of the 1940s, when the raw materials of the earth in effect became circulating media for the economy, renewed with each season and monetized on par with wages and capital costs.

Certainly money had to be produced by the same body economic that consumed it, and all schemes that sought to negate this truth contained the seeds of disaster.

There is, I argued editorially and in my *Last Word* column, a par requirement when the gifts of nature enter the scene. Every transaction in the economic equation appears to be a wash—man debited, man credited—except one. When we take raw materials from nature, fish from the sea, stone from the quarries, wheat from the fields, the raw materials are a gift, except for the cost of capturing them. But these gifts must be turned into money, monetized, and the costs of harvesting those gifts must first be recovered before there is a profit to the economy. Man debited, nature credited—that's the equation, and nature is not paid back! If energy is harvested from the cosmos, it too is a gift—man debited, nature credited, and nature has no repayment requirement.

Thus through Pfeiffer and Albrecht and all the rest, the role of the farmer became real. His costs were always manufactured by every other sector in the economy, by the machine maker, the gasoline producer, by the teachers, doctors, service industries, even by the legislator who creates taxes.

I cannot recall even one issue of *Acres U.S.A.* I didn't like. This has been true even when the news wasn't pleasant. When the month's work was done, it seemed that everything fit and blended itself better than envisioned at the outset. The old agriculture was dying, and all of America was stressed because of the ultimate debauchery of farming. It took decades to bring this fountainhead of wealth to its knees—but it took only moments each month to report developments as both running history and "happenings." Withal, I think an uplifting message figured in each issue.

The nation's political, economic and scientific giants, after all, were no less than the Founding Fathers—Ben Franklin, who imported soybeans one hundred years ahead of their time, Thomas Jefferson, who air-conditioned his home a century before Carrier; Washington, who knew the value of land and the raw materials of earth. They decreed that Congress shall coin the money and regulate the value thereof. They were naturalists, these Founding Fathers, and they understood that money could fulfill its role only when consumed. They would even have agreed with Albert Carter Savage that *"People can be fed to live peaceably or fight, to think or dream, to work or sleep, to be virile or pathologic, physically, mentally and spiritually developed or retarded, and for any possible degree of advance or variation, within the mechanical limits of the organism."*

But early in the 1920s, great economic forces decreed something different from Albert Carter Savage's brightest visions. This attack on the quality of human life came long before the debauchery of farm technology had been made complete.

Behind agriculture, food retailing is the nation's largest industry, larger than steel, larger than most manufacturers. It was during the 1920s that today's leading chains achieved a prominent place in food retailing, usually through acquisitions, but also because public policy was hard at work wiping out a more efficient system, namely thousands of corner grocery stores. During the great depression, the supermarket was introduced by the independents, largely as an answer to the chains. The main weapon was price competition and *shelf life*. And shelf life in the grocery store became an attack on quality of life for the consumer.

From that moment on strange words in type too small to read became an indispensable part of almost every label. First came the emulsifiers and stabilizers—carrageenan in cheese spreads, chocolate products, evaporated milk, ice cream and dairy products. All evidence of mutagenicity, carcinogenicity and teratogenicity remained neatly tucked away in the scientific literature. Dioctyl sodium sulfosuccinate became a wetting agent of choice, even though infants suffered gastrointestinal irritation and reduced growth rates as a consequence of its use.

There are also dozens of flavorings and colors other than Red No. 2 and 4, all inimical to sustained human health. Aspartame is a sweetener with approximately one hundred sixty times the sweetness of sugar. The problem is that persons with phenylketonuria can't handle it. It accumulates in the system and causes mental retardation and even death. Cereals, chewing gum and gelatins are loaded with it.

As shelf life for foods improved, strange anomalies in the population multiplied. The public prints became filled with reports of bizarre crimes (youths dumping gasoline on old ladies and setting them on fire, for instance) and asylums for the insane became a growth industry, finally to emerge with credentialed practitioners and a new nomenclature, mental health. Did shellac—a food grade version of furniture finish—used as a confectioner's glaze have anything to do with this? Or xylitol, a sugar substitute that is a diuretic, and causes tumors and organ damage in test animals. Or propylene glycol alginate, or oxystearin (a modified glyceride), or calcium peroxide, or glycerol ester of wood rosin, or guar gum! All annihilate lesser life and whittle away at human health a bit at a time.

It would take pages and pages to list these disgraces to a civilized society, and I have used pages and pages of *Acres U.S.A.* to do just that over a decade and a half. During this entire period my pet antipathy continued to be what I call plastic coffee creamer, which is loaded with shellacs, varnishes, anti-freezes and compounds better used in the embalming trade than in grocery stores. None of these things are likely to make people live in peace, think and fulfill great dreams.

At the 1984 *Acres U.S.A.* Conference I read the following prayer from the podium, and I usually keep a supply of printed cards on hand for instant use. It was taken from *Moment in the Sun* by Robert Reinow and Leona Train Rienow.

"Give us this day our daily calcium propionate (spoilage retarder); sodium diacetate (mold inhibitor), monoglyceride (emulsifier), potassium bromate (maturing agent), calcium phosphate monobasic (dough conditioner), chloramine T (flour bleach), aluminum potassium sulfate (acid baking powder ingredient), sodium benzoate (preservative), butylated hydroxyanisole (anti-oxidant), mono-isopropyl citrate (sesquestrant); plus synthetic vitamins A and D.

"Forgive us, O Lord, for calling this stuff bread."

I am sure Albert Carter Savage would have added, "Amen!"

10

FOR WHOM THE BELL TOLLS

I saw them tearing a building down,
A gang of men in a busy town:
With a "ho-heave-ho" and a lusty yell,
They swung a beam and the side wall fell.
I said to the foreman, "Are these men skilled?
And the men you'd hire if you had to build?"
He gave a laugh and said, "No indeed,
Just common labor is all I need.
I can easily wreck in a day or two
What some have taken a year to do."

So I thought to myself as I went my way,
Which of these roles have I tried to play?
Am I a builder who builds with care,
Measuring life by the rule and square?
Am I shaping my deeds to a well formed plan,
Patiently doing the best I can?
Or, am I a wrecker who stalks the town,
Content with the labor of tearing down?

I doubt that Arnold Paulson ever concluded a speech without reciting Frank Baer's inspirational poem. I met Paulson when I first met

NFO, and our friendship survived both of our breaks with that organization.

Paulson was both my teacher and my student. His forte was the spoken word, mine the verbal fare consumed best in silence. As a speechmaker he parted company with almost all of his colleagues in that there was real substance in every presentation. I often marveled at the diligence with which he pursued facts, background history and the vital connection upon which his talks depended. Arnold Paulson would become so engrossed in the pursuit of a point, a proof, a clinching argument, he sometimes abandoned good judgment, such as the weekend he missed his own twenty-fifth wedding anniversary because he and Butch Swaim were caught up in a torturous bout of ratiocination.

On the hustings he served as a largely unpaid ambassador for NFO, breaking open hostile territories, melting away opposition because he said the right thing in the right way at the right time. Over the years I came to know Paulson better than I would a brother. And after I left NFO, and Paulson endured in good graces, I watched with disbelief as NFO cut him down. The device used was simple. Acting on orders from Oren Lee Staley, Butch Swaim caused field operatives to set up meetings atop Paulson's, thereby draining away support. It was the cruelest cut of all, considering how much of himself Paulson had given to make Swaim's job a success. But Paulson made no outcry, a point I stressed in double italics when some years later I gave a memorial address to mark his passing.

Our friendship endured because we both wanted to understand. In our most cynical moods, we observed that governments—from the smallest village to the greatest parliament—were really proficient in only four areas, namely killing, stealing, lying and making woodenheaded decisions. We had no doubt that most of the mischief came about because of a total misunderstanding of the nature of coin and currency.

In societies with a simple exchange equation, money was nothing more than a creation of individual actors based on a commodity. Precious metals followed, and somewhere in the eighteenth century fiat money was introduced to the fiat world. It was the scam used by the priests of Baal all over again, namely money being created out of thin air. Generally speaking such money wasn't worth the paper it was written on, but it had behind it the clout of government and banks and a reserve of hard money, or metals as common denominator commodities. As economies became too complex for detailed bookkeeping, money achieved nebulous status. Lost in the equation was the mundane business known as the nation's lifeline.

Ehrenfried Pfeiffer said it all, and he said it well, although neither Paulson nor I—nor any of the people in National Organization for Raw Materials—managed to identify that simple homily while he was alive. Few really understood how to regulate the value of money as demanded by the U.S. Constitution. This made parity one of the longest continuing stories in a decade and a half of *Acres U.S.A.* reporting. Dealing with the par exchange requirement was front burner stuff in the very first issue in 1971, and it will likely remain a prime topic as long as *Acres U.S.A.* is published.

In our many private meetings Paulson and I wondered whether future historians would look back on the years between 1776 and the present as an accidental time during which real freedoms existed. We wondered whether they would footnote the discordant voices that spoke common sense when a nation and its leaders no longer had the mental acuity to listen or understand. At the time of the American Revolution, one of the orders that went out to all the British generals was, *Smash those printing presses!* The printing presses were tearing the guts out of the British, and the best military minds couldn't cope with them. Something was happening to the people in the colonies, and that something had been traced to the fact that messages could be reproduced and scattered to the winds. The world has since come to wonder and marvel at the *Crisis Papers*—at *Common Sense* in particular.

Common Sense was signed simply, *Written by an Englishman.* In terms of population it enjoyed the largest circulation of any book in American history. I compute that a book today would have to sell twenty-five million copies in three months to do as well. It is safe to infer that everyone who adhered to the cause of independence either read *Common Sense*, or had it read aloud. In addition to booklets in print, sections of *Common Sense* were printed in every patriotic newspaper in the country. It made Thomas Paine the pamphleteer of the Revolution.

Common Sense was only forty pages long. But it said it all. Paulson and I determined that's what we'd better do, say it all! Somewhere, someone had to express the cause in terms that all could understand. This had to be done in forty pages or less, and it had to be read by all farmers, to be abstracted and printed in as many papers as possible, debated on as many TV screens as feasible, and circulated so as to touch all men of goodwill between the ears. I drafted the forty pages and ran them through *Acres U.S.A.* before printing a booklet styled, *Parity, The Key to Propserity Unlimited.*

Only 100,000 copies of *Parity* managed to see print, and possibly another 100,000 impressions were added via farm papers. A few thousand more impressions were accounted for when the entire text was printed in government hearings papers. The intellectual godfathers for *Parity* were Carl Wilken and Arnold Paulson.

All the bases were touched in *Parity, The Key to Prosperity Unlimited.* In a manner of speaking the booklet was really a condensation of *Unforgiven* with a few updated items added. The opening fifteen pages were standard stuff, the kind of paragraphs either Paulson or I would use in speeches when we changed the audience, but not the text. The real clout of *Parity* was contained in a recitation of questions people were asking, and tightly reasoned answers. These questions and answers are recited here because they should be warehoused, reviewed when there is plenty of deep-think time, and held ready for instant retrieval.

There is a lot of criticism concerning parity because it is old and based on 1910-1914 = 100. Is this criticism valid?

No, this criticism is not valid. There is usually agreement that 1910-1914 was a golden age for agriculture, that there was relative balance between the price of what a farmer sold and what he bought. But—look at how things have changed! Look at agriculture in 1910-1914—dirt roads, a horse and oats economy, jolt wagons, few tractors, no milking machines, awkward headers, few combines, no electricity. Well, this is true, but it has very little if anything to do with it. Parity is a yardstick, a measuring device. The foot is sometimes dated back to King John, sometimes to the ancients who built the pyramids. Obviously a measuring device does not suffer because of its age if indeed it does a good job.

Does parity as a measuring device do a good job?

Of course, if the premises are understood. Unfortunately these are not well understood by most of the press, politicians and Congressional leaders—certainly not by USDA, if we accept what they are doing as being intellectually honest. The governing factor is the base period. It has to be properly selected, and this requires correct economic information and an understanding of logic. You can find one of the best rationales in Thorold Rogers' *History of Agriculture and Prices.* Now what do we mean by a base period? In history, you have the birth of Christ. Everything is measured backward and forward from this base year. In economics we select a base year to equal 100 with certain considerations in mind. Such a year has to hone close to an era in which there is no debasement of money and no rupture of the price structure through imports, and few if any inequities between different sectors of the economy. Thorold Rogers, for instance, used 1541 as a base period in one study—1541 = 100. This happened to be a year before Henry VIII debased the coins. In those days they didn't have computers, so the rascal prince simply shaved the coins when he wanted to cheat the public. Nowadays we punch a few figures into a giant computer at Culpeper, Virginia and create federal notes, bills and bonds, and float these out into the financial community so reserves can follow a certain formula, and money can be created via the creation of loans. When you create money this way you inflate to the extent this money isn't answered by earned income. This is our modern method of shaving coins. Even as far back as Henry VIII, the index based on a sound base period revealed prices moving from 100 in 1541 to 213.5 in 1556, a fifteen year period, or inflation.

How did parity (as a measuring device) make a transition to the American scene?

Economists understood it when the Founding Fathers were active. If you want to look at it that way, the Revolutionary War was really a monetary war. England was exploiting raw materials producers and delivering manufactured goods at a price differential. The colonies didn't like this. They smuggled. They evaded the law. One of the final straws was when the Bank of England forced British pounds on the colonies. Up to that time the locals coined their own money based more or less on commodities, or warehouse receipts. But in the modern context, parity got a toehold in the American language when George Peek wrote *Equality for Agriculture* shortly after WWI.

How did Peek define it?

He called it a "fair exchange value." In other words, the American economy was no longer a one wheel economy. It now had plenty of division of labor, and continued prosperity under a condition of division of labor depended on an appropriate division of income between the several sectors of the economy. The buying power of a crop should be on par with the buying power of factory labor, services, professions, taking these things in terms of broad spectrum averages. Without the balanced exchange equation, a shortage of buying power would sooner or later short-circuit the system. That's why they went back to 1910-1914 = 100. There is an assumption here. And that assumption is that technology development will benefit the several sectors of an economy about the same. Sure, they had jolt wagons in 1910, but the factory wasn't computerized either. In the 1920s and 1930s many factories still ran with a central power plant and lots of pulleys and belts running all over the place. Picture it now—an automobile rolling off the assembly line every eighteen minutes. All these arguments against the parity measuring stick suggest that farm technology has outrun factory technology in efficiency, and therefore farmers ought to constantly express their efficiency advantage in terms of lower prices. This is fiction.

What kind of calculation did George Peek come up with?

In terms of a 1910-1914 index, corn sold at 64.2 cents a bushel. Wheat came to 88.4 cents a bushel. To compute true parity prices for any year, all one had to do was take the 1910-1914 figures and multiply times an average of the things a farmer had to buy. The government has commodity indexes, processed food indexes and the like. We know how these have increased. Simply take that figure and multiply. For instance, it is now generally agreed that the big bull market in stocks peaked in 1966 in terms of stable dollars. At that precise point the commodity index stood at 240%. Thus the multiplier became 340 for that year since you have to add the base period of 100. This meant that corn parity for that year should have read this way: 64.2 cents x 340% = $2.18. Wheat: 88.4 x 340% = $3.00. Total income in 1910-1914 averaged $33 million per year. The industrial wage was 23 cents an hour. It took several hours of wages to buy the equivalent of a bushel of wheat in those days. It took about 25 minutes to pay for that bushel in terms of the national wage average of $5.68 circa 1978. In 1982, the nation's wage average stood at $8.34 making a bushel of wheat worth approximately 30 minutes, illustrating that the individual wage average is also below parity.

This seems simple enough, assuming that we have accurate figures on how the rest of the economy has fared. Would it be possible to move the base period a little closer to modern times—just to satisfy the doubters?

Of course—provided, however, that a year was selected in which there was relative balance in the exchange equation between rural and industrial America. The year 1926 could be used as a fair base period = 100. An even better one is 1946-1950 = 100. During the 1946-1950 period, farm prices averaged—all things considered—at 99.5% parity. Corn averaged $1.54 a bushel and wheat averaged $2.01 a bushel. If you follow through on what we've illustrated, you'll find that your consumer price index adjusted 43% upward between 1946-

1950 and 1966 (the point of reference cited earlier). So if you multiply $1.54 corn x 143% (the 43% increase plus the base of 100), then you get $2.20 corn. Wheat on the same general basis comes to $2.87. This is a penny or two different from the 1910-1914 projection, but that isn't bad.

If this is the way it works, what's the big hang up about using this yardstick for farm prices?

The whole thing started getting goofed up in the very beginning. Take the tobacco crop. They decided not to use the 1910-1914 base period because it was considered out of line. So right off they used a base period of 1919-1929. This could be questioned. Then there were special concessions for soybeans. Here was a crop all but unknown in 1910-1914. In 1937 the pre-war base for milk was routinely questioned. As a result Congress gave the Secretary of Agriculture the right to decide milk prices in federal order markets. In 1940 they changed the base period for tobacco to 1935-1939, to Depression years, if you will, and all this kept the parity equation dancing around stage center in a chorus of question marks. By 1944 USDA was computing parity figures for some one hundred fifty-seven commodities. No more than sixty-one were on the 1910-1914 base period. The sixty-one, however, did account for 82% of the farm crop values. At that time seventy-three commodities had a 1919-1929 base, twenty-one made use of various combinations drawn from the 1920s, and two used 1935-1939. So you can see, the simple yardstick wasn't so simple the way the government did it.

Yet you say it is simple?

Basically, it is, that is if you keep a sound base 100 in mind. Under the War Stabilization Act of 1942 and the Steagall Amendment, farm prices were maintained at relative parity for approximately ten years *by the market.* There were war years and there were years of peace involved. You see, it was economic stupidity that kept the United States in a depression during the 1930s. The administration told the public that there were farm surpluses. Henry Wallace even burned the pigs and corn to short the supply. At the same time we imported more than we exported during each of the Depression years. We imported more than we exported during each of the war years—just to catch up. After the war we got Mr. Truman for president. The War Stabilization Act and the Steagall Amendment had been written so that 90% parity for farmers would end two years after the war, which could be ended by Congress or by presidential proclamation. Well, Truman took that step on the last day of 1946. Had he waited until the next morning, farmers would have had another year of 90% parity automatically.

Why 90% parity? Why not 100%?

It was reasoned at the time that the farmer produces a year in advance—which is true. It is his economic function to store the crop inventory. At 90% of parity at harvest, with storage added, it turned out to be very close to 100% of parity.

Truman ended the war in 1946. Is this the reason there was a farm bill problem in 1948?

Yes. As you know, the Republicans met in convention in Philadelphia that year. At 5:00 a.m. on the day the convention started, Congress finally came up with a farm bill. It continued the 90% parity bill for one year, and also enacted the 60 to 90% of parity idea into law as soon as that one year was gone. Truman signed this legislation. The decision had been made that agriculture would henceforth be the shock absorber for the rest of the economy. When the 1948 law was passed for agriculture with a 60 to 90% of parity law provision—it contained a mandate that the parity base year would be moved forward every decade. So you had this situation: 1947-1949 might be a fair base period—relative balance in much of the economy! But a decade later 1957-1959 = 100 became the base period because of this law. Under the earlier base period, corn was $2.04. When 1957-1959 became the updated parity base year, they simply reduced corn to $1.55 and called it full parity. They took 49 cents off a bushel of corn with a lead pencil this way. You have here complete dishonesty and this very dishonesty is used to discredit the parity yardstick.

Has the parity base period been moved since then—to 1967-1969, for instance?

Yes. And to 1977-1979. And each time it has been moved, they've called everything even at 100. In other words, when they move the base period they rig the figures and call whatever the prices are for that year 100, even though they might have been quite lower. They do this *after the fact.* This is the reason farm prices are expressed at 77% of parity when they're actually at a lower par with the rest of the economy.

Can this be proved?

There is a book called the *Economic Report of the President of the United States.* The year 1962 produced a relatively honest array of statistics. The next year they changed many of the figures for every year clear back to 1929. This has been going on ever since. One of the tables in that book carries the all commodities index and the farm products index and the processed foods index. Using the 1962 report,

112

these are figures for 1947-1949, for instance:

Year	All Commodities	Farm Products	Processed Foods
1947	96.4	100.0	98.2
1948	104.4	107.3	106.1
1949	99.2	92.8	95.7
Total	300.0	300.0	300.0
Average	100.0	100.0	100.0

By dividing the three years, one can see that they average 100, suggesting a very balanced base period. Now using this same source of reference, let's take the situation ten years later—1957-1959.

Year	All Commodities	Farm Products	Processed Foods
1957	117.6	90.9	105.6
1958	119.2	94.9	110.9
1959	119.5	89.1	107.0
Total	356.3	274.9	323.5
Average	118.7	91.8	107.8

Obviously prices were not in balance when the first move was made to the base period in compliance with the 1948 farm act. You can see farm prices were 36.9 lower than all commodity prices, and 16.0 lower than processed foods expressed as an index.

Does this suggest the national statistics are being rigged?

I think the record can do the suggesting. It is really an education to compare, say, the 1962 report to later reports for the same years. In August 1965 they made a lot of changes, for instance. In one maneuver, interest was transposed from one side of the income equation to the other, thus raising corporate profits from $57.0 billion in the old report to $64.5 billion in the new. The corporations never got these profits and never paid taxes on them, yet there they are in the statistics.

How can the 1977 *Economic Report* show 100 for 1967 period, and still show 100 for the 1957 period on, say, all commodities?

It doesn't. Each decade, they just change all the figures back to 1929. So your 1982 report shows farmers getting 100% for 1977, even though farmers drove tractors in protest in 1977 because of low prices. In the 1966 *Economic Report*, they show it this way:

Year	All Commodities	Farm Products	Processed Foods
1957	99.0	99.2	97.2
1958	100.4	103.6	102.9
1959	100.6	97.2	99.2
Total	300.0	300.0	300.0

You see, it averages out at 100 as if by magic. Now if you look at the 1977 *Report*, you'll see that all commodities index at 88.6 for 1957, not 99.0 as it appears in the 1966 *Report* data for the year 1957. Agriculture hasn't had a balanced base period since 1946-1950, and computations have to be made from a balanced base to be valid.

Yes, but the people in government argue that parity for agriculture costs too much.

Parity doesn't cost at all in an economic sense. It supports the national income on an earned basis. We're paying more to the interest mill than we're paying to the farmer. It is the interest mill that is feeding inflation into everything, even into cans on a shelf manufactured years ago. They can manufacture national income by inflating the money supply, but these are watered dollars and borrowed dollars. They get bottled up in the capital pool and are not drawn out to be circulated on an earned basis. When used, there is interest—and interest compounds itself chain letter style. This is the reason that bank liquidity—which is where 66% of the operating money is kept—goes down as farm income goes down. Today there is little bank liquidity. The banks are in fact loaning out the float. The only time bank liquidity jumped a little was when the Russian grain deal triggered parity prices to most of agriculture for a few months. Once this temporary farm prosperity passed, bank liquidity started down again. If common citizens understood what parity prices meant to the economy, and not just farmers, they'd be out at the farm gate with shotguns and prevent the farmer from letting his production go to market at less than parity.

If the figures are rigged, how can you use government data to compute honest parity?

You really can't. You have to come at it another way.

Which is?

Using your own data. Up to recently, there were indexes that had not been rigged. *Wall Street Journal* carried a Dow-Jones Futures Commodity Index and a daily Dow-Jones Spot Commodity Index based on 1924-1926 = 100, a fairly decent index. This umbilical to a stable period has now been cut. Reuters of the United Kingdom has traditionally used 1931 as 100. The *Associated Press* index has been 1926 = 100. You have to know what the base period is to understand what it means. Now these are commodity indexes. The problem is that with all this rigging, we no longer have a good *all commodities index*, or a good *processed foods index*. About all one can do is take figures from the President's Economic Report and strike a new multiplier based on differentials in the rigged figures. It would be preferables, of course, to structure a new index based on actual *all commodity* prices and all processed food prices, with a few other composites thrown in. Arnold Paulson of National Organization for Raw Materials has made some of these computations. Remember, he didn't have the computer time or the resources to handle this the way it might be handled. Yet he came up with parity figures based on a 1955 update and a 1910-1914 = 100 that were quite close.

Now look at your *Wall Street Journal*, June 1, typical year-wheat in Kansas City, at $4.0675, corn in Chicago, $2.585 and so on. You don't have to be a figure wizard to know that $4.0675 wheat divided by $10.30 (1910-1914 = 100) is 39%. Just about all farm crops, some specialties excepted, were less than at half parity, and they are worse now. And that's the reason the countryside is being emptied, and why it is taking over 25% of the national income just to mount relief agencies and so-called social programs. This explains why Reagan can create billions of new money at a whack and be called conservative.

Are the economists really that out of tune with requirements of the parity concept?

Most of them are. We don't know whether this is their ignorance speaking, or thoroughly informed self-interest. Back in 1946 they had a contest in the American Farm Economics Association on the subject—*A Price Policy for Agriculture Consistent with Economic Progress that will Promote Adequate and More Stable Income from Farming*. This one drew 317 papers. If you want a real look at how theory period instruction ruled the roost, this is a good example. Of the eighteen winners, fully 100% agreed that 1910-1914 as a parity base period represents a grossly distorted pattern. It ignored shifts in population, technology, on and on, so they argued. Not one of the professors accepted the idea of par for agriculture. They didn't all agree on one thing—whether there ought to be a relief check over and above what international commodity prices allowed or whether farmers ought to take it on the chin all the way. Lawrence Simerl suggested a loan rate at 55 to 75% of parity. This way agriculture could absorb a lot of shock for the rest of the economy. He wanted a 1935-1939 base period for "equals 100." One professor came up with the Brannan Plan in the contest—a relief check for agriculture. Not one of the economists understood that this nation got 1% of unemployment for each 1% farm prices remained below parity during the Depression years.

The common sense public thinks it is to its advantage to have low food prices. At least six administrations have agreed, and for this reason the nation has a cheap food policy. Is it really in the self-interest of consumers to have cheap food?

No. The housewife pays a terrible tariff for the fiction of low food prices. Let's illustrate this. The family spent about 25 cents of its dollar to feed the family in the 1946-1950 era. At that time taxes took about 25 cents of the dollar. Today it takes about 16 cents plus to feed the family. But because the farmer has not been getting paid, the exchange equation has faltered. This has prompted the government to cover up by structuring all sorts of agencies to employ the people, all sorts of relief programs. Because the farmer was short-changed, it took debt and war spending and fear of communist aggression and foreign give-aways to sustain the prosperity. As a consequence it takes 44 to 45 cents of the dollar to feed the tax collector. Now 16 cents for food and 45 cents for the tax collector adds up to 61 cents, not the 50 cents when food cost a bit more. If there isn't proper division of income between different sectors, then the sectors can't consume each others' production. Generally, when there is farm parity, there are surpluses in the treasuries of taxing units, and there is liquidity in the banks. We're told that if farmers get a parity price it means inflation—and it may mean higher prices temporarily as the economy adjusts itself. Farmers got parity prices briefly in the 1973-1974 era because of the Russian grain deal. This meant about 10% inflation, but remember there were other factors. There was a well choreographed oil crisis. The Fed kept on pumping money into the economy the same as if farm prices had not climbed. One thing is certain. As debt creation continues, public and private debt will double each decade, as it has since 1950. This has meant a public and private debt of $4 trillion by 1980, and will mean $8 to 12 trillion by 1990. Congress may think it has voted stability for the Social Security System, but this is simply whistling Dixie. President Carter could have balanced the budget if he got behind farm parity, but a balanced budget without parity raw materials was impossible.

If parity for agriculture and other raw materials is the only non-inflationary course to take, why is this so?

There are only three ways to bring money into circulation. You can directly issue the money via government as provided for in the Constitution. This leads to inflation. You can tax money from people and circulate it, or use the credit mechanism, such as we do through the Federal Reserve. This leads to bankruptcy because it dissipates the savings and future earnings of our people and sets up debts that cannot be paid. The only sound way to bring money into circulation is through the production and sale of raw materials. These dollars draw on the capital pool, are earned, and return to the capital pool with each cycle. The sale of 1,000 bushels of corn at, say, $2.50, draws on the capital structure to the tune of $2,500. If corn is $1.00, only $1,000 is drawn and earned into circulation. When the producer spends the dollar received for his product from nature, he passes the purchasing power to the next man and the next. The units of raw materials—new wealth—are transformed by industry into other forms of wealth and become permanent assets of the society. This isn't true of either the dollar of issue or the credit dollar. Since the gross farm income dollar represents something like 70% of all new wealth income and largely gauges the industrial demand for other products of new wealth, the relationship of agricultural income to national income on an earned basis becomes the governing factor of the economy.

Well, don't the economic advisers know this? Don't the bankers know it?

Unless we take the position that these people are stupid, we have to assume they do. It is probably the most important discovery since the signing of the Constitution. It is the key to the economic democracy. It is also the key to undoing economic democracy.

How so?

Knowing this relationship makes it possible for a few men who control speculative markets of the world to lower raw material prices to a world level. This forces a nation of over 220 million people to exist by borrowing from their savings and placing a mortgage on future income. It forces inflationary issue of money. Since the American public does not comprehend this fact, they accept the idea that an economy can use agriculture for a punching bag while compounding debt. Government programs hand off inflation on a chain letter basis.

Let's recap. Explain the consequences of moving the base period in parity computation forward as required in the Farm Act of 1948.

The Republican convention was to open June 20, 1948, and it was generally agreed by both political parties that a farm bill had to be passed ahead of the convention. The full parity program was to come to an end December 31, 1948, because the war had been ended on December 31, two years earlier. There was no general agreement on the ten year moving average simply because it was an unsound device to circumvent a sound base period for parity computation. Congressman Steven Pace of Georgia correctly observed that a moving average imposed on an imbalanced base period would lower farm prices methodically—never to absolute zero, but well below honest parity while at the same time holding up an inaccurate parity figure as real. The consequences of the revision, and the public policy called 60-90% of parity that became effective under Ezra Taft Benson, was to bring American farm prices down to a world level. This is where they have been ever since, except for 1973-1974, when the Russian grain deal resulted in par prices for agriculture very temporarily. The temporary par period in 1973-1974 was either the result of an accident, or a device used to knock out the last of the farm programs. The answer to this point has still to surface. Incidentally, the carrot of supply and demand on the international level delivering good prices to farmers will be dangled again. Farmers will be told to just hold out, that the rainbow's end is in sight. This is cruel fiction, and those who make such statements are doing a terrible disservice to agriculture and the nation.

To continue a recap—parity is much more than a price comparison?

Of course. It is a measuring unit that distills into one index figure production costs, the state of the arts in terms on inventions and technology, economic well-being, and income. It assumes and absorbs into its composites the historical reality that technology will not likely benefit one sector of an economy more than another. It is true, parity as a concept has limitations. It is not easily comprehended by economists who often deal with it.

Wouldn't parity hurt exports and therefore America's balance of payments?

Under condition of full parity, it would require 40% less exports to return the same dollars in terms of payment balance. Cheap and free exports do very little to repair the international exchange imbalance.

Why do some businessmen fight farm parity?

Many businessmen believe that all gain is not really earned, but achieved at the expense of others, and they therefore believe that in

118

denying parity to agriculture greater gain will be achieved as business profits. They forget that business principles are not economic principles—and that economic principles requiring par exchange ultimately govern over business principles one way or another. Par exchange is a natural economic requirement. The only way to conquer a natural law is to obey it.

But if grain prices are at parity, won't this hurt the cattle rancher or feedlot farmer?

No. Parity for the six or seven basic crops that constitute 75% of the harvested acres has a self-adjusting effect on the rest of agriculture without regimentation of men, capital or production resources. Cattlemen get in a bind not because grain prices go up, but because they go down. Demand dries up long before the market is saturated. Moreover, the cattle situation is distorted by import invasion. Approximately 1.3 billion pounds of red meats, processed and boned, were imported annually during the 1970s. Much of this was produced on $1.00 an acre land. Each pound displaced seven pounds of grain on the average. Without this import invasion farmers would have to produce an additional three million 1,000 pound slaughter animals. This would require an additional cow herd of approximately 3,500,000 head, plus an additional 100,000 bulls. It would mean the need for an additional one million mother cows to produce those animals. The cowman cannot be hurt by parity grain prices. He can only be hurt by lack of farm parity because a lack of parity authors poverty and makes it impossible for the population to eat properly. One key to low farm prices has been dislocation between farm commodities. Such dislocations disappear promptly once the basic crops get to and hold at parity.

Won't parity prices for agriculture create unmanageable surpluses?

No. This is not possible when farm raw materials are priced at parity because full parity prices set up the credits with which the population can consume the production. The only time there aren't surpluses is when prices are at parity for farm raw materials. The big surpluses have all been piled up when prices were at less than parity. At less than parity the income needed to consume the production is not created. Supply without effective demand cannot be consumed. Notice how people find it possible to consume steak whenever raw farm commodities are at parity. This is because a flush of earned income is churning through the economy.

How can the farmer get parity?

He can only get it with the aid of Congress. Congress should pass a law that mandates payment of parity prices as raw commodities enter trade channels. This is not unlike a minimum wage law. It simply would keep the trades from stealing farm production at the tailgate. It would not be necessary to regulate all crops. A computed parity on six or seven stable commodities that account for 70 to 75% of the harvested acres would do the job. Crops that spoil quickly—vegetables, certain fruits—could not be used in any formula. Such a base would permit the play of the market to function for minor commodities, keeping them very close to parity. Parity must be maintained at the market. This is not too difficult. Senator Robert Dole's state of Kansas requires all whiskey makers to sell Kansas wholesalers at the same floor price they charge all other wholesalers in the nation. The primary suppliers post prices at their parity. The state goes even further. It requires retailers to add a certain markup. This is done to maintain trade stability even though the *Statistical Abstract* give figures to indicate that never in history has there been as much whiskey in the warehouses. If Kansas and the other forty-nine states can require each pint of whiskey entering trade channels to have a parity price, then surely the powerful federal government can pass a law to keep the trades from literally stealing raw farm production.

Why not a loan program or a subsidy?

The loan program concept embodies a fundamental error. It permits buying power to be brought into existence and farmers to spend that money without the goods actually moving through the system. When the so-called stored surplus is eventually sold into trade channels, the farmer has already been paid for it, and he has spent the money. All he now gets in payment for the surplus in a loan program when it is sold is the price difference between the loan received and the market price at that time. Under a sound parity program, the farmer must be paid full parity for production only when it enters the marketplace, and not one minute earlier. The loan system is a fundamental error because the farmer gets a loan price but in the end gives it away through inflation, or he creates stored inventories (because of distorted and shorted buying power) that hang over the economy and ultimately destroy the parity program. It can be fairly stated that government programs have been used to insure cheap farm prices through loans and have forced perpetual expansion of debt, and these programs have at the same time assured built-in inflation. Parity can apply only to commodities that can be used. This is why the price must come from the marketplace at the time of the sale, not from loans or from subsidy payments. Only by passing through the market at full parity can farm crops generate a multiplier effect. A government that can set rail rates and prices on a pint of whiskey can also name the price at which basic raw farm commodities can enter trade channels. As for the subsidy concept, it represents little more than frustration economics—the tawdry business of keeping farm prices at a world level and giving a relief check to farmers to pace the rate of farm bankruptcy. The idea of the subsidy is to throw the farmer a bone so he won't get too restless for government comfort.

Can you summarize?

The present type programs all were brought into being under the theory that it would be better to give the farmer a relief check to keep him satisfied politically than to permit him a proper price at the market. Farmers who understand economics are not asking for loan supports. They are asking for parity at the marketplace. It is realized that to pay for exports of manufactured goods, financiers import many products from their acquired sources of production in other lands. These imports displace our own farm crops enough to create a spot surplus. Yet farm prices could be maintained by maintaining a price balance between six or seven of our basic crops—corn, wheat, barley, rye, soybeans, cotton, the foundation of all farm production—and the prices of finished goods as reflected in some normal period. If the general commodity index, which reflects industrial prices, moves 10% above a base period, then farm prices must also be adjusted to that index base. The big bugaboo about parity is "surplus," and the argument that agriculture will produce in excess of the economy's requirements. A good merchant maintains a price on his products. If he develops a surplus he has a sale and then spreads the markdown over the whole. He doesn't let the small overage set the price for the entire inventory. Even so, there is little evidence that a surplus could develop under parity conditions. Parity for agriculture follows the other economic indexes. After an initial adjustment, full parity has a stabilizing effect because it takes bites out of the real cause of inflation—debts pretending to be earnings, and interest compounding debt chain letter style. Parity has been scuttled during recent decades largely as homage to free international trade. Yet exports below production costs really subsidize foreign buyers. Exports going into the Common Market often deliver more in taxes to foreign countries than the American farmers get as a price, and then those taxes are used by foreign governments to subsidize import invasion into the United States to further debase American farm prices. Opposition to full parity is based largely on conjectural economics and perceived self-interest. The only ones who profit from less-than-parity prices are the great lending institutions that profit by keeping the economy trapped in ever-expanding debt.

But the government economists all say you are wrong, that parity won't work. What do you say?

Perhaps it would be more to the point to talk about track records. The government economists have had their way ever since the 1950s. As a consequence there hasn't been a balanced budget since the Truman years, when indeed farm raw materials last enjoyed parity for any period of time. If these gentlemen are so correct, then why is the American economic system poised at the brink of hyper-inflation and/ or collapse? What we're talking about here has worked whenever it has been tried. What they're talking about has never worked, and it has been tried countless times throughout history. It seems to us that economists who object to full parity for agriculture are letting failure go to their heads. It should stand to reason that nothing—not hummingbirds, bacteria or money—can compound itself chain letter style *ad infinitum.* At some point in time there will be a clash between mathematical ambition and physical possibility. If the present policy towards raw materials is continued, we will have between $8 and $12 trillion public and private debts by 1990, possibly $39 trillion by 2000, assuming the chain letter game could last. Inflation has to follow public and private debt expansion as a direct ratio. Historically debt is the mechanism used to take the wealth of a nation from the many and put it into the hands of a few. It is not likely that this present economic policy can be followed much longer without having it preside over fantastic adjustments in political and institutional arrangements in this country. To put it bluntly, this means the nation will go into receivership. In political language, receivership is simply dictatorship, and when it happens it will come because economists have thirty years of failure under the belt.

If we have reached the point of no return, doesn't this in effect annihilate the concept of parity?

No. The economy will slide into a depression. This cannot be stopped. It will wash out a lot of debt and set the stage for recovery. But there can be no real recovery without parity. That's the lesson history has taught. In fact, 1980 was probably the point of no return because the debt structure at that point could no longer be adjusted to a sustainable basis. According to the Office of Management and Budget, borrowings for 1982 were computed at near $206 billion. Yet national net savings were only some $223 billion. Net borrowings simply have to take over 100% of national net savings. The word here has to be crisis! Only farm parity can start undoing the damage accomplished over the last thirty years. Unfortunately, in the words of Dr. John L. King, a Wharton graduate and publisher of *Money Matters*, "the establishment economics that is taught in universities, proliferated in journals, regurgitated in councils of government, with all of its mountains of published output, has not advanced our capacity to control our economy beyond what it was in the late 1930s."

What would be the effect of farm parity prices for agriculture on industrial imports?

Parity for agriculture would secure parity for labor by bringing into focus the problem of import invasion. As it stands now, cheap goods flow to the high markets of the world. This import traffic has the same effect as importing cheap labor, and disemploys the American labor force. Thus the requirements of a parity equation for agriculture also make mandatory tariffs sufficient to make imports enter U.S. trade channels on par with goods produced at the American wage scale. Parity and structural balance cannot pertain only to agriculture. They must govern all sectors of the American economy, labor included, if full employment and a secure food lifeline are to be maintained. The impact of import invasion and resultant unemployment on the American labor force is substantial. Massachusetts Institute of Technology has estimated that approximately 25,000 jobs are eliminated for each $1 billion of direct private U.S. foreign investment. This would suggest that 6 million American jobs have been handed over to low cost employees the world over, chiefly in Asia. Workers thus unemployed pay out in more than lost jobs. A Johns Hopkins professor has computed that a 1% increase in unemployment rates increases 36,887 more deaths, 4,227 first admissions to mental hospitals and 3,340 commitments to prisons. In 1980 U.S. firms increased their investments abroad by $8.2 billion (to a new total of $52.7 billion). Wages in some of these countries are 50 cents an hour. Over 238,000 people were employed in the manufacture of electric and electronic equipment in low wage countries. Low wages and even lower farm prices have resulted in out-migration from farms in these countries. As a consequence, there has been a demand for farm crop exports from the U.S. *at low prices* to accommodate the wishes of the multinational exploiters of labor and agriculture.

Then in order to stabilize the money and regulate the value thereof, Congress must achieve structural balance or parity. Are the two synonymous?

Yes, they are. Parity is not just something for agriculture. There has to be a parity for labor, for business, for interest. This is what is meant by structural balance. For all practical purposes, an economy based on structural balances is one based on par exchange. Unfortunately the economic managers now refuse to evaluate this requirement of the exchange economy. For the time being, the interest mechanism is being used to fly another mini-cycle across the economic landscape. This distortion of logic has invaded every area of society.

Reports on economics that surfaced in *Acres U.S.A.* would fill several books the size of this one. And yet it remained the one area for which reader comprehension lagged. Over the years I had long conversations with Carl H. Wilken, Arnold Paulson, and Nebraska bankers Vince Rossiter and Ray Dykeman about this. The average person simply couldn't handle the abstractions involved, it seemed.

And yet the answer to this dilemma is contained in *The Age of Inflation*, by Jacques Rueff, the French economist. Rueff pointed out that the rules for the individual were exactly opposite the rules required for an economy. It was in the interest of the home owner to get cheap electricity, but electricity too cheap soon reduced the power and light company to insolvency. Cheap food seems something devoutly to be wished for the population, but cheap food soon means hungry people. The parable can be extended *ad infinitum*.

"Farm income has a duality that other types of income do not have," I testified before a House sub-committee, reciting words and sentences that had been pushed through *Acres U.S.A.* several times before. I was leaning on Vince Rossiter and an analysis he had made a decade earlier when these concepts were equally a mystery. Ten years of added instruction, it seemed, should make the mystery come clear. "It serves as the basic operating income for the farmer, obviously. And it provides the foundation income for rural townspeople who provide services to the farmer as a consequence of the division of labor. But farm income means much more than that. Farm income is the biggest share of the total new wealth created by an economy in any given year, and it therefore accounts for the total addition to the existing money supply. It—with other raw materials income—is the source of investment for expansion and the foundation for the total savings of the economy.

"In truth, our national capital fund was built from a virgin country. It took generations—each adding annually the gross value of raw materials production—one year atop the last—to bring on savings. And these savings—savings which reflected a holdback from consumption—built so many homes, churches, highways, permanent capital improvements. In earlier times people waited for the next crop to come in to finish a project. We've learned to borrow against future earnings since then, and so we can have it now—but we still owe for it.

"But no capital or savings are generated if raw materials entering the cycle are not monetized at par with wages and capital costs."

I asked the Congressmen attending that session to read *The Age of Inflation,* and then I quoted from it. "Inflation does more than complicate the work of parliaments; it makes them a laughing stock and discredits them." And then I added on my own: "It causes legislatures to sacrifice freedom to sooth the indigestion caused by a lack of par exchange between farm and city, between city and state, and state and nation. Always, the so-called beneficiaries of Fabian measures become the first victims. Witness the cries of retired persons, social security recipients, and the receivers of transfer payments."

This declining rate of profit for the economy (because the farmer was not being paid) was accommodated by inflation these many years, and by unions pressuring for inflationary increases, and by business enterprise accommodating the accommodators despite the fact that industry did not have the ability to pay the asking price. And farmers basked in their own ignorance by simply blaming the middleman.

When I first started to attend college in 1946, the United Auto Workers settled a four month strike for 18.5 cents an hour—this being five cents over what they had been offered—not a very big increase. At that time United Auto Workers President Walter Reuther said, "Wages are limited by a corporate ability to pay, and by our ability to produce without raising prices." And he went on, "I'm not interested in negotiating the wooden nickels of inflation." Not only Reuther, but the AFL approved of this. Some even criticized Reuther because they thought 18.5 cents an hour increase was too much.

When hearings were held in 1946 on the Employment Act of that year, Walter Reuther said he understood that labor could not have more of a parity than agriculture without bringing on inflation and a declining rate of profit and future investment. Yet when I asked Leonard Woodcock, his successor, about this, he couldn't recall this testimony and he saw no relationship between agriculture and labor and business profits.

A few years earlier, according to Opinion Research, Americans believed the average profit margin in industry to be 20% of sales, and they believed this to be too high. At the time of that testimony they believed it was 33%. Yet industry at large got something like 4.5%. Opinion Research Corporation said Americans believe that for every income dollar split between labor and stockholders, labor got twenty-five cents and stockholders got seventy-five cents. This was arithmetic illiteracy, if not complete madness, yet this is what people thought.

Withal, it was the nature of coin and currency that baffled the fools and fooled the wise. For most people, money simply is out there, like air and water, a fixed supply workers struggle for the way a victim of emphysema gasps for air. Few people—including most *Acres U.S.A.* readers—managed to handle the money bit, and thus they were forever viewing economics much like the affairs of a small business raised to the *nth* power, or as some big mystery.

A question often posed, "What did parity cost the American economy?" was answered routinely in *Acres U.S.A.*, meaning several times a year. It cost nothing, not one dime, not one penny, not one brass farthing. By requiring new wealth harvested from nature to enter trade channels at an indexed par exchange, the economy generated enough earnings to pay for WWII, for instance. That's how it works, I told *Acres U.S.A.* readers over and over, and it won't work any other way for very long. An economy has to monetize—that is, turn into money—the production taken from farms, mines, stone quarries, even the pre-Cambrian harvest of energy called oil, and fish from the sea. It takes price to turn corn into money, nothing else—not tax rebates, not cheap interest, not relief checks, not soothing words from Senator Bob Dole, not sermonettes about free international trade or the right to go broke.

At a Chamber of Commerce meeting one day I asked the lecturing economist how come Truman was able to balance several budgets, and no one else has been able to do this except by statistical manipulation ever since. Was Truman a genius? I asked. The answer would have qualified for a Shirley Temple tap dance. I had the floor and I could have explained that Truman balanced those budgets because parity agriculture earned the national income that made it possible. But without a few weeks of prime instruction, this would have been lost on the group, the mystification of economics was that complete.

Frequently farmers called my office. "What's the catch with this parity idea? Come on, level with me."

I will now tell you exactly what I have told each and every caller. There is only one flaw. When there is par exchange, the producers of real wealth prosper. They pay off their debts. They enjoy the earnings of the just. And then I had to recite the rest of the equation. The speculators take a beating. The bankers go hungry. The international flim-flam men lose their base, and the munitions makers find their profits eroded by peace. When basic raw commodities—beyond certain specialties—move across borders at less than equity of exchange, armies follow, either to staff the killing grounds or to stand guard as constabularies.

In 1979, Arnold Paulson and I met with representatives of the General Accounting Office, an agency that serves Congress with expert information. The agency had been mandated to study NORM's brand of parity and the principles contained in *Unforgiven*, and we outlined the necessary model. The researchers did a fine job, but before their findings could be published the hatchet men—meaning the peer review people serving the powers that be—removed the logic, the syllogism and the substance of that report.

Without a political outcry from agriculture, without a rationale from the economists, the job of bleeding agriculture proceeded through the '50s, the '60s, the '70s, and through the 1980s. If a farm was completely paid for in 1980, and the farmer didn't have sense enough to quit, and there was no off-farm income, the chances were 90% that by 1985 the farmer would be mortgaged out as far as Farm and Home or Land Bank would let him go. The chances were 90% that this farmer had listened to wild optimism about feeding the world, about that Earl Butz payday just around the corner. And then one day or month or year, while he slept, the farmer's equity evaporated. Land values fell. And commodity prices fell even faster. And the professors who had told him to mortgage out, to borrow to the hilt, softly whispered, "Bad manager." The farmer was somehow to pay for inflated land with deflated commodities. And in the wings stood Farm Bureau telling the trapped farmers to get out of the way, their acres were needed in strong hands. President Reagan was saying, *Keep the grain and export the farmers!* And Senator Dole was advising farmers on how to suffer.

One morning it came to me that the *Acres U.S.A.* brand of reporting was no longer entirely unique. The public prints were covering the mortgage foreclosure story, but they couldn't seem to understand cause and effect. Nor could the policy paper writers. They talked about world markets, but they failed to explain how these markets were to generate the wherewithal to buy. They gloried in PL 480 programs and all sorts of credit devices to enrich themselves in this international system, but they never explained to themselves or to the world how this bloodletting of American agriculture could be made sustainable now that the frontier was gone.

The flack I received was only moderate when I commented on a paper styled *Bishop's Pastoral*. It had been written for the signature of

127

the Catholic Bishops and was filled with moral sentiments that answered many of the prime bankruptcies that faced the nation, chiefly the spiritual and managerial bankruptcies, this abandonment of God and morality in business dealings. But there was not one footnote on par exchange, without which there can be no strong internal economy. There was not one word for equity of trade, without which it is impossible to fashion the fabric of help for the world's needy. I offered the advice that the pastoral be dropped into the garbage can, and that the Bishops vote instead on two paragraphs in Pope Paul VI's encyclical on *Peoples and Progress*. For Pope Paul wanted equity of trade, or international parity at an appropriate level.

Some people—including all the newsletter writers of the nation, Arnold Paulson excepted—would come up fighting from their chairs when I suggested a political solution to the farm problem, a mandated parity equation such as we have for a minimum wage law, an indexed regulation for basic storable commodities not unlike the index system used to determine telephone and utility rates. No, they would scream, the holy of holies, the market must decide. And so they became married to the breath-taking absurdity called free international trade, as though there existed a rational basis for trade between a dollar a day country and an $80 a day labor country. All they knew was that hustlers ought to be free to plunder the earth without answering to anyone. As a result, the concepts revealed in *Acres U.S.A.* rated no consideration whatsoever at monetary conferences, where the newsletter fraternity met. The prize was simply there—like a mother-lode of gold—and the actors had their roles, which in any case would deliver the greatest good to the most people—never mind the sins of erosion, a growing inventory of the world's impoverished, and the wasting away of mental acuity on the broadest scale in history.

This was the problem Ken Stofferahn faced in his South Dakota Senatorial campaign. The market, unfortunately, is merely a world government of grain. By common consent, no more than five major international firms own millions of serfs called farmers, and the governments that ought to protect their own do nothing except recite sayings that belong in stories that begin with "Once upon a time . . ."

In the mid 1980s, *Acres U.S.A.* published a comment by Charles Luxem, a Minnesota business consultant, and a one time NORM speaker. It would not be long before the insanity of our situation would become apparent to even the slow thinkers among us, he said. And then would come a time of fear, anger, and despair. "Those who remain will have to choose between God, the government and the gun. If we choose the gun we will perish by the gun. If we depend on government alone, we will suffer terribly, for government has only legislation, taxation and coercion at its disposal. But if we turn to God, we can find an economic turnaround," he said.

The parity story handed off by *Acres U.S.A.* deserved complete codification beyond what I had accounted for in *Unforgiven*. I had always hoped Arnold Paulson would do this. But he couldn't.

At the 1980 meeting of NORM at Dodge City, Kansas, Arnold Paulson retired to his motel room, doubled over with pain. Later he rose above his agony to conclude the meeting. A few days after that he checked in at the Mayo Clinic in Rochester, Minnesota. Too soon the word came back. Arnold Paulson had cancer, and it was in an advanced stage. The doctors said they could do nothing and suggested he do nothing. But Arnold fought on. He flew to Las Vegas and checked in at the Degenerative Disease Center on the Strip. The DMSO treatments relieved the pain, but little more. To the end he received visitors and "held court," the medical staffers told me. Finally, they sent him home to die.

A year later NORM met at Dodge City again. I was selected to present a memorial eulogy. Accordingly I repaired to my room at the motel and wrote out a message in longhand. I recalled the great men I had known and I compared them to Paulson in my mind. I recalled the wounds Arnold Paulson had suffered at the hands of his friends, and how he refused to make denunciation—how his silence shouted to the world. It took over an hour to write that draft. It is reproduced here exactly as spoken, January 16, 1981.

Your presence here tonight—at this annual meeting of NORM—is the finest tribute anyone could pay to Arnold Paulson. Had this evening been otherwise, had a dozen Executive Committee members and a few Board Members arrived here—and no more—it would have been a sad tribute. It would have meant that we could not carry on, that Arnold Paulson had failed to do what he had set out to do.

So now, with your presence here, we know that you heard the bell toll on that crisp morning almost a year ago. And we know you stood by as associates and relatives carried our friend to his resting place.

Perhaps we said too little at the time. We all knew he loved us more than life itself, that he was a man for all seasons. Words would not come easily. But now time has intervened, and perhaps we can correctly evaluate the enduring quality of Arnold Paulson.

Nature has decreed that the wisdom, tolerance and fortitude accumulated during the lifetime of one individual cannot be gifted to those he leaves behind. It is a wise provision. For who among us could bear the crushing burden of Arnold Paulson's greatness?

He lived at a time when it was easy to bury the body of a murdered conscience without risk of detection, yet he kept his alive at great personal cost. He had gone the route of the businessman—the Chamber of Commerce spokesman—content to get and spend, buy and sell, but his soul hungered for more. He listened vainly, but with thirsty ear, for the wondrous wisdom that a nation needed, but found wanting. And so he set out to seek the cause of the cause the way a saint seeks God.

In the early 1960s, Arnold Paulson made a classic study at Granite Falls, Minnesota. He searched for the source of the income that supported his community—and finally he found it. He found it on the farms serviced by rural mail carriers, and he found that city prosperity was an illusion without a supporting rural prosperity. His life was never the same after that. In the fullness of time, he became Carl Wilken's most capable student. Others heard and studied Carl Wilken, but we are well within our mark when we say that Arnold Paulson outpaced them all—always opting for even greater understanding first—and then unity in essential things, liberty in nonessential things, and charity in all things!

There were times when a yawning chasm developed between Arnold Paulson and the leadership of other organizations he loved, but he did not feel compelled to go about the countryside making public denunciation of any betrayal. And in these tests of conscience, his silence shouted louder than the fervent approval of a thousand lesser men. "It isn't difficult to stay in good graces," he said. "Just don't make trouble."

But if truth meant trouble, he seemed to say, *So be it.*

Now that our friend and teacher is gone, we see too clearly others who saved themselves with a word, a wretched compromise, a momentary closing of the eyes, a barely discernable shrug of the shoulders.

These things were not for Arnold Paulson. He enjoyed the cerebral life, and he would have agreed with the prayer of St. Francis—*Lord, that I may seek more to understand than to be understood.* To live up to this prayer—that was Arnold Paulson's trial. He enjoyed the rapture of understanding, and he suffered the curse of not being understood. Yet in the end he knew he had succeeded beyond his wildest dream.

When Carl Wilken passed from the scene a decade ago, he left only Arnold Paulson with his lessons in tow—and perhaps a few others!

But when Arnold Paulson departed less than ten months ago, he left hundreds if not thousands—including the leadership of American Agriculture Movement, and NORM—who understood parity, the role of raw materials income in the solvency of an economy—hundreds who knew the joy of understanding and perhaps the agony of awaiting a new convulsion on the curve of history.

And so it seems the book was not really closed when the bell tolled, but that it was reissued, just as Arnold Paulson would have wanted it.

For All Mankind is of one author and one volume, the poet has said. When one man dies, one chapter is not torn out of the book, but is translated into a better language. And every chapter must be so translated. God employs several translators. Some things are translated by age, some by sickness and suffering, some by war, some by justice, some by failure, some by success. But God's hand is in every translation.

We have been told about Arnold Paulson's last ordeal. But there was a brighter side to the life and death of our friend and associate.

We have a feeling Arnold Paulson knew he had done his work quite well—that he had passed the torch to a new generation, and it was now their responsibility to carry on, to extend and expand the lessons and the wisdom, for surely what had been written and translated with the pen could not be removed with a hatchet. When Arnold Paulson was already shod with stone and gloved with the leaden look of a fading life, he found a great personal joy. He wrote to his minister about his life, his trials, his almost unbearable pain, and the pain suffered by his wife and family—and about his victory!

"Oh, but what a victory! What joy! It's the greatest thing that has happened to me in all my life! I had no idea of the peace and joy and comfort Christ could give me during these days of strife," he wrote.

But what about the others, the people who heard, but did not listen. What about the leaders in Washington who trundled Arnold Paulson's statistics and advice into a lower drawer or a wastebasket? What about the marathon failures who continue to glory in their failure? What about economists who know no answers and know no questions? To them the message is as clear as only the poet John Donne could make it clear.

"No man is an island . . . every man is a piece of the continent, a part of the main. If a clod be washed away by the sea, the mainland is the less. Any man's death diminishes me because I am involved in mankind. And therefore never send to know for whom the bell tolls. It tolls for thee."

11

MEN WITHOUT PEERS

Lee Fryer always struck me as an iconoclast, a scribe with reverence for humanity, and a perceptive student of government. He is also a fine agronomist and a passable humorist. He is probably the nearest thing to the ritually uncircumcised philosopher, Phil Allen, who I mentioned earlier. Although I have never been able to make the parity connection for him—I have seen him wince with pain when I tried—he stood for that principle as a USDA official, and literally sacrificed his career over the issue of the family farm during the Orville Freeman administration. Yet for all his wisdom he reserved for himself certain bulletproof myths. When I thought I was using a cannon, he would use these myths to make my artillery pack all the wallop of a BB gun.

When I ran a series of articles on the Kervran effect—the business about transmutation of elements under microbial power—I could see Fryer's eyebrow raised all the way from Kansas City to Washington. I titled that particular story, *Nature's Atom Smasher*, not because Kervran used the terms, but because that language best translated biological transmutations into common language. The Kervran effect was a natural for a paper like *Acres U.S.A.* It gave me an opportunity to examine many imponderables. For instance, a chick at birth has a skeleton of bones. And the bones are composed of calcium. Yet there is not enough calcium in an egg to account for the appearance of bones. In fact a chick at birth has four times more calcium than can be found in both the yoke and the white of an egg. Research has demonstrated that the calcium does not come from the egg shell.

Take the dairy cow. This animal secretes more calcium than she ingests. In fact the cow has a negative balance sheet for both phosphorus and calcium. Weights of these elements for dairy animals "are noticeably inferior to the quantities of these elements which leave the animal's body with the milk." Obviously the cow has other uses for these elements, such as maintenance of her own body. These uses, together with the milk excreted, exceed the intake of those same elements via food. There has to be an indigenous production of phosphorus, but the rules of chemistry say this is not possible.

Take the terrestrial and marine iguana. Some species secrete a liquid containing up to one hundred ninety times more potassium than there is in the blood plasma, and they do this at a rate of one hundred ninety centimeters per hour.

Indeed, nature is chock-full of phenonema for which there are no questions, and questions for which there are no answers.

Why is it that whenever limestone is missing on lawns, daisies spring up as if by magic? Experienced folk gardeners know that daisies mean limestone deficiency. And yet when Ehrenfried Pfeiffer analyzed the ashes of daisies he found them to be rich in lime. Pfeiffer could not answer from whence came the lime. Indeed, Pfeiffer raised so many questions for which there were no answers, the process may have caused chemical agriculture to bypass his astounding biodynamic findings. When told that the oak tree indigenous to regions where limestone is missing contained limestone in the wood and bark (up to 60% lime being found in the ash test), the orthodox turned and walked away.

Louis C. Kervran was a noted French scientist, and at the time of our reports he was Chief of the Department of Hygiene in France. It was his theory that nature—operating with its microorganisms—in fact smashes atoms to make new elements. Allowed to operate, nature has many ways of preventing a deficiency, but nature can't operate if microorganisms are driven from the soil by certain salt fertilizers, phenoxy plant killers and toxic rescue chemicals.

Kervran said that insufficient production of the enzymes that carry out transmutations was the real culprit. The implications were clear. Increasingly, fertilization had to take on the task of building life into the soil system, rather than replacing elements, and this made technology that deals with carbon, humates, bacteria and soil life an important contribution to eco-agriculture. It also made obsolete the fertilizer laws of all states, and explained again why sovereign governments ought never to write laws prescribing what is science, and what should be ruled from the field. Kervran's message was as clear as anyone could make it. Either switch to biological agriculture, or starve!

It may have been overkill, but the *Acres U.S.A.* reports presented formulas and revealed how under proper life conditions isotopes came unhinged, reached for a new balance, and formed a new simple element. Biotic life did this atom smashing, so to speak, and this made microorganisms nature's prime mover in maintaining balance. It also put to pasture the concept that *balanced crops* can be grown hydroponically, in sterilized soil or in chemical systems devoid of nature's smallest workers. Without biotic life in the soil, crops became partially matured, carbon-based production that appear like food, but lack in the fundamental health necessary to ward off fungus and insect attack.

In response to these reports, Lee Fryer—ever the gadfly—wrote a letter—"I'll bet you took chemistry in high school." In time Lee Fryer came to have more than amazed interest in Kervran, but there was more fringe science on scene. Much of it had been described in *The Secret Life of Plants*, by Christopher Bird and Peter Thompkins. Lee could not identify with much of it, and he positively suppressed an inner merriment when—once upon a time—we visited Karl Schleiker's Mankind Unlimited in Washington, D.C., a not-for-profit operation which warehoused just about everything ever written about fringe science. I was therefore dismayed the day Phil Callahan's *Tuning In To Nature* dropped in over the transom, courtesy of Lee Fryer. For Callahan's story seemed to belong in a class with Kervran, dowsing, sound-inspired growth and audible whistles from the stomata of a leaf.

Frankly, I was arrested and chilled by Lee Fryer's icy intellect. I had met him in Kansas City at a conference he was staging to recover from his Freeman fiasco. He was fishing for a rural-urban coalition long before Jesse Jackson, albeit unsuccessfully. I lost track of him after that, largely, I suppose, because he had disappeared into Washington, D.C.'s ghetto outback, if the term can be permitted. There he met a fine young woman who was good enough to be interested in him, and about the time *Acres U.S.A.* came off the drawing board in the early 1970s, Lee Fryer surfaced with a new family and company and a book called *Earth Foods*. I have never been able to tunnel too far beneath his immense literary talent. If an emotional turmoil slumbered in his soul, it did not show on a face, which was usually as calm as sculptured stone.

Fryer seemed to say that economics was too interactive and too resistant to controlled experiments for anything meaningful to emerge, and for this reason the world bumbled from convulsion to convulsion, and there was really very little one could do about it. Didn't Lincoln say that without public opinion nothing could be accomplished, and with it nothing could fail? The problem was that too much public opinion was badly informed public opinion, and it was failing the nation.

Lee was really a surrogate political man. This role was assumed not because of snobbery, or an unwillingness to endure pizzas and meatball heroes, such as usually staff the leadership posts in farm organizations, but because he led best from the wings. With sardonic good humor, he could evaluate the usefulness of the Wobblies and true believer communists, never for an instant taking fright of their potential for mischief. They stimulated activity between the ears, but they were forever tormented, he said, by the fear that the social order would correct itself and steal their planks and deprive them of the glories that revolution would bestow. I had the feeling that Fryer viewed *Acres U.S.A.* that way, as a hedged upstart touched slightly by that same malaise.

I would issue no confirmation or denial. The human mind is too intricate, too wondrous, too rich for the analyst's scalpel. I am certain a hidden scar called the dust bowl and the Great Depression affected my thought processes, ergo the *Acres U.S.A.* output. But also I have been certain that *Acres U.S.A.* was a socially appropriate exercise, and those who come later would be able to appraise the rest.

Fryer was a conventional agronomist, a bit uneasy with some of the man-made molecules of poisons, but not at all certain that the LD_{50} system—the make-it-to-the-door-system—wasn't somewhat valid. But here was Fryer on the phone and by letter apparently accepting Phil Callahan, the biggest heretic to come down the pike in many a year.

Our coverage on all this assumed blockbuster status from the start, and it hasn't died down yet. For years people like Albrecht, Pfeiffer, Fenzau and Joseph Cocannour had known that insects and plants communicate with each other. Observant farmers had long wondered aloud how come insects knew just which plants provided the fare they wanted. Don Hart, a Texas panhandle farmer, had passed on the question for which we all sought answers. Greenbugs would invade one field of alfalfa, but not the next—or they would consume the crop to a knife-like division in the field, one defined by weed patterns, fertilizer mishaps, or changes in the geological makeup of the soil. What was it in nature that commanded the bugs to feast on one field, and not the next? How did the codling moth know where to go? Now Phil Callahan answered. Insects and plants send out frequencies in the infrared.

In order to understand this, a view of the full electromagnetic spectrum is required.

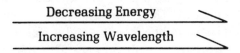

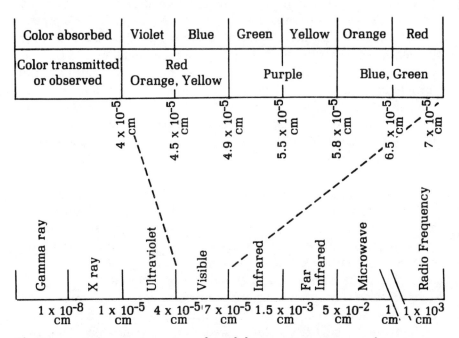

Electromagnetic spectrum in order of decreasing energy and increasing wavelength.

This diagram illustrates the division of the electromagnetic spectrum in order of decreasing energy and increasing wavelength. The bottom scale has the whole package. Dotted lines take the reader into a breakdown of the visible part of the spectrum—the one we're all more familiar with.

Using instrumentation available only recently, Callahan proved that insects emit a coded infrared signal, and it contains a unique navigational message. When insects fly, they vibrate their antennae at the same frequency that they flap their wings. Insect antennae pluck the signal out of the air.

"The female moth, for instance, emits her signal from the scent gland at the top of her abdomen as she vibrates her wings. During emission her temperature increases 6 to 16 Fahreinheit above that of the surrounding air space. This means that as the scent drifts through the air pushed by the gentle breeze, it cools and decreases in concentration. The scent flows along in the water vapor of the gaseous atmosphere which is the carrier gas," Callahan said. Close to the female, wavelengths are long. A few hundred feet away they are short. In electronics this system is called "concentration tuning."

Insects use short spines (sensilla) to resonate to short wavelengths, longer sensilla to read the signals as they close in. There are spines for tuning in to sex scents—a part of nature's mating game. There are sensilla for detecting infrared radiations from the food supply. Plants, after all, have odors, and odors are governed by health or the lack thereof, regardless of whether pathology is gross or, say, the corn plant is simply subclinically ill.

Callahan proved that the moth is programmed like an orbiting satellite to respond to a series of frequencies. There are seventeen micrometer pheromone lines present in the candle. "Thus the candle mimics the moth body-wing-modulated signal because the flickering of the flame in the air modulates the candle blackbody radiation between six and twenty-five micrometers—exactly what the moth is programmed to respond to."

Picture the scene. A female cabbage looper moth releases a pheromone scent from the tip of her abdomen. It is a complex molecule composed of alcohols and acetates hitched together as a long chain. Free in the atmosphere it is a complex trace element in solvent because of water vapor in the night air. This pheromone is pumped along by other trace elements in the air. Insect sensilla pluck these signals right out of the evening mist. "The drifting plume of pheromone not only gives direction to the flying male but also the distance from the female by reference to the wavelengths at specific concentrations and temperatures in the air," said Callahan.

Do plants transmit the signals that call in cutworms, cabbage loopers, moths or earworms? Even those who agree in principle tend to disagree on specifics, but at least one school believes that daily life rhythms are timed from the body. If this is so, then the makeup of the plant—the enzymatic and hormonal balance as governed by soil fertility, nutrients and balance thereof—determines whether these microminiature transmitters attract or repel.

I figured it was well within reason to suggest that a subclinically sick plant would have an altered wavelength. Is this why insects attack the undernourished plant, the one with missing trace nutrients? If so, then the questions have been answered by the eco-farmer who has discovered the bio-chemistry of immunity not only in genetic engineering, but also in fertility management.

All this made wonderful reading for *Acres U.S.A.* It also infuriated Callahan's contemporaries that a scientist of note would publish without peer review, and then further sully the profession by writing articles for a paper such as *Acres U.S.A.* Callahan responded, "A man who is the first to discover something has no peers." He might have added that by going into print again and again without the blessings of peers, he foreclosed on them the possibility of their stealing his findings.

Callahan in fact continued to write about what pleased him. His biography appeared in that hauntingly beautiful book, *The Soul of the Ghost Moth*, but I really did not get to know the soul of Callahan until he led an *Acres U.S.A.* sponsored tour of Egypt. Of a sudden his visions about Irish round towers, pyramids and low-level energy came clear. The Egyptians were naturalists, and likely they used principles found in nature to slide giant obelisks into place, hoist railroad engine-sized stone blocks atop pyramids, and perform the other wonders of the ancient world. My son Fred was handling the manuscript of a short book by Phil Callahan at the time. I suggested the title, *Ancient Mysteries, Modern Visions*. Phil asked Fred to write the foreword. It turned out to be a superb message, one that put into perfect focus the man and the scientist.

Science [wrote Fred Walters], perhaps to an extent unparalleled in any other field of human endeavor, has a very peculiar set of standards, norms, expectations, dogma and even rules. For instance, freshman science students are repeatedly hammered with the philosophy of the scientific method. The scientific method, a deductive form of reasoning, was designed to provide science with a foundation and framework into which all of the assorted bits of information could fit to form an integrated area of knowledge. It reaches not only into the cataloging and collecting of bits of information, but into actual discovery. It is also drawn upon by scientists to provide a logical way of finding the answers to problems.

The first step in applying the scientific method to the solution of a problem involves carrying out a series of experiments designed to gather all facts about the particular problem being investigated. Then a simple generalization is formulated to correlate these facts. If successful, this generalization becomes scientific law. A jump such as this is seldom made, however, without an intermediate stage—the hypothesis. This is, for the lack of a better term, an educated guess. It is one idea that may serve to join the various facts observed. An hypothesis will be subjected to further experimentation in the attempt to find a flaw. If generally unrefuted, the educated guess will earn the status of theory, where it will likely remain for fear someone will find an exception. It is far more acceptable to disprove a theory than a law.

There is a second scientific method that, although unwritten, has far greater impact on scientists and their findings. This is the reality of project funding, peer review and the publishing of scientific papers. These subjects were discussed in the scandalous book, *The Double Helix*, by James D. Watson, one of the discoverers of the structure of the DNA molecule. He rocked the scientific world by discussing the behind-the-scenes power plays and the jealousy and fighting for funding. But Watson offered these as an aside, showing that scientific discovery is a very human process, not a cold, mechanical ordeal filled with test tubes and microscopes. Discovery relies on a vision.

Like Watson, Phil Callahan has not let the various bureaucracies and administrative tangles taint his love for science and life. Phil Callahan left Louisiana State University at Baton Rouge because he wanted to study biological methods for insect control, whereas the system told him to study pesticides. Many of the discoveries explained [in *Ancient Mysteries, Modern Visions*] are still being bandied about by the scientific community. In fact, Callahan actually has a letter that states, "You went too far," implying that he discovered too much. His discoveries, however, are now a matter of public record, and the right of discovery cannot be denied Phil Callahan. But the implications of Callahan's discoveries are too earth-shaking for a professional journal to risk its reputation in covering.

Phil Callahan does not rebel merely against the formalities of the unwritten scientific method, but against the formal scientific method as well. He openly states that both are ridiculous concepts. A good scientist does not make a discovery through the process of deduction. On the contrary, he discovers through induction. *All great scientific discoveries*, says Callahan, *originate with observing something in nature. Then you try to explain it.* But to utilize inductive reasoning and gather facts from all sources, a scientist must be a generalist. He must be crossed-trained in all fields. Modern practice dictates specialization and fields of expertise. Unfortunately for these scientists, nature knows no boundaries. Her wonders traverse all areas of science.

In earlier times, scientists were literally called *natural philosophers.* They were naturalists and generalists. No one seems to ask why the great discoverers were often experimenting in fields outside their area of expertise. They were often great artists, observers of nature, as well as engineers and scientists. For all of their specialization, famous universities, in general, do not produce Nobel laureates. They hire them after the fact.

Phil Callahan is a natural philosopher of the same school as da Vinci, Galileo, Newton and Tesla. His formal training reads of degrees in literature, ornithology and finally a Ph.D. in entomology, the study of insects. He accumulated his informal training as he walked from Japan to Ireland, stopping to observe people and nature along the way. He meditated in the great temples of bygone eras. He lived with the Bedouins in the desert. He ate insects to survive. And he slept in the great stone cathedrals that are now roped off from tourists. It is from this rich background and broad base of experience that he draws far-reaching conclusions that only a cross-trained natural philosopher could account for.

It is exactly because we live in a society of specialization that ancient peoples are misinterpreted. Hieroglyphics in Egyptian temples are misidentified because archeologists do not study entomology. Tales of monks floating in the air are dismissed as folly because anthropologists and historians do no understand natural forms of magnetism. History tells us about wars and death on the battlefield, not about agriculture and the lives of people. Probably the greatest reason for error in our analyses of ancient civilizations is that we relate their lifestyles to our own preconceptions. Phil Callahan is a naturalist, just as ancient peoples were naturalists. He is a 4,000-year-old man who has somehow found himself perfectly comfortable with computerized instrumentation. It is this rare mix that the world does not see enough of, and perhaps it is because men like Phil Callahan are thought not to exist that they frequently go unappreciated.

But Phil Callahan is not unappreciated. Instead of embittering himself to the world and fighting for peer acceptance, he is writing of his discoveries in language that ordinary people can understand, no clouding the wonders of nature with technical hocus-pocus. He is helping us all understand the very nature of life and how it relates to man, his religions and his agriculture. For this we owe Dr. Phil Callahan a very great debt."

I liked the line, "a 4,000-year-old man," and I always suspected that Phil was pleased with it. The ability to understand peoples in terms of their times is rather special, and it fit in the pages of my unique journal because so many of our readers saw our good news in exactly the same light. The cast of characters that has paraded through the pages of *Acres U.S.A.* has meant good news to thousands of readers, but few have enjoyed the rapport bestowed by common consent on the lanky, bearded, balding entomologist, Phil Callahan.

Word for word, however, it fell to Lee Fryer to channel perhaps the most quality copy through *Acres U.S.A.* It was Fryer's vision that reasonable men could live in both worlds. For this attitude he was often seen as a point man for the Fertilizer Institute, and by the Institute as a man whose intellect had collapsed into folklore unsupported by science.

This was less than justice from both sides, but it managed to be ironed out as the readership matured and took on the happy duty of doing its own thinking. More than most, Fryer taught "your own thinking," especially when he released *Food Power From the Sea.* His *Bio-Gardener's Bible*, extracts of which filled the pages of *Acres U.S.A.* for months, was really a better book, but for our readers it was sullied by the gardener's handle, which was strictly a publisher's choice, since the book dealt with management of a farmer's soil system.

After a decade and a half of reporting the many ramifications of the eco-farming story, *Acres U.S.A.* could take pride in having the largest readership in the country that could read between the lines—our lines included—and think for themselves. And so if a great debt was owed to people like Phil Callahan, Louis Kervran, and the followers of Ehrenfried Pfeiffer and William A. Albrecht, an equal debt was still on the books to Lee Fryer.

12

A PIECE OF PAPER

Judy Piatt seemed too frail and used for her age when I first met her at an Environmental Protection Agency hearing in Kansas City. I had brashly read into the record a short statement that both stated the premises upon which *Acres U.S.A.* had been founded, and ended by reciting anew the proposition that there was no place at all for toxic genetic chemistry in agriculture. The gale of silence that followed my testimony could have sunk the battleship Missouri, it was that deafening. Standing in the back of the hearing room, Judy Piatt alone applauded. It was the gesture of a queen.

A few years earlier she and a partner built a large indoor horse arena with seventy stalls, a restaurant, a saddle shop, seating for the public, and offices, all under one roof. She named it Shenandoah Stables. Business consisted of training and boarding and selling horses, and maintenance of quality breeding stock for the purpose of raising registered quarterhorses. She purchased two famous quarterhorse stallions and several mares with quality bloodlines. Shortly before the "accident," one of the stallions bred forty-one outside mares. Judy's two young daughters became successful in showing their ponies and horses. They did their own work such as feeding and grooming and exercising their animals. Because of the arena's success, Judy contracted with one Russell Bliss for an oil product to hold down the dust. The material he used contained a dioxin contaminant, a byproduct of a now defunct maker of toxophene near Springfield, Missouri.

The early warning system went into effect almost immediately. Birds that flew across the arena fell out of the air and died. The resident cats lost their hair. A couple of weeks later Judy's little poodle became sick. She took him to the vet hospital. There his condition worsened. A few days after that the unknown malaise touched human beings, right and left. Judy's partner suffered soreness in his joints, and found it difficult to work. Soon she found herself working eighteen hours a day with constant headaches. And then the horses started dying. A junior stallion suffered terribly for fifteen days, then died, and was taken to the University of Missouri for necropsy. When Judy Piatt returned she found blood in the kitchen and in the bathroom. Her youngest daughter had been hemorrhaging. With that St. Louis Children's Hospital and the Center for Disease Control, Atlanta, got into the act. But there were still no answers.

Judy Piatt informed the people who boarded their horses that the experts could not identify the problem and told them to board their horses elsewhere. That weekend the boarders left, and with them went the income needed to support the stables.

"The following three years we lived our lives in a constant state of wondering," Judy told *Acres U.S.A.* "We watched helplessly and in total frustration as sixty-two registered horses, twelve cats, four dogs and two fed billygoats died horrible deaths. We lost a good reputation that we had earned." There was more. She lost the ability to make money as her business developed a reputation for dying animals. The best stallion was no longer popular, but a horse that had weighed 1,300 pounds and now weighed 650 pounds. She was forced to give up her home and stable and lost all but three of her animals. Within three years she did not have one single mare or one single foal. Those years also brought ugly facts to her daughters. They watched with horror as their beloved ponies and show mares died. "The most difficult thing I had to bear through it all was their naive questions of, *Mom, if there is a God, why did he let our animals die?* I could only tell them that God would make it all better some day."

The chemical contaminant that caused all this mischief was dioxin. And because an illiterate oil salvage operator lied about his load, and the scientific establishment couldn't even make an educated guess for years, dioxin continued to fill the dumpsites and lace the dust cover of village streets, its damage seldom to be measured.

When Judy Piatt recited her story before an *Acres U.S.A.* conference, there was hardly a dry eye in the place. If ever there was cause to remember Rachel Carson, this was it. "If the Bill of Rights contains no guarantee that a citizen shall be secure against lethal poisons distributed whether by private individuals or by public officials," Rachel Carson had written, "it is surely only because our forefathers, despite their considerable wisdom and foresight, could conceive of no such problem."

Indeed, they could not, otherwise George Neary of Chico, California would not have become a continuing report over several years in *Acres U.S.A.*

Scabies is a nutritional disease. It is generally brought on by an excess amount of zinc in the mineral ration, and this zinc is almost always in the wrong form. Copper often is balanced to start, but as soon as too much zinc enters the picture, the copper is complexed.

Cowmen who know their business never confuse credentials with having an education. Education comes from observing that ration minerals often don't do their job. They are frequently not assimilated by the blood system of the animal. They stay in the rumen and then pass out through the feces. Forage, feed, even computerized rations that do not contain zinc in chelated form, set up an animal for disease conditions such as scabies. Regardless of contact or migration potential, scabies cannot endure when proper metabolism is taking place in the animal.

Informed cowmen know that trace mineral nutritional balance determines all disease. It is the institutional experts who want to make excuses for incredible eradication programs or toxic cures by pointing to pathogens and parasites when in fact it is a weakness in the nutritional system that makes animals susceptible. The great French scientist and farmer, Andre Voisin, writing in *Soil, Grass and Cancer*, was among the first to point out that the dust of cells is the dust of the soil, and that if these dusts "have been wrongly assembled in plant, animal or human cells, the result will be imperfect functioning of the latter." Cells that do not function properly invite opportunist organisms and parasites, and cells that function properly, Voisin argued, make it impossible for organisms and parasites to endure and function. Dr. John Whittaker, a veterinarian who wrote over a hundred columns for *Acres U.S.A.*, expanded on this topic by making the bad nutrition-mold connection.

In Neary's case, the problem was that California Department of Food and Agriculture gumshoes hadn't read Voisin, or even *Acres U.S.A.* for that matter. And so they came unglued when someone computed that one hundred eighty cases of scabies existed in North America's 120 million beef cow herd. This meant chemical treatment, possibly because of the handsome balance sheet it delivered to chemical firms.

And so they came to Neary's ranch while he was away. The

objective—to cure the beef cow herd with toxaphene. Each animal was forced into a cabinet that was built like a carwash—a six-sided box big enough to hold a cow. Animals were run up a ramp with a hotshot, always nervous and hyperventilating. The coffin was then slammed shut and a four hundred pound per square inch jet spray from a mass of nozzles raked the animals for two or three minutes—body, eyes, ears, nose and anus. In a totally oxygen-deprived atmosphere saturated with toxaphene, the animals got a lung full of the neurotoxin.

In about three minutes the animals stumbled out, eyes bugged after irritation by the astringent material. They staggered into the corral and started dying. Before it was over, more than four hundred animals expired in agony.

In covering the story I used the present tense for a few paragraphs.

The cows die hard. Some of them go into labor. They squeeze their uterus out in chunks. Some of them have massive cerebral hemorrhages. Blood spurts out their eye sockets and nose. The dead are everywhere. Although animal bodies are opened, tissue samples taken, raw visera exposed, temperature 70 degrees, there are no maggots or flies. A dog eats some of the meat and makes it about 100 yards. A fox does not make it that far. A vulture starts to fly away, but crashes in the field. The animals do not decompose. They just lie there, embalmed.

In the meantime the government people started covering their tracks. Three times—two times to Neary personally, once on TV—the state people admitted they'd given Neary a release order to take the poisoned cows to slaughter, even though they knew the animals were carrying 212 ppm toxaphene in their tissue. In trade channels, meat would pass to consumers. The cancers would get started in human beings, but the vets, the Food and Ag people would be off the hook. This would enable the health people to keep their jobs and go on to greater glory—perhaps dipping people for dandruff.

To get rid of the evidence, the Food and Ag people dumped some 4,000 gallons of toxaphene in various dilutions into Neary's water supply. The overflow went across salmon spawning grounds and into the Sacramento River.

When Neary arrived home from his trip, the first cows were dying. The veterinarians had an answer. It was anaplasmosis, they said. In an interview, Neary related how he handled the situation.

"Look, friend, I'm a cowman, and you're just a bunch of rummies who graduated at the bottom of your class in vet school, and like all losers, you ended up working in some public agency. That cow's dying of radical neurotoxin."

The government people came back with a verbal counterattack. One supercilious federal twerp—to use Neary's words—started to bluster. This brought on an ultimatum, Neary speaking.

"Here's your options. You're going into that gawd-damn spray box, the lot of you, and I'll give you two or three minutes. And if at the end of that time you're still alive, well, you'll probably die of anaplasmosis. Or you can hop into your cars, leave this unit here—I'm seizing it as evidence—and cut out. Do what you're good at and get out of here. The third option is, stand still and I'll shoot the lot of you." With that Neary got his rifle. The government people used good judgment for the first time and split.

In the early 1970s, when the first issues of *Acres U.S.A.* snailed their way through the mails, the publication was called "underground" and accused of fanning the fires of alienation. Underground it was not, except that it had a basement office for a time. It was duly incorporated and registered, and complied with all the laws that man has fallen heir to. If it fanned the fires of alienation from established insanity, that was something else. Some people called our brand of journalism muckraking, some called it investigative journalism. We called it *on-the-table-journalism*.

For years "better living through chemistry" had rivaled Hallmark's slogan, "If you care enough to send the very best." Who would question a technology that yielded hardly a demerit for the public prints? In fact, the makers of the hard stuff boasted that deleterious effects from their products rarely made the news because, if used as directed, there was nothing dangerous about farm chemistry. It may be that others pointed to the faults in Madison Avenue's slogan, but no publication ever hammered at it like *Acres U.S.A.*

One day while I was interviewing a fine old gentleman named Harold Pratt—who had invented Green Life and sold it to Victor Irons—Mrs. Pratt gave me a book entitled, *Sue the Bastards*. It was written by Billie Shoecraft, a diminutive lady who remained as tough as Arizona leather even though a cancer timebomb was ticking away in her bones.

That cancer had arrived one morning when Billie was standing on the porch of her mountain home at the edge of Pima National Forest near Globe. As she shook her fist at the spray helicopter, the pilot dumped an extra flush, saturating Billie, her pink chiffon nightgown, and the planks beneath her feet with Agent Orange, a mixture of 2,4-D and 2,4,5-T. It was the same material that U.S. Forces had been using in Vietnam, causing a news agency to comment that not since

146

Rome salted Carthage had any nation taken such pains to visit the effects of war on future generations. It contained the same dioxin that had turned Judy Piatt's life into a nightmare.

Billie Shoecraft took her fight against the spray planes to the state legislature, to House hearing rooms in Washington, and to the airwaves over the radio station her husband owned and operated. Victor Yonnaconne, the eminent California lawyer, had commented that there was no future at all in standing toe-to-toe with Highway Patrol headbreakers, or Sheriff's deputies, or officials of any ilk. Lie down in front of their engines of death, and they roll over you, he said. But hand any of them a piece of paper with a court's seal on it, and deputy, highway patrolman, spray plane flyer or Dow Chemical executive all dutifully obey and present themselves in court. In other words, *sue the bastards!* Mike Brown, a Kentucky-Utah based paralegal, inventor, and sometimes writer in *Acres U.S.A.*, explained the process in more colorful words. "I'll take a nick of the wrist," he said of the legal process, "if I can leave your intestines in the sawdust on the floor."

Unfortunately, legalese is seldom colorful, and the courts—a fantastic invention in King John's day—are hardly an instrumentality for dealing with chemistry's deadly molecules. The epitome of legal decision is still the smoking gun. Catch a man with a smoking gun over a corpse, and you have the culprit and the proof. But how do you identify a smoking gun that went off ten or twenty years earlier, invading the protein of a chromosome, sending into incubation a cancer cell that would be harvested years later? Billie Shoecraft answered the depositions and complied with all of the law's paperwork, but the cancer time bomb moved fast. Dr. Granville Knight, also an *Acres U.S.A.* writer and conference speaker, treated the little lady in her losing battle. After she died, Dow Chemical settled the case, and it appeared that her fire had simply spent itself, leaving the polluters and absconders in command of the field.

Not so! Billie Shoecraft assembled whole cabinets full of literature on the phenoxy herbicides, some of it from the pen of Dow Chemical scientists. The toxic clouds would never be viewed the same again. I fielded quite a bit of static over the Shoecraft reports, a memorable one coming from a chemical distributor.

The points raised had to be answered, and I did this, paragraph by paragraph, page by page. It was a technique I had used in handling the DDT issues. DDT was banned and discredited, but it continued to walk the planet like one of Bram Stoker's un-dead. Shortly after its demise I found myself answering one government official named H.

Rex Thomas, paragraph for paragraph, page for page that way because this government man said *Acres U.S.A.* had published a number of erroneous statements. I stood accused of saying Dr. Paul Mueller got the Nobel Prize for his discovery of the insecticidal properties of DDT in 1939. Actually I did not say he got the prize in 1939, but that the discovery was made that year. Nitpicking wouldn't wash, not when I resorted to the debate in print technique, and after a while the chemical shills stopped arguing, not a gesture of reconciliation marking the end.

The scientific establishment, once perceived to be the guardian of absolute truth, had become saddled with myths from which it dared not retreat. For the makers of farm chemicals this was understandable, given the penchant for pure businessmen to turn a buck at any cost. One and all they could take a $5.00 gallon product, and move it into the market at unconscionable prices, charging the farmer sixteen times the cost of production. The planet probably hasn't seen anything this profitable since tough sea captains transported black slaves—fetched from the jungles at near zero cost—to the new world at a fantastic per pound price. What was more difficult to understand was that men and women with credentials and standing in the scientific community would sully their profession with lies that seemed to achieve an art form. It was difficult to say whether it started with press releases or in the laboratory.

The newsmen who served the wire services and the news magazines didn't help very much. They were competent to witness the great wrecks in history, but they never seemed capable of identifying the carbuncles in the neck of society. Use of aldicarb in the potato fields and malathion to battle the medfly—as examples—relied on fraud and myth, not necessarily in that order of importance.

Fraud wasn't often documented. Still there was the case of Industrial Bio-Test Laboratories. The firm was one of the nation's leading testing facilities. It became a household word when a federal grand jury found three of its officials guilty of defrauding the government and certain pesticide and drug manufacturers. This was a euphemism for saying the officers covered up inaccurate research data used to gain federal registration.

In the twenty-six years of the company's operation, it conducted more than 22,000 studies—almost half of which were the basis for federal drug pesticide and food additive approval. The specific items that brought about the conviction were the herbicide Sencor, a pesticide Nemacur, an arthritis drug Naprosyn, and a soap additive trich-

148

lorocarbonilide. While these products have been retested and approved, thousands of other tests the company performed through the years have not been reevaluated, and will probably never be backed by proper scientific data.

In the legal case, the government argued that because the lab's client companies were very aggressive and eager to bring their products to market, laboratory procedural errors were covered up, rather than rechecked. This amounted to saying, "Oops!"

The world's greatest salesmen didn't even say "Oops!"

In 1974 there was a hearing in San Diego to deal with the Japanese beetle. Some people were concerned because chlordane—since banned—was to be used to eradicate the pest. Sevin, a highly toxic carbamate, was also to be used. At that time one of my reporters, Ida Honorof, was informed by an ag employee that the beetles had been planted in the traps to sell products. Laura Tallian, in *Politics and Pesticides*, published affidavits substantiating this fraud. A grand jury met. Guided by the coverup artists, it found no wrongdoing. And then the record was sealed to make certain the press and history found no wrongdoing on the part of the chemical shills.

While in California some years later, I was told the same had been done in the medfly caper. Guardsmen were called out. Over the radio people were told that their organic gardens had to be sprayed. Fruit had to be stripped from backyard trees—"and I have still to see my first fly," a guardsman told me.

And malathion sales skyrocketed.

Sales had been poor the year before that, and a year before that, too. Iowa farmers were blamed because they weren't doing as much "insurance spraying." The weather wasn't right for California insects, and sales were down. But with a well financed program, it took only an insect or two in a trap, and that valuable revelation was good for a sales ticket covering at least another country or two.

Mythology was clearly in charge. Carefully, and with propaganda worthy of Joseph Goebels himself, the body politic had been led to believe that Father Washington was standing guard. On the street and in the grocery store, little old ladies purchased preparations that could send a child into convulsions, all on the premise that pesticides registered with EPA had passed stringent health testing. In 1972 Congress set up health testing standards based on the Stone Age system called LD_{50}. But a decade later not one pesticide on the market had been reregistered after meeting health testing standards. The law, an amendment to the Federal Insecticide Fungicide and Rodenticide Act, charged EPA with reviewing and re-registering some 35,000 pesticides with registrations that carried over from previous regulatory agencies, as well as registering new pesticides. Re-registrations were to be done only after tests on animals indicated that the pesticide was unlikely to cause cancer, mutations, birth defects, sterility, neurotoxicity, or many less dramatic injuries.

If there have been cancellations, they can be counted on two hands. The bottom line is simply that EPA hasn't subjected chemicals to health effects testing, and has no answers whatsoever to the matter of mixed ingredients which appear when formulations are combined at the time of application, although it is well known that chemicals interact synergistically.

Trained liars also like to hand off the conceit that a no-observable-effect-level (the so-called NOEL factor) can be determined for any pesticide. The problem with this myth is that NOEL is different according to test, route of exposure, and animal species tested, and is therefore generally meaningless. More to the point, a NOEL effect on a hamster might be near zero, yet 100%, perhaps 800% higher for a human being, as was the case with thalidomide. Furthermore, there is no safe level for any mutagen or cancer initiator because these injuries are not repaired between exposure and are therefore cumulative throughout life.

The granddaddy of the myths is "safe if used as directed" concept. This is a claim made by the chemical firms, not by EPA. In fact EPA calls that statement "false" and "misleading" and the agency cites misbranding statements that include claims as to the safety of the pesticide or its ingredients, including statements such as "safe," "nonpoisonous," "noninjurious," or "nontoxic to humans and pets" with or without qualifying phrase as "when used as directed."

All pesticide labels are still based on the lethal dose after brief exposure concept, and a low LD_{50} citation has absolutely nothing to do with risk of low dose, cumulative or unrepaired damage such as nervous system injury or loss, and mutations which may not appear for generations.

Merriam Doucet Schoenfeld, a frequent contributor to *Acres U.S.A.*, and an expert witness in Canada whenever pesticide controversies arise, was the prime resource person when a South Okanagan study group prepared *The Other Face of 2,4-D*, which ran as a series in *Acres U.S.A.* In helping the group background a study having to do with milfoil eradication in the Okanagan lakes, she researched the scientific literature for definitive connection between size of dose and injuries to future generations. The conclusion that surfaced was so at variance with official statements one had cause to wonder whether both ends of the controversy were operating on the same planet. From the literature it was determined that low doses are often more lethal than high doses in terms of mutagenicity, teratogenicity and the other mischief that man-made molecules account for.

Phil Callahan explained it to me in terms of solid state physics while we were crossing the Atlantic.

"If you cram molecules together, they tend to jamb each other because they oscillate. Too far apart, they fail to achieve concentration tuning. In weed control, too-far-apart is never a factor, so it becomes a matter of heavy doses versus light doses. And the light dose will more likely achieve the concentration tuning that affects cells." Callahan compared this to a violin with strings too close or too far. Too far, the sound from each string acts on its own. Too close, the sounds jamb each other and produce a discordant noise. Spaced just right, the sound waves have the optimum effect.

The biological explanation, Merriam Doucet Schoenfeld pointed out, was simpler. In low doses 2,4-D and 2,4,5-T were able to perform without tipping off their activity to the body's defenses—all this according to the EPA's own experts.

The Veterans Administration, faced with a lawsuit from angry GIs who had fathered kids with cleft palates and mental and physical problems, simply ignored the above information and told the public that "there is no scientific evidence" that there was a connection between these unhappy circumstances and use of Agent Orange in Vietnam.

When people who didn't understand the grammar of the subject asked questions, scientists could explain away just about anything. It took almost a decade and a half for Missouri to take seriously the matter of dioxin after Judy Piatt's tragic encounter with the substance. When the *Missouri Dioxin Task Force* submitted its *Report*, it handed off a preface that—for most people—made light of something being dumped into the environment with reckless abandon. There were really seventy-five possible chlorinated dioxins, the *Report* said, and twenty-two isomers of tetrachlorodibenzo-p-dioxin (TCDD). The *Report* studied only one, presumably the worst, meaning the others were presumably safer, more or less!

I cannot possibly recite here the dozens and hundreds of tragic case reports handled as "happenings" by *Acres U.S.A.* One of my gardening columnists, a peppery lady who grew up in Madagascar with a name many readers liked to mispronounce and trill over their tongues—Bargyla Rateaver—turned these happenings into optomistic case reports, always illustrating how refreshing results could be achieved by following her advise on eco-gardening. She would tolerate toxic genetic chemistry in the environment even less than the editor who marked up her copy. Bargyla often handed off her lessons as questions and answers, with trees, leaves and even roots exchanging comments much like a Plato dialogue. Much the same was true of Harold Willis, an entomologist and botanist, who wrote *The Rest of the Story About Agriculture Today*, and *The Coming Revolution in Agriculture*. His well illustrated and poignant lessons made eco-farming so convincing and so reasonable, one had to wonder why the poisons and harsh fertilizers still enchanted main-line agriculture. Readers often confused Harold Willis with Harold Wills, another *Acres U.S.A.* scribe and commentator, and former wheat trader. It was Wills who divided agriculture between cellular farms and plantations. The cellular farm, he wrote, was one that is self-contained and properly referred to as the family farm. A plantation is a commercial enterprise where labor, hired or otherwise, does the work for an owner or owners who may not live on the land. Dixie and the huge cattle ranches of the west are good examples of plantation agriculture. Throughout history, noted Harold Wills, "America has wavered between adoption of cellular farms and plantations as its model of agriculture. Todays big farms are a hybrid of both and contain elements of both. Their size, so dependent on toxic chemistry, is both a blessing and a curse. They are too big to become cellular and too small to become corporate investment units. They have existed on a cushion of debt and periodic high crop prices. Their value has been based on land appreciation, which, at the beginning of the 1980s became reversed." Both of these farm styles were simply production units with no control over pricing, marketing or competition. People like Marvin Meek, of American Ag Movement, and Wayne Cryts, the fellow who made headlines by liberating his soybeans from a bankrupt elevator, understood some parts of this equation, but never the real role of toxic genetic chemistry in bringing countless farmers to ruin. In more than one case report, *Acres U.S.A.* was able to illustrate how debt and toxic chemistry brought farmers to early deaths. It illustrated how little the average educated person knows when first coming in contact with products from the devil's pantry.

Ralph and Rita Engelken of Greeley, Iowa were often cited in the pages of *Acres U.S.A.* for their contributions to clean agriculture. It wasn't always that way. During the first nine years the Engelkens farmed, Ralph was probably the worst chemical man in Iowa. "I went all the way," Ralph told me. "I was the first to own a spray rig in my area," the northeast corner of the state. "I was the first to put on everything the chemical world had to offer. I followed the advice out of Extension, and then I started losing livestock. That was bad enough. The worst thing of all was when the children developed all kinds of rashes and sicknesses. We went to five doctors. Nothing helped. Some of the kids had knees as big as footballs."

Engelken's voice seemed to strain as he spoke softly into my small tape recorder. After a year of doctoring, Ralph wanted some answers. He called the state vet, who told him there wasn't a thing in 2,4-D that could be used safely around human beings.

"My wife was the worst," Ralph said, "probably because she handled and washed clothes. She was constantly covered with salves that looked like black gun grease. Before we changed to eco-farming, she probably hadn't washed in water for a year and a half. It was always a case of *put on salve, take off salve*, she was that sick. If our ailments didn't keep us awake, then the muffled cries of our children did. Farm chemistry gave us a man-made hell. So when we got an explanation, we started backing off."

As with most people who back off, Ralph and Rita knew very little about ecological farming. The Engelkens had just bought a farm, one that had been savaged with just about everything "better living through chemistry" had to offer. They realized that the family had become so sensitized to toxic chemistry it was no longer possible to invoke moderation. For them there was no safe level, no tolerance level.

A kindly old priest helped them farm differently, and from his revelations new lessons took form. As the years went by, Ralph and Rita literally educated themselves. They did their own research. The big breakthrough came when Brookside Laboratory told them something about soil balancing, cation exchange capacity, and the general philosophy Dr. William A. Albrecht had brought to Brookside in the first place.

Having "done" with hard chemistry did not mean chemistry was done with Ralph and Rita Engelken. One day a neighbor laced his cornfield with the hard stuff only hours before a gully washer. By evening the contaminants had reached the Engelken's water supply. And the cows started aborting and dying. Those that didn't die wouldn't settle. In the end the Engelkens lost the entire herd.

To crutch his way into another season, Ralph borrowed money, and faltering commodity prices said the loan couldn't be serviced or paid. Chapter 11 bankruptcy followed, and one day the mail brought a piece of paper that said Ralph was in contempt of court. He had contracted to feed cattle without permission from the judge.

Ralph sat in stunned silence most of that day. Not even his wife could guess what torment he must have endured, not being too familiar with the ways of the court. By 7:00 p.m. he was dead. The medical people couldn't put a handle on that death. Rita could. He was a victim of worry—and toxic genetic chemistry! He had worried himself to death.

13

THE ENERGY GAMBIT

Solid lead editorials became workaday stuff in *Acres U.S.A.* from the very beginning. At times it seemed serendipitous how the backbone reports, the editorials, even the letters to the editor became coordinated with little or no planning. Each issue seemed to gather together the loose ends that said "to be economical, agriculture has to be ecological," and made them into a whole. In no major story did this surface with such strength as in our treatment of the energy gambit.

The crisis itself became the basis for a series of articles by Harry Lobel, a researcher from Omaha, Nebraska. Lobel in turn picked up his drive, he said, after reading *Unforgiven* and an *Acres U.S.A.* report, *Of Fats and Oils*.

In fact I had a chapter entitled *Of Fats and Oils* in *Unforgiven*, and I think I made a good case that there were interlocks between international grain companies and the fats and oils crowd, and it all had something to do with prices down on the farm.

Lever Brothers, Inc. had an affiliation with Lever Brothers, Ltd. of Great Britain and Unilever N.V. of Holland. Unilever N.V. had been spawned by the old Margarine Union of Europe. The several combines operated in thirty-seven countries, had four hundred subsidiaries, and eight hundred factories. Through the sale of soaps, shampoos and perfumes, Unilever N.V. enjoyed an affiliation with the distributors of drugs and sundries. Unilever also sold paper, candles, lye, copra, fish, cattlecake and fertilizer.

The most important facts about the Unilever combine surfaced during WWII. Charles Luckman, then president of Lever Brothers, was named chairman of the Edible Oil Division of the Food Committee of the United States. His annual company salary was reported at $300,000, a very handsome figure in those days.

As the Allies drove Italy and Germany out of North Africa, Lever Brothers Limited of Great Britain acquired millions of acres of palm oil plantations. And as American troops drove Japan out of the South Pacific islands, Unilever N.V. of Holland took over the coconut groves on Guadalcanal, in the Solomons, New Guinea, Malay and Indonesia.

Indonesia produced as much coconut oil as the rest of the world combined. The survival of a large part of Asia depended on coconut oil from Indonesia. The fats and oils people moved fast as World War II ended. They not only cornered the palm and coconut oil market, but also set out to corner the animal fat market of the United States.

The invasion of American markets by a flood of imported fats and oils actually started during the depression of the 1930s. Three conduits were used to pour nearly 3,000 tons of fats and oils into the U.S. a day. One route was through the paint and varnish and floor covering industry (the drying oils). The second route was through the food industry (cooking oils, shortening, oleo margarine and salad oils). As A.M. Loomis of the National Dairy Union pointed out at the time, "The powerful opponents of any concerted effort toward national sufficiency in fats and oils are the selfish industrialists who prefer to make big profits from cheap jungle fats, rather than pay fair domestic prices for domestic fats."

Loomis was somewhat on target. Tropical oils such as palm and coconut oil are the cheapest and the most common of the oils. They have the least value industrially and are "unsuited" for feeding livestock or human beings. Most of the people in under-developed nations depend on tropical oils for food and cooking.

A higher quality oil is produced in the temperate zone. Such oils come from corn, soybeans, cotton seed, peanuts, flax. These oils are more valuable both industrially and nutritionally. They are useful for livestock feeding operations, and they make good margarine.

The economic goal thus presented itself—how to cause human beings to eat fats unsuitable for nitro and rubber making, thus freeing edible fats for industrial use at cheap prices.

Hard on the heels of WWII, the Unilever combine launched an attack calculated to depress the price of animal fats, in effect making animal fats cheap and tropical fats more expensive. This attack included a massive publicity campaign correlating animal fat with atherosclerosis (clogging of the arteries) and arteriosclerosis (hardening of the arteries). Ostensibly, either condition resulted in coronary failure, or heart attack.

There are in fact three main theories on heart attacks. The first is the impedance mismatch theory—coronary spasm. This "cause" accounts for 60% of the coronary failure cases, according to some experts. A second theory holds that heart attacks result from blood clots and ulcerations. Either can be confirmed at autopsy.

The third theory is the one promoted by Unilever. It is based on the premise that animal fats raise blood cholesterol, and that this condition results in arteriosclerosis and coronary blockage, hence heart attack.

Lubricated with money, science soon found itself favoring the theory that delivered so well for the international fats and oil crowd. Well-aimed publicity on the animal fat theory resulted in the price of lard being depressed from twenty five cents a pound to five cents a pound almost overnight at the end of WWII. For each cent that the price of animal fats was made to decline, the price of chops and steaks raised a cent. Similarly, dairy farmers found milk under attack so that butterfat could be stripped away and watery stuff sold on the premise that 2% butterfat milk was better for growing kids and adults.

The depression of animal fat prices was carried out at a time when the Secretary of Agriculture had declared a world shortage of fats and oils, and General Lucius Clay was screaming that "there is a perfectly tremendous demand for fats. The need is desperate. The fat crisis is here."

But fats and oils were kept dammed up in the U.S. because it suited Lever Brothers and the others with coconut groves to have cheap fats and oils. Administration of government controls, staffed largely by experts with business interests, first drove fats and oil prices below the OPA ceiling, then toward the pre-war price level.

The propaganda about animal fat being related to heart failure was one of the most effective brainwashing campaigns in advertising history. It led to the publication of such nonsense as "hardening of the coronary arteries may begin when a newborn baby takes its first breast feeding." One can excuse the cited absurdity because it appeared in *The Omaha World Herald* and was written by a typical newspaper journalist. The attitude of the average news reporter has been show by military expert Howard Silber (". . . the people would become confused if there were more than one theory of heart failure") and by Mary McGrath, a medical expert ("It is not necessary to understand science to be a science writer.") If this sounds like, "Last week I didn't know what a science writer was, now I *are* one," well, that's the way it is.

Money makes it so.

Dr. Charles D. May put it all in focus in the *Journal of Medical Education* in 1961 when he pointed out that the Unilever combine, through drug and sundry distributors, was spending $750 million each year on promotional activities alone. It has now been made a matter of record that Tino DeAngeles, the salad oil king who was convicted of embezzling $25 million, had been pressured into paying vast sums to heart scientists and heart officials for the purpose of advancing the cholesterol theory.

While Harry Lobel was involved as a researcher at my alma mater, Creighton University, Dr. Charles Wilhelmj, the Creighton Research Director, received up to $250,000 a year in research grants. The strings to the money required him to publicize the "finding" that animal fats were the chief culprit in causing high blood pressure. Dr. Cecil Wittson, the chancellor of the Nebraska Medical School, a consistent opponent of the impedance mismatch (coronary spasm) theory, received grants of over $1 million a year, a sum big enough to keep almost anyone friendly.

The scope of the fats and oils campaign was only hinted at in *Prescription Only*, which stated that science editors were paid up to $10,000 for planting news stories. *Time* got $50,000. Wrote Morton Mintz, who quoted the Kefauver hearings—"all of the news media has been caught up—the great wire services, the daily newspapers, country weeklies; magazines, health columns, radio, television . . . what Senator Kefauver uncovered about this abuse of the press . . . was the most under-reported story of 1962."

There is more to this fats and oils thing than the story that came out of the South Pacific at the end of WWII. *"Do not damage coconut trees for the United States government must pay $50 each for each tree injured,"* read the signs, according to ex-servicemen. Just who runs the United States? asked Georgia Commissioner of Agriculture Tom Linder at the time. "These American boys were giving their lives to defend these coconut groves belonging to the Dutch Company to save them from destruction by the Japanese, yet the U.S. taxpayers were to pay $50 for each tree that our boys might injure."

As the 1970s got underway, the energy gambit shifted from one oil to another. First President Nixon slammed down the gold window, a prelude to the creation of pure fiat money. It was a perfect point in time for the fossil fuels crowd to make a grab.

The international oil people did this by discerning that in some few hundred years there would be an oil shortage. They then translated that into a crisis *right now*, this week, and they choreographed the Arabs and Iranians to give substance to the OPEC cartel. In a series of articles by Harry Lobel we quietly demolished the myths and correctly predicted the life of the cartel. Lobel even warned me that substitutes for fossil fuels would not survive. This ran with *Acres U.S.A.* projections in some ways because I viewed—in editorials, and in think-tank sessions—the long haul, and shuddered at the trap being set for farmers alcohol and for the family farmer.

The root word for *debt* is *death*, and economic death was waiting. The Mennonites, Amish and Hutterites would not likely fall into the credit trap, but the meeting-going farmers who listened to the likes of Don Paarlberg, Luther Tweeten and Howard Hjort, economists, would be walking into a snare like a blinded sable. Too many variables were nipping at the heels of the farmer to ignore alternative home-grown fuels.

Thus there surfaced several fundamentals from which *Acres U.S.A.* refused to retreat. I argued long and repeatedly that no total farmer ought to buy his nitrogen. His soil system and his mix of technological skills ought to see to it that he fixed his own nitrogen in abundant supply. I also said that no farmer ought to buy his protein from a rigged market. With a natural nitrogen cycle and a natural carbon cycle working, a farmer's home-grown protein would be superior to any he could buy through trade channels. Finally, I said the farmer ought to raise his own tractor gas. To do otherwise would be to come off low man on the totem pole of foreign trade, that international exchange of bundles of warm, moist air.

I wasn't talking about raising hay for horses, as the Amishmen still did. I was talking about farmers alcohol, which may well be the oldest invention of man. I had a hunch that the wheel or eyeglass or even the runcible spoon were come-lately entries compared to the fact that water boils at 212 Fahrenheit at sea level, whereas alcohol boils and vaporizes at only 170 degrees. For here was a fact of chemistry. Take a fermentable substance—grain, grapes, potatoes, anything with sugars and starches—add yeast to convert natural sugars into alcohol, and that 42 degree spread in temperature does the rest. The beer is boiled off and vaporized. Other solids and liquids are left behind.

An *Acres U.S.A.* interview with Donald Despain, the author of *The*

One and Only Solution to the Farm Problem, was a reprint. I had handled it several years earlier for another publication, and felt justified in reprinting it. When I last talked to him, his vocal cords had given out, and he was dying. But he blessed the project, and readers of *Acres U.S.A.* ultimately gained a fair background of fuel alcohol because of it.

Over the years—starting in 1964—I had written no less than two dozen major articles on alcohol. I had heard all the objections, and answered them. Some of those reports were read by Nebraska farmers who prompted the unicameral to set up an alcohol program. Thus it was time to recapture that story and recycle news that had been mislaid or forgotten.

I asked *Acres U.S.A.* readers to listen anew to Dr. Leo M. Christensen of Iowa State College, speaking at the height of his career: *"Alcohol is not a substitute for gasoline. It is an ingredient of a superior fuel already in use. It competes with the several materials or processes employed to improve the qualities of gasoline. With this in mind, we can proceed to an economic analysis of the use of agricultural alcohol."*

And proceed he did because he had the know-how. He was standing on the shoulders of giants, not in the shadows of the military and political hell-raisers who usually hog the pages of history. Christensen knew that men who dream dreams and see visions light the fuses that detonate historic events—Wohler's transformation of ammonium cyanate into urea in 1828; Adolf von Baeyer's conversion of coal tar into indigo in 1878; Hilaire de Chardonnet's revelation of the silkworm's secret in 1889; Haber's fixations of atmospheric nitrogen in 1913. The madmen in authority are something else, I wrote, and so they took Fritz Haber's gift of nature revealed, rammed it into a cannon and launched World War I. They bypassed Boss Charles Kettering's obvious hint when he said we are running automobiles by solar energy seasoned some forty million years in the ground. "Maybe we can learn how to pick up our sun-energy direct, instead of going along on that long-drawn-out process," Kettering said. "I'm not worried about what we are going to do so long as the sun keeps on shining, because we can grow enough fuel. I'm sure we can grow all our fuel after a while because all of the fuel that we have has been grown."

I asked our readers to listen to Dr. William J. Hale. When this man spoke, the ground thundered and statesmen listened. "Let's grow more and more until every acre is trapping sunshine and until every employable human being has a job and is adding the value of his labor to the things which nature provides so abundantly." They didn't call

Dr. Hale "Chemistry's Dizzy Dean" for nothing. In 1915 the Rochester Section of the American Chemical Society cancelled a talk by Dr. Hale because so few American chemists knew anything about organic chemistry.

Who was Dr. Hale? Just an American boy who went to Germany for post-graduate study and came back with insight still denied most of our leaders. He got to know Dr. Herbert Henry Dow when he returned. Dow—it will be remembered—perfected an electrolytic process for extracting valuable chemicals from Midland, Michigan's brine wells. He set up a plant to make chloroform by reacting sulfur chloride with carbon bisulphide and then treating the resultant carbon tetrachloride with iron in the presence of water. When WWI came, Dow's factory grew because there developed a big demand for phenol (carbolic acid), chlorobenzene and other organic chemicals herein before produced by the Germans. Billy Hale helped Dr. Dow drag magnesium out of the Midland brine so that star shells could illuminate death on the Western Front. They combined chlorine and alcohol and sulfur—dichlor-di-ethyl-sulfide—mustard gas. Dr. Hale didn't like this apeman use of superman's gifts. And thus was born his life-long love affair with farmers alcohol.

In the 1920s and the 1930s, Dr. Hale concentrated on farmers alcohol as the key-log in the jam that kept the exchange equation from working for the benefit of all. Farm production, he held, simply had to flow into industrial trade channels. A proper exchange would see to it that the fruits of the industrial society would flow back to millions of operating farms.

Alcohol could be more than a motor fuel. It could become a plentiful source of acetic acid. His interest in this common stuff centered on direct oxidation of ethyl alcohol by means of water. Further, Hale proved that isoprene and butadiene, resulting directly through dehydrogenation and condensation of alcohol molecules, would afford the cheapest possible source of synthetic rubber—and this would be better than natural rubber. The time would come when men would find ways to introduce metal atoms into the molecular latticework of plastic structures, he said, and the metallo-plastic age would be born.

The oil cartels didn't mind dreams so much. What brought them up fighting from their chairs was the suggestion that farmers alcohol could be used to power tractors and automobiles. At the technical sessions of the era, there were always funded professors and company chemists to refute alcohol-gasoline blends.

In a whole series of articles on farmers alcohol, Dr. Hale spoke again—

"When the apologists for the petroleum industry try to tell us that alcohol-gasoline blends are not satisfactory, they seem not to recognize what the organic chemist knows, namely, that in feeding gasoline into a motor we are already using alcohol for fuel." The aliphatic hydrocarbon, gasoline, begins combustion (under high pressure and by blending with oxygen) by the production of a hydroxylated compound of the same chemical order as alcohol—and so to the organic chemist, gasoline is alcohol in that split second when the electric spark detonates the vaporized gasoline-oxygen mixture into horsepower.

Early in 1935 Dr. Hale joined Dr. Christensen and other interested parties—hundreds of farmers included—in touching off the farmers alcohol battle, a battle that surfaced again as *Acres U.S.A.* gained maturity. They concluded:

1. An unfailing source of farmers alcohol was needed.

2. This alcohol would have to be completely anhydrous in order to perfectly blend with gasoline.

3. This alcohol would have to be adulterated to remove it from the highly-taxed category of beverage alcohol.

4. It would have to be cheap enough to compete with premium gasoline.

5. An unfailing source of gasoline would have to be found, a source where officials would not oppose blending.

Remember, this was during the 1930s. Because of international manipulations, farmers were perceived to be swimming in surpluses. The state of Nebraska passed a law to rebate taxes on alcohol-gasoline blends, and across mid-America, independent producers agreed to cooperate with Hale and Christensen. By 1938 the Atchison Agrol Company was producing farmers alcohol on a commercial scale. In one year business increased 1,500%. Running on barley, rye, corn, grain, sorghum and Jerusalem artichokes, the plant erased crop pileups in the general area. The distillate was rendered anhydrous, adulterated to make it unfit for human consumption, and blended with gasoline. The remaining fiber was converted into concentrated stock feed—40% protein, 90% digestible—and returned to farmers.

All of a sudden bands of experts roved the countryside. They had a little gadget to prove that gasoline and alcohol didn't mix. The oil companies used every gimmick in the books to run Agrol's cost higher by six to eight cents a gallon. And, finally, Phillips Petroleum started erecting massive polymerization units at Kansas City and Borger,

Texas—producing octane, if you will, 100% anti-knock. This made for more efficient use of raw crude, and stretched the supply.

Banking, monopoly power, and centralization of ownership combined during that day and hour to put farmers alcohol to death. The chemists were coming into their own by then. They could juggle the molecules of hydrocarbons and produce from coal and petroleum the byproducts Dr. George Washington Carver and Dr. Hale and others expected only from vegetable or animal sources—paraffin, wax, asphalt, fuel oil, alcohols and their denaturants, medicines, and so on.

True, there was a lot of oil in the world—but the American continent didn't have title to it, Dr. Hale said. "The cracking of petroleum merely to secure gasoline is one of the most wasteful deeds of man," became his conclusion. Besides, asked Hale, "Is there a direct connection between the growing incidence of lung cancer in the United States and the fact that the high polymers of gasoline, known to possess carcinogenic properties, are constantly poured into the atmosphere by exhaust vapors of gasoline-powered vehicles?"

When farmers alcohol was reborn hard on the heels of the energy crisis of the early 1970s, a clarion call for more research was heard, on signal. In Nebraska the gasohol program was delayed for years while professional study people reinvented the wheel, so to speak. The college people were learning anew that there were protein values in distillers' feeds. The name of the game became *get a grant to learn what had been learned before, then use that grant to get another grant!* Bundles of research from the United States Brewers Association and the Distilled Feeds Institute were quietly ignored.

The farmers alcohol story unfolded in chapters and verses too numerous to mention. Front and center, always, there was the call for still more research. It thundered much like the other cliches and myths of modern science. If "poisons are safe if used as directed" and "there is no scientific evidence" had become a sing-song chant, they were now joined by a chant for "research" on the use and effects of neat alcohol and gasohol.

Dr. Hale's words were less considered than remembered. "Alcohol is the only outlet in mass form for farm products with sugar and starch, the only permanently renewable resource we have to replace the steadily disappearing and diminishing natural resource, gasoline. There is nothing in all the farm products of corn, wheat, sorghum, rye, rice, barley, potatoes, or fruits that contains such a usable, invaluable chemical product as alcohol—the most valuable of all chemical compounds."

In telling the farmers alcohol story I came across a letter by George E. Johnson, General Manager of the Omaha Alcohol Plant during WWII. Johnson also served on the Advisory Committee of the Chemical Branch, War Production Board.

"During the war the principal opposition to the construction of the alcohol plants was the oil companies. For more than a year, Mr. Frank Robinson and I put more than one-half of our time to get the allocations through. In so many places we found the oil companies had interlocking directors and financial arrangements where they were controlling the activities of a large part of the research being done by the Department of Agriculture as well as other Departments.

"We found Secretary Ickes had from thirty to thirty-three advisers, who were officers in the various oil companies and who either had indictments pending for violations of the federal laws, or who had been found guilty of violation of the federal laws. These were the principal men advising the Secretary on the Liquid and Solid Fuel Program during the war. Their influence extended far beyond the work they were scheduled to do."

And what did these men of great stature tell Secretary Ickes? As it filtered out of the Chemical Branch of the War Production Board, *there was no place in the war effort for agriculture except to feed the people.*

I simply had to ask our readers to picture the irony. When a young fellow falls afoul the law several times over, the agencies call him a police character. He is shunned and spends much time in lineups when a crime is committed. But here we had corporate police characters—men accused of criminal conspiracy many times over—put on a pedestal and honored and obeyed.

In reporting the alcohol story, I tried again to suggest that there was no basis for free international trade—or "protectionism" for the traders. Cheap foreign oil was too costly to the American economy. To illustrate the point I recited a little parable.

At the end of WWII, we were buying Swiss watches at $15. The economists were arguing this was good business because it cost $30 to make the same watch in the U.S. This made it possible to spend the second $15 in the U.S. for other merchandise. But there was a fallacy in the equation.

First, we had to use $15 of other income to buy the Swiss watch because, certainly, we couldn't use any of the income generated by production of the watch simply because it wasn't produced here. Next, because it wasn't made here it cost the American economy $30 of income—income lost because we didn't make the watch ourselves. And what did that watch cost the American economy? The answer was $45.

It could easily be seen that alcohol produced at double, even triple the foreign price was still cheaper in the United States, even without factoring in the cost of higher polymers of gasoline, "known to possess carcinogenic properties, that were constantly poured into the atmosphere by the exhaust vapors of gasoline-powered vehicles."

And I used another parable, one recited earlier in this book.

During the debates over tariffs during the Lincoln administration, the question came up—*Why not buy the rails for the transcontinental railway from England? They had the factories and could make them cheaper!* And Lincoln's answer was so profound and yet so simple even a child could understand it. If we buy the rails from England, we will have the rails and they will have our money. But if we produce the rails here, *we will have both the rails and the money!*

If we made the fuel alcohol in the U.S., obviously we would have both the fuel and the money. The international flim-flam men pretended not to understand this principle, but grass-roots supporters of farmers alcohol did. While William Schiller of the University of Nebraska was conducting his million mile road test, grass-roots supporters of gasohol assembled enough money to set up a National Gasohol Commission, and to hire Bob Soleta of Minnesota as executive secretary. Soleta's first official act was to give a talk at the NORM meeting in Amarillo, Texas, January 1978.

I interviewed Bob during the meeting, and in due time his taped remarks appeared in our regular conversations section. Soleta understood the goals and the pitfalls for fuel alcohol. At ground level the movement was being supported by thousands of farmers—and by a few friends such as Bill Holmberg and Tina Hobson in EPA—but the benefits were all accruing to the grain companies and big operators, such as Archer-Daniel-Midland, and the oil companies. Farmers who hoped to make home-grown fuel tried everything from fence post stills to sophisticated units with computerization. For their efforts, they received little support from the government, and cheap alcohol from Brazil was ever biting at their heels. USDA, charged with bringing farm stills on-line, simply drug heels and refused to make appropriated money available.

The farmers alcohol story became so big that for almost four years the *Acres U.S.A.* staff digressed into the publication of *Gasohol U.S.A.* I still don't know how we got the work done. I allowed that magazine to die peacefully in its sleep, having put it to bed for the last time just as the OPEC cartel was faltering, and gasohol as a name was dying.

Gasohol died because the oil companies decreed that it must die. A generic name was not acceptable, they in effect said, and until it departed the scene incorporation of alcohol into gasoline either as an additive or a fuel extender simply would not happen. Dave Hallberg, formerly an aide with Congressman Berkley Bedell of Iowa, assessed the situation correctly. Accordingly, he formed a Renewable Fuels Association, went to big ticket operators for funding, and with that the movement made the transition from grass-roots to big business. And the National Gasohol Commission as a grassroots organization started going down hill.

Almost lost in the shuffle was the real connection with agriculture. In the end Lee Fryer made the connection for everyone by causing to be printed in *The Washington Post* the ad on the facing page.

An institutional ad of this nature could not have been justified on the basis of instant impact. It was the mileage that counted. Reprints and editorials and letters followed, and the image itself was kept alive for many months running via reprints to see if the anointed leadership would find the connection. If any of them did, the feedback did not arrive back at *Acres U.S.A.*

The heady days of one-thousand-person meetings departed as quickly as they came, and hardly a hundred mature industrial giants remained in command of the field. The farmers who first beat the drum for home-grown fuel took to fighting among themselves.

The first president of the organization, Nebraska farmer Holly Hodge, stepped aside. He and his secretary both abandoned large families, and formed a new one—a happening that would be ruled from fiction, it was that bizarre. He was replaced by former Illinois Department of Agriculture Energy Chief, Al Mavis. Al Mavis had his vision—meeting the energy crisis through substitution, not denial. Single handedly he brought the first alcohol to Illinois, proved its worth and set the hearts of farmers afire with a desire to help themselves.

National Gasohol Commission, in special session, removed President Al Mavis from office a few months before his term was to expire anyway—a fantastic exercise in vindictiveness—and when it was all over the grassroots support group took out bankruptcy. Mavis stood accused of not keeping proper rein on the organization's executive secretary.

The USDA experts who made all the meetings and gave so many speeches retired from the field, a practiced smirk on their collective faces. None of the money commanded by USDA had been put into the

The Washington Post

(Reduced from 2/3 page)

President Carter:
The Administration:
Members of Congress:

let's stop fertilizing our national energy crisis

U.S. farmers can release over 200 billion cubic feet of natural gas per year... enough to heat 4 million homes.

If that sounds incredible, consider this:

America's agriculture currently uses nearly 500 billion cubic feet of gas annually to make it's nitrogenous fertilizers, despite the fact that alternative energy-saving technologies and products are available to produce full yields of farm crops at lesser costs. Using these energy-savers will release large amounts of vitally needed gas.

We urge the new Administration to move vigorously on the farm energy problem by taking the following actions:

1. Launch new research further to validate energy-saving fertilizers and practices for producing the Nation's food and fiber crops.

2. Obtain funds for doing this by curtailing less essential research, farm payments and services of the Department of Agriculture.

3. De-emphasize farm research projects promoting petrochemical-based fertilizers and systems of farming.

4. Help to amend State laws that favor gas-made fertilizers, and that discourage sale and use of alternative energy-saving products.

These steps are essential. They mean heat for our homes, gas for industries and nutritious, reasonably-priced food supplies for everyone.

LEE FRYER, Author & President
Food & Earth Services, Inc.
Suite 302
1345 E. Street, N.W.
Washington, D.C. 20004

LEONARD BLANTON, President
Plant Food Enterprises, Inc.
Adamsville,
Tennessee

JAMES WAGNER, President
Earth & Sea Products, Inc.
Watsonville,
California

Dr. JOHN G. SALSBURY, President
Sea Born, Inc.
Rockland Road
Charles City,
Iowa

CHARLES WALTERS, Jr., Publisher
ACRES, U.S.A.
Raytown,
Missouri

ORVILLE NABER, President
Crop Boosters, Inc.
Kiester,
Minnesota

field to help farmers simply because USDA did not want farmers alcohol muddying the waters for client grain traders, the Milo Minderbinders who were putting the family farm to death.

The farmers alcohol story dropped out of *Acres U.S.A.* not long after that, but I have a hunch there will be more on the subject. In the meantime it will be enough to remember South Dakota Professor Paul Middaugh cooking alcohol on the Washington Mall; Dale and Al Snipes of Montana running her alcohol powered cars from coast to coast and from Canada to Mexico, and making pancakes from distillers grain to boot; Indy 500 driver Janet Guthrie and Mo Campbell taking fuel alcohol to the race tracks and into the headlines; astronaut Gordon Cooper converting aircraft to alcohol; petite Marilyn Hermann braving a Department of Energy peer review like a modern Joan of Arc and issuing a positive report on fuel alcohol out of that government agency; Richard Merrill, living like a monk, yet almost singlehandedly keeping farmers alcohol afloat in Congress; Argentine ex-patriate Richard Blaser putting the final touches to his Beta Engine.

I even took *Acres U.S.A.* to Brazil hard on the hunt for alcohol news. There Sergio C. Trindade, a guiding voice in Brazil's alcohol program, said it all. Farmers alcohol couldn't fly in Brazil either, he told me, without a public policy that made it possible. The U.S. still has no such public policy.

14

RETREAT FROM REASON

"An accumulation of venom, pseudo-science and breath-taking arrogance" was the way I put it in a lead article styled *FDA's Retreat from Reason*, a front page story that told about a *Federal Register* entry FDA Commissioner Charles C. Edwards had accounted for. *Acres U.S.A.* was not alone on this one. James J. Kilpatrick, the syndicated columnist, called the then new food and drug regulations "the most autocratic, most arrogant, most infuriating orders ever decreed by a federal agency," and he went on to score Edwards for taking scientific matters under dispute and establishing what was false under pain of law.

Based on solid ignorance, Edwards had boldly asserted that mineral nutrients in foods were not significantly affected by storage, transportation, cooking and other forms of processing, even though in many cases minerals were entirely removed. Moreover, he established by decree that the vitamin content of foods was not affected by the soil in which they were grown, as if to relieve chain grocery stores of the nibbling competition by some 3,500 health food stores selling organic produce.

In the early 1970s, Edwards and a number of then present and past employees of giant pharmaceutical and biologic houses determined, and caused to be cast into law via the bureaucratic procedure of publishing in the *Federal Register* the intelligence that "there is no rationale for allowing or encouraging the promotion and sale of dietary supplements of vitamins and of minerals to the general American population for the purpose of treating, preventing, or curing diseases or symptoms."

Also, "Lay persons are incapable of determining, by themselves, whether they have or are likely to develop, vitamin or mineral deficiencies."

Also, "Vitamin or mineral deficiencies are unrelated to the great majority of symptoms like tiredness, nervousness and rundown condition."

Also, "Scientifically, it is inaccurate to state that the quality of soil in the United States causes abnormally low concentrations of vitamins or minerals in the food supply produced in this country."

It was not clear to discerning people by what magic Charles C. Edwards made these assertions scientific fact. Admittedly, there were experts who stated these things. And there were experts with standing and credentials in the academic community who said exactly the opposite.

Why, then, this retreat from reason?

Obviously, it had become the convenient self-deception of Dr. Edwards to take up the chant of the food manglers presiding over the diet, as if to prevent, by law, the people from separating scientific information from propaganda masquerading as such.

Obviously, if Charles Edwards could turn non-science into science, then the overprocessed carbohydrates called snacks were no longer lacking in essential vitamins and minerals, presumably on grounds that preservatives and food grade plastics and varnishes provided nutrition. Kids could go on eating butyl-hydroxy-anisole and butyl-hydroxy-toluene because everything is chemical anyway. Chickens that never touched the ground, whole flocks of which died routinely of hemorrhagic disease, were excellent fare after all if they appeared at the friendly chain. Water, sugar, a dollop of citric acid and a little fruit juice with vitamin C was gung ho stuff because it was so profitable.

When it came to reporting what was happening at the grocery and sickness end of agriculture, most of the stories we had to carry would have been ruled from fiction, they were that incredible.

There was the attack on practitioners in the health care field. Dr. Carey Reams was spending most of his time and dollars in court defending himself for giving nutritional advice when I first made contact with him and veterinarian Dan Skow, and their system of soil analysis. After one particularly vicious go-round of court battles, Reams closed his clinics and settled for teaching courses in soil management. He died in 1985, with most of his knowledge unrecorded for fear of official reprisal.

Others fled to Mexico and still others bankrupted themselves fighting for justice that was no longer within reach.

Dr. Cliff Robertson, the Kentucky osteopath and author of *The Health Explosion*, made the mistake of letting one case report appear in the public prints. This brought his brand of success to the attention of medicine's policemen, and the agents of those who profit so handsomely from the sale of coal tar derivative drugs. These firms, of course, pick up most of the tab for medical meetings, publications and printed information physicians receive from detail men—meaning salesmen. Even the osteopaths have allowed themselves to be swept into chemical gambit, and thus Cliff Robertson became fair game.

The Robertson case concerned a little girl scheduled for chemotherapy to combat leukemia. Robertson somehow managed to keep that form of bottled death better than arm's length away. Instead he subjected the girl to a program of detoxification and counseled sound nutrition. The little lady recovered and even passed the sternest tests modern medicine had to offer.

This so infuriated the head of the local medical board—a man who distinguished himself by sewing up a patient without first removing an instrument and sponges—that he went for Cliff Robertson's hide. This meant taking his license to practice.

Once the deed had been done, Robertson had to change his telephone numbers. Nearly a thousand patients were beside themselves, some of them offering to meet the doctor in Mexico or Canada for his life and health saving advice—all this while Robertson was forced to spend his substance fighting to undo that capricious act.

There was the fluoride story.

No controversy in modern life has drawn and thrown as much fire as fluoridation. Indeed, never has a single subject taken on such an air of religious fervor. It was, therefore, not surprising that an unpublished paper on the subject should turn up among the papers of Dr. William A. Albrecht. After *Fluoridation of Public Drinking Water* was circulated to a few friends in mimeo form, Albrecht's attention was drawn to a paper, *New Concepts in Bone Healing*, by Lewis B. Barnett, M.D. [*Journal of Applied Nutrition*, 1954]. Dr. Barnett, as a practicing physician in Deaf Smith County, Texas, presented that paper before the Orthopedic Section of the annual meeting of the Texas Medical Association, Dallas, Texas, May 6, 1952.

It was at his suggestion, said Dr. Barnett, "that Dr. Edward Taylor of the Texas State Department of Health and his staff made an extensive survey of dental conditions in that county. The results of that survey were first reported in the *Journal of the American Dental Association* in August 1952. At that time, the school children of Deaf Smith County had the lowest rate of dental decay ever reported in a civilized country. Following the report, the U.S. Public Health Service Department did an extensive survey on water in the high plains area. From their findings, it was deduced that this unusually low rate of tooth decay was due to fluorine in the drinking water. It was considered that the Deaf Smith County area had the optimum fluorine for good dental health. It is on the basis of this study that the American Medical Association, the U.S. Department of Health, and other similar groups and agencies approved the fluoridation of all drinking water in the United States. "To some of us it was apparent that factors other than fluorine were, at least partially, responsible for these findings," said Dr. Barnett.

Dr. Albrecht's comment was equally to the point. "That such a highly tenuous correlation of fluorine at one part-per-million in the drinking water and the low dental caries per child should be considered cause and prescription of the former for the latter, would certainly be hesitatingly taken as the universal logic among members of a professional society, according to which alone we can be born, or can die, legally. Yet it seems that it is on the basis of such fallacious logic, considering no other factors affecting dental health, that the fluoridation of public drinking waters is premised, and legally enforced."

The profitable truth that the inorganic chemical element, fluorine, in well waters was responsible for good teeth in Deaf Smith County, Texas was embraced by the aluminum and phosphate industries. For a time "The Town Without a Tooth Ache" became copybook maxim, but it was a fallacy, said Albrecht. It was not the first time Albrecht had annihilated a commonly accepted truth. He, of course, had reported to the farm community that limestone to remove soil acidity was simply supposed science, that the real role of this dust on the fields was to nourish crops with calcium and magnesium. Bordeaux Mixture as a plant spray was not a poison, really, but copper for the crop so that it could grow its own antibiotic. Blue vitriol for stomach worms in sheep did the same thing. Epsom salts as a purge functioned by exchanging magnesium for calcium in the intestinal wall and bloodstream until the latter was restored to established intestinal conditions. Brucellosis was said to be a contagious disease, yet good soil treatment eliminated both the infection and the abortion, causing Albrecht to say brucellosis was about as contagious as the stomach ache.

"We make the mistake in reasoning that the fluorine in the water is the cause of the better teeth, when we should look to the presence of liberal amounts of the calcium-bearing and phosphorus-bearing apatite putting more calcium and more phosphorus in the foods at the same time that by decomposition it is putting fluorine into the water percolating down through the soil."

What Albrecht was saying was transparently obvious. Fluorine was the most soluble of the three elements. It had a single valence, or combining power. It was highly soluble. As a consequence it departed the soil's surface easily and percolated into the wells and underground water supplies. Calcium represented a double valence, phosphorus a triple valence. As fluorine left the apatite rock, it left behind the calcium and phosphorus to combine with each other to be both more readily available to crop plants than these two essential elements were in the original apatite. By draining away the fluorine, calcium and phosphorus stayed on to nurture mineral-rich, high protein crops by which healthier bodies were built, with better teeth as exposed parts of better skeletons. It was the presence of calcium and phosphate in the soil that was the logical reason for good teeth rather than the fluorine in the drinking water.

Albrecht's science was brushed aside, just as has been the science of thousands of others in the literature.

One of the finest reports published in *Acres U.S.A.* on fluoride was written by John R. Lee, M.D., a California physician. Dr. Lee had joined the fluoride fray because of an upcoming debate in his local medical society. In researching his role, he discovered that both those for and against fluoridation of the water supply used the same technical data, each reading science in a different way. This brought him to attention. It did not seem likely that science—the arbiter of such controversies—could not furnish an answer.

Lee found that fluoride was a uniquely potent enzyme poisoner, in fact the most powerful one of all elements. There are several reasons for this. In the table of elements, fluorine belongs to the halogen family, sharing chemical properties with its close relatives, chlorine, bromine and iodine. As ions, reacting with other particles, they all carry one negative charge. As the halogen having the smallest atomic weight, fluoride is naturally the most active. It is extremely active in combining with any element or molecule having a positive valence, such as the mineral ions (enzyme co-factors). It decomposes water to form hydrogen fluoride which readily attacks glass. It actively replaces its sibling halogen, chlorine, in any solution, including the hydrochloric acid within our stomachs, or any chlorine-containing molecule within our blood or our intracellular fluid.

Fluoride's negative charge and atomic weight of 19 is almost identical to the negative charge and weight of the hydroxyl group (OH), 17.008, which is vitally important to the chemical composition of innumerable substances throughout the human organism. It is, in fact, such interchangeability with the hydroxyl group that is cited as the reason for increased hardness of the apatite crystal of tooth enamel when fluoride is involved.

Unfortunately, and all too obviously, this structural change is not confined to teeth, but occurs elsewhere in the body as well. Fluoride poisons enzymes. The book, *Fluorides*, published by the National Academy of Sciences, 1971, lists nine enzymes involved in the breakdown of sugar (glycolysis process) that are fluoride sensitive. The halogen inhibits many enzymes by tenaciously binding with the metal ions they require in order to function. It inhibits others by a direct poisoning action of their protein content.

But the ultimate shocker is the toxic effect fluoride has on genes. Painstaking research at the International Institute for the Study of Human Reproduction, Columbia University College of Physicians and Surgeons, as well as at the University of Missouri, have proved beyond doubt that fluoride is mutagenic, *i.e.*, it damages genes in mammals at doses approximating those we humans receive from artificial fluoridation exposure.

Such a statement ought to clear the air, but this has not happened. The continuing story has maintained a presence in *Acres U.S.A.* for fifteen years, with in-depth research by Gladys Caldwell, Dean Burk and John Yiamouyiannis—the last both Ph.Ds.—and George L. Waldbott, M.D. in collaboration with Albert W. Burgstahler, Ph.D. and H. Lewis McKinney, Ph.D. the authors of *Fluoridation, The Great Dilemma*, all supporting our reports.

In covering the fluoride story, I tapped many of the 50,000-plus articles on the subject that have been parked in the scientific literature. Over a period of time, I developed a morgue of material on the subject so extensive it made fluoridation the biggest file at *Acres U.S.A.* Included was a statement by retired U.S. Army Colonel Lindegren that has ever caused radio and TV announcers to chortle. Lindegren told me that in the early 1930s, Hitler had his scientists hunt out an odorless drug that could be unobtrusively administered to the German people to make them more docile and open to suggestion. Accordingly,

174

chemists at I.G. Farben came up with sodium fluoride. Lindegren said that "In the rear occiput of the left lobe of the brain, there is a small area of tissue responsible for the individual's power to resist domination. Repeated doses of infinitesimal amounts of sodium fluoride will in time gradually reduce the individual's power to resist domination by slowly poisoning and narcotizing this area of brain tissue. In large doses, sodium fluoride causes paralysis and death. The drug allows a muscle to move one way, but blocks it from a corresponding reaction or contraction. But when an individual continually receives minute doses of it, the next effect is a marked weakening of the will."

Colonel Lindegren went on to accuse the shadow government of the United States of pushing fluoridation for the same reason Hitler did. I.G. Farben's record was partially revealed at Nuremburg, and its interlock with Standard Oil of New Jersey, David Rockefeller and Exxon is too well known to merit discussion. More important is the fact that the first Secretary of Defense strongly opposed fluoridation of water supplies on military posts. He died on May 22, 1949, ostensibly of self-defenestration. Many informed observers believed, however, that he was thrown from his hospital room window. One of them was Wesley C. Trollope, an FBI agent. According to Trollope, Forrestal was very much opposed to the dociling of servicemen. He said reports revealing this effect were available from the House Committee on Un-American Activities, volumes 7 and 9, *Reports of the Special House Committee on Un-American Activities in the Armed Forces*, Hearings of the 77th Congress.

Unfortunately, these hearings have disappeared off the face of the earth. No art of journalism, no Freedom of Information request, no intervention by Congressman or Senator can free up these hearings, and therefore the cited information became available to *Acres U.S.A.* readers via testimony only.

Equally unavailable until I finally located its "author" was the so-called *Liberty Study*. The *Liberty Study* refers to Liberty, Missouri, and usually consisted of arrays of figures that seemed to prove that there was a steady drop in cavities after fluoridation came to Clay County. In fluoridation battle ballot fights, dental societies and other pushers ran full page newspaper ads citing the *Liberty Study* which "revealed" how fluoridation reduced dental caries from 70% in 1955 to 25.5% in 1977.

The study became suspect at *Acres U.S.A.* for two very logical reasons. First, the Liberty school system has never had as many students as the "study" says were checked. Second, the actual "study" simply wouldn't surface. It took a special trip by Dr. Al McCone to Jefferson City to get an "official" copy of *The Liberty Study*, the one being passed out by state officials. In the meanwhile, misrepresentation of the study's character backgrounded a fluoridation election in Kansas City, Missouri.

I met up with the solution in the person of Ann Wilson. She told me how she developed a unique dental hygiene education program in the six school districts of Clay County, North Kansas City excepted. Her data had little to do with Liberty, although she officed in that community. Ann Wilson said she was surprised to see her figures used to promote fluoridation since fluoridation was not a part of her program. She said she never gave her figures to anyone and she never published them in the professional literature.

Drs. John Yiamouyiannis and Dean Burk delivered what should have been the end to the fluoridation of the water supply concept by taking death certificates, and paring cities of like size, demographic makeup and age groups. Cities that had been fluoridated for a decade showed a remarkable increase in deaths over cities that had not availed themselves of this halogen. As *Acres U.S.A.* reports were being rendered for issues beyond the scope of this book, a similar pattern was emerging in connection with AIDS.

In his book, *Fluoride, The Aging Factor*, Yiamouyiannis detailed the ultimate horror story. In the village of Kizilcaoren, Turkey, the young looked and felt old. All had brown teeth, a consequence of fluoride poisoning. At age thirty a man was ancient. Women produced dead babies after pregnancies that too often lasted four months. Not even the cattle enjoyed good health. Dr. Yusuf C. Ozkan, of the University of Eskisehir identified the cause of all this suffering—the high content of fluorides in the water. The better fed tolerated the substance best, but those forever on the edge of starvation paid this intruder with their health. This pattern is repeated in slum sections of major U.S. cities. The well fed can endure a lot of abuse to their metabolism, the others bow to that fabulous enzyme inhibitor. And still the Public Health Service, the dental profession, and science politicians stay the course, which is to continue using the water mains as a disposal system for a substance only slightly less difficult to get rid of than atomic waste.

On the front page and in the editorial columns, the fluoridation story gave way to the irradiation story only a year or two ago, and I suggested that a replay of the fluoridation scenario was unfolding. In the case of irradiation, the surplus product that needed disposal was radioactive waste.

There was nothing new when in 1984 broad-spectrum approval was sought for irradiation of all types of food. The foundation for the procedure was put down with the discovery of x-rays by Roentgen in 1895. Work with nuclear radiation by Curie and Rutherford added to the body of knowledge, as did Thompson's work with cathode rays in 1897. The arrival of the atomic age rounded out missing links in the technology for use of irradiation.

Soon after WWII in 1945, industrial firms and their captive scientific institutes in various nations, chiefly in the U.S., kicked open the door. The Atomic Energy Commission marched in. By 1953 a large scale program for irradiating food was started by the U.S. Army. Soldiers became uncomplaining guinea pigs. Now, with hotboxes ready to go, all industry needed was FDA approval.

In *Acres U.S.A.* I objected because the scientific literature said I ought to object. And with chapter and verse I explained how foods, proteins and amino acids disintegrate, how lipids produce dangerous breakdown products, and how carbohydrates produce substances which injure cell division and hereditary structures. Most of the objections to irradiated foods paled into insignificance when compared to the radiomimetic factor. The very process of irradiating foods forms radiomimetic chemicals. These are chemicals that ape the character of radioactivity. All enzymes have metal keys, and radioactivity heads for metal the way a duck goes to water. The result—radiomimetic terror.

In reporting this story I cited dozens of scientists who warned about some of the consequences of eating irradiated food: embryonal damage, reduced digestibility, malignant lymphomes in mice, changes in organs, and more. Since the after-effects of the consumption of irradiated foods on living tissue are similar to those of direct radiation, the relevant problems, which include an eventual reduction of the resistance against infectious diseases, AIDS included, deserved attention, but the Svengalis of science defended that irradiation was cheap.

There was the cancer story.

The victim of cancer might well be the victim of farming practices as well as the end product of environmental contamination and near total debauchery of the food supply, Dr. Donald William Kelley said, speaking into my *Acres U.S.A.* tape recorder. According to Kelley, cancer is the result of the inability of the body to digest its protein intake, just as diabetes results from the inability of the body to metabolize sugars and carbohydrates. The human body depends on pancreatic enzymes to digest food, but our food intake is loaded with preservatives and chemical residues. Chemicals attach themselves to the enzymes and render them helpless to do their work. Dr. Kelley contended that malignant tumors were symptoms of cancer which could grow only when the pancreatic enzyme function was not adequate.

In order to learn more about Dr. Kelley and the controversy that surrounded the cancer industry, I tripped to Grapevine, Texas for a very special interview. Dr. Kelley turned out to be a young, soft-spoken, intensely dedicated man who believed in the dictum, "Physician, heal thyself." He had done so. "I had cancer three years and seven months before it dawned on me," Dr. Kelley said. Physicians in effect wrote him off when the horror of horrors was discovered. "This even hit me harder than the average because I had been studying and researching the details of cancer." As an orthodontist and clinical worker, he ran a bio-chemical test on his family when he discovered his own terminal cancer. The results were shockers. His wife, two of his children and his mother had cancer. Dr. Kelley decided not to accept his fate. He concluded that malignancy was never normal tissue gone into wild proliferation, but normal primitive germ cells growing normally in the wrong place.

Kelley suggested several reasons for cancer—toxic genetic chemicals, injuries, too much protein, stress, obstructed pancreatic ducts. The direct cause was the changing of an ectopic germ cell into an ectopic trophoblast cell.

"Let's start at the beginning," Kelley said. "You have this human life cycle. The male sperm unites with the female egg. If this fertilized egg would grow directly into a baby, then we would have no such thing as cancer. Nature isn't that simple. If it were, the newly formed baby would fall out of the uterus. Nature has in fact developed a way to attach the embryo to the wall of the uterus and a way to feed it. Therefore, this fertilized egg gives rise to three kinds of cells—the primitive germ cells, normal body cells, and trophoblast cells. The egg is fertilized by the male sperm in the fallopian tube of the mother. In the three days that follow this egg falls into the uterus. During the three days and for several days thereafter, the trophoblast cells—or cancer cells—grow rapidly and surround the primitive germ cells and normal body cells. This baby will fall out of the uterus unless something happens fast. It does. The trophoblast cells metastasize to the wall of the uterus. After this happens the baby can't fall out of the uterus, but it has to be fed. The trophoblast cells continue to grow and form the placenta. Thus attached and fed, the baby continues to grow until birth."

The connection between this process and cancer fell into place, according to Kelley. The placental cancer mass grew until about the seventh week, and then the baby's pancreas developed. It was the baby's enzyme production together with the mother's enzyme production that stopped the growth of placental trophoblastic tissue.

Since this baby is formed from normal body or somatic cells, the primitive cells multiply. When the baby has developed to the proper stage, the primitive cells stop multiplying and proceed to migrate to the gonads—to the ovaries or testes. Not all these cells reach the gonads. Of the some three billion, about two for each area the size of a pinhead are dispersed in the entire body. Any one of these germ cells is a potential cancer site. This means that cancer is a normal growth of placenta due to development of the basic germ cell in the wrong place, or outside the uterus. It is the function of pancreatic enzymes to remove these cells that are growing in the wrong place. This is not possible when the pancreas no longer digests the protein intake. When this happens the pancreas no longer disposes of cancer cells.

What Kelley was saying was damning in its finality. It meant that a researcher such as Dr. John Beard of Scotland was right when in 1903 he discerned pancreatic enzymes as the key to cancer control. And Ernest Krebs, identified with laetrile, was far from the fool the medical establishment believed him to be. Kelley sought to deal with the scourge of cancer gently, with diet, rather than with surgery, radiation or chemotherapy, the approved AMA tools. This was heresy, and the establishment struck back.

It may have been happenstance, but it is a fact that at one time no less than seven government agencies landed on Don Kelley, all at the same time: the state dental society, the medical society, the state income tax, the federal income tax, the licensing board, state sales tax, and the local licensing authority.

Harold W. Manner, Ph.D., Loyola University, Chicago, Illinois, was Professor of Biology and Chairman of the Biology Department when he became part of the cancer story. For months on end his experiments with amygdalin (laetrile) made the pages of *Acres U.S.A.* Using standard scientific procedures, Dr. Manner tested the Krebs' theory that the cyanide content of the laetrile molecule would be released only in the presence of the enzyme "beta glucosidase." It had been the Krebs' theory that this enzyme was present only at the site of cancer.

On the other hand, the theory held, healthy cells are protected by another enzyme, rhodenase, which Krebs asserted was plentiful in healthy tissue but not present with cancer or trophoblast cells. It had been the Drs. Krebs-Beard concept that cancer represented the proliferation of the trophoblast cell, a cell which is produced in the body when estrogen stimulates total life cells to produce growth in the healing process.

It had been the conceptualization of laetrile proponents that when trophoblast cells are not killed by the body's pancreatic enzymes, they proliferate—cancer. Dr. Krebs held that laetrile works as a backup mechanism to kill cancer cells when the pancreas fails to do its job.

Up to the time of our *Acres U.S.A.* reports, the scientific establishment more or less refused to consider the theory. Dr. Manner's experiments served to break the log jam. Here are the words Dr. Manner left behind on tape after a brief meeting with *Acres U.S.A.*

"I was opposite a representative of the FDA—a man by the name of Dr. Young," Manner said. "I spent more time with him than I spent with my own wife. I knew everything he was going to say, and he knew everything I was going to say. But this time something was different. We had finished those toxicity studies. We had shown laetrile to be non-toxic. It was published and copies of the published reports were sent to the FDA, to the National Cancer Institute and to the Sloan-Kettering Institute. And then at the next state legislature meeting I heard Dr. Young say to the Senators, *Gentlemen, the FDA cannot support the use of laetrile becauses laetrile is an unsafe substance.* And I looked at him and said, *Dr. Young, how in the world can you say that? You have my report. You know that it is non-toxic.* He said, *Oh, I didn't say that it was toxic. I said it was unsafe.* He said, *We mean by unsafe that if a person uses laetrile that person might not use orthodox therapy, and so for this reason FDA considers it unsafe.*"

To learn more about therapy that did not rely on the burn, the cut or hard chemistry, Manner journeyed to California, Mexico, Jamaica, Hanover.

"I found that each of the regimen were a little different," he said. "But the one thing that was common to all of them—and I don't know how this escaped me, and how it escaped people at Sloan-Kettering and NCI—was that never was laetrile used by itself. It was always used in conjunction with a complete therapeutic program." A complete therapeutic program, it turned out, could save countless cancer victims, just as had been the case when Dr. Max Gerson was alive, and when the Hoxie Clinic beat back degenerative metabolic disease with vitamin, mineral and nutritional therapy.

For a time "Manner-type" clinics sprang up, but in the end Manner failed to get the approval of the establishment he believed pure science had earned, and the old way of handing off chemotherapy—"bottled death," Hubert Humphrey called it—stayed in command of the field.

There was the swine flu story.

The swine flu program began in January 1976 when an outbreak of influenza took place at Fort Dix, New Jersey. Most of the Fort Dix flu had to do with a common virus. Three cases, however, involved an agent styled *swine influenza*. This flu agent went from pigs to man, but only rarely from man to man. Once the New Jersey strain was identified, the Communicable Disease Center director came to Washington for a meeting with the Assistant Secretary for Health in Health, Education and Welfare. The theory being entertained had it that there was a connection between the New Jersey strain and the flu epidemic of 1918-1919. This information was taken to the Office of Management and Budget in the White House, and ultimately it got to then President Ford. The President made an announcement in March that year that he would like to have the American population vaccinated for swine flu since this might save millions of lives.

In the meantime it developed that the New Jersey strain was a very mild agent, that the disease posed no great danger. President Ford nevertheless sent to Congress an estimate that it would take $135 million to carry out a program that might save millions of taxpayers from premature death. HEW organized workshops to determine how a program was to be carried out. All sorts of problems developed, including the fact that children got very ill when vaccinated. Most important to the bureau people was the fact that the strain out of New Jersey was not suitable for vaccine making. This information might have scuttled $135 million appropriation, a price the bureau people did not want to pay.

Hearings were held in the House. The highest health official in the nation testified that a safe and effective vaccine could be produced using present technology—a clearly false statement. Manufacturers agreed they could produce the needed vaccine. Insurance firms were more reserved. They did not care to assume the risk involved. They said such a program had never been undertaken before in the history of man, that associated dangers could not be calculated, that taking the history of immunization into consideration, they could not insure against risk without going broke. Not mentioned, but equally real, was the history of problems connected with measles vaccination that had been recently published in the *Mortality and Morbidity Report*.

There was some reluctance on the part of Congress to pass the program or assume insurance risks. But unfortunate cases of Philadelphia Legionnaire's disease rescued the scam. At Senate and House hearings, it was stated that medical men didn't know whether Legionnaire's disease was indeed swine flu, but if it checked out that way, then these might be the first cases of swine influenza in the country associated with death. Congress dissolved into panic. The $135 million bill was passed.

Dr. Richard Shope, who used to work for the Rockefeller Foundation, had recovered influenza virus from pigs in 1931. Once he got that agent firmly established via experimental procedures, he went back and got blood from persons who were living in 1918-1919, persons who had survived influenza. In addition to getting those bloods, he had in the serum bank bloods that were taken in 1918-1919, and he tested those bloods for the presence of an antibody against the swine virus he got out of pigs in 1931. He found that those persons had antibodies against pig virus. Therefore, on that information, he made the assumption that the 1918-1919 epidemic was caused by the same virus he got of pigs in 1931. That might be a valid supposition. It might not be valid. He never said it represented "truth." He said this represented "possibility."

The agent that came out of New Jersey in February of 1976 was shown clearly to be different from Shope's 1931 virus—weeks before President Ford made his announcement. But no one ever brought this to the attention of the President. He still believed that the New Jersey agent was related to the agent that caused that 1918-1919 epidemic when this was no longer a feasible position to take because the evidence was in.

I wanted to track the swine flu disaster ever since I made the decision not to have my family immunized. There was something that didn't add up. For instance it had been a matter of record in the professional literature for ten years that a consequence of untested vaccines was Guillain-Barre. People literate in the subject knew this as recently as when I was handling an editorial pencil at *Veterinary Medicine*. And yet the establishment was ready to inoculate an entire population with a vaccine that had been conjured up during the previous three or four months.

I caught up with Dr. William Morris at a meeting in Los Angeles. It was one of the most difficult interviews I've ever managed. There we were in the hallway, a steady cacophony of noise in the background, and not infrequent interruptions from well-wishers and passers-by. I had to get answers immediately because from here he was headed to the airport. Dr. Morris had tried to blow the whistle on the swine flu fiasco before it started. His reward was termination in a manner brutal even for "cover-up" Washington.

He arrived at his office one morning and found the door locked. All the workers were gone. They had been reassigned. He had mice that had been on experimental procedures for three years. These mice had been destroyed. He had mice that were developing mammary tumors following inoculation with other vaccines. These were gone. He had been studying a contaminant of early Salk vaccine called SV-40, or Simian virus 40, which had turned up originally in monkeys. It was a small virus and relatively uncomplicated, but its effects had proved puzzling. It caused cancer in mice and hamsters. It had been shown to infect laboratory preparations of normal human cells, making them act cancerous. Millions of people had been inadvertently injected with SV-40. Yet as far as was known, no harm had resulted from its use, according to government reports.

That was a true statement in 1960. It was still true in 1965. But in 1969—twenty years after that vaccine had been used—SV-40 was picked out of the brain of two persons at Johns-Hopkins Hospital. These people had a very rare disease called PML—progressive multifocal leukoencephalopathy, a degenerative brain disease. This meant SV-40 was rearing its ugly head, and it was capable at least of being associated with a human disease condition. The annihilation of Dr. Morris' test animals suggested that the bureau heads didn't want to know.

They certainly did not want to know enough about the swine flu vaccine being readied for the American people because an election was coming up.

"Vaccines are made by putting virus in chicken eggs," Morris said, responding to my questions. "It grows there, and infected fluids are harvested. You inactivate this with formalin, then you neutralize the formalin, and so on. That's essentially how the vaccine is made. In order to do this, the influenza virus must mulitply in those eggs. It did multiply, but slowly—too slowly. In the normal course of events, you should be able to get three or four doses of influenza virus vaccine out of each egg. If the growth is so slow you only get one dose, that means you have to use three and four times more eggs. When you're trying to make 200 million plus doses of vaccine, that's a lot of eggs. It is also a lot of time. They could not make enough vaccine fast enough with that slow-growing agent to carry out what the President said he wanted done, that is, get all the people vaccinated [before the election]. To overcome this difficulty, they gave scientist Ed Kilbourne a job. Ed

Kilbourne had developed a technique by which he takes the nucleic acid out of the lipid surrounding the virus. The nucleic acid is surrounded by fat—your lipid—and on top of that there is a layer of protein. And on that protein you have spikes representing different antigens. That's what an influenza virus looks like in simple form. You put one in a chicken egg, and get out a million two or three days later. But the New Jersey strain grew very slowly. Now, the growth characteristic is determined not by the coat, but by the nucleic acid. He put this thing in detergent. The detergent dissolved the fat. This freed the nucleic acid and left a coat of protein floating around. He ended up with a new inside, and a New Jersey strain on the outside. Now you have this new agent. When you put that in the egg it grows fast. This is a man-made agent, and he called it X-53. It has nucleic acid derived from the lab, and a protein coat derived from the New Jersey strain. The vaccine is made from this recombinant. This is a new agent. It does not occur in nature, and it confers no protection against anything."

In other words, the swine flu vaccine program caused the American people to be inoculated against a disease that did not exist. It did, however, make the nation a warehouse full of tortured Guillain-Barre victims.

No one knows what causes Guillian-Barre. But one of the precipitating factors is a vaccination procedure. Sometimes the tingling and numbness goes away, and the body handles its own protection. But sometimes it proceeds further.

"The basic morphologic change in Guillain-Barre is demyelination of the nerve myelin," Morris said. "Your nerves have a covering over them, like an asbestos covering over a hot water pipe. You have a covering over your nerves that's made out of myelin, a myelin sheath. It is sort of an insulation for your nerve fibers. The first thing that occurs with Guillain-Barre is that the myelin sheath disintegrates. That's a manifestation of hypersensitivity. Now if that tingling continues, and progresses, the arm becomes paralyzed. You can't move the arm. Legs become paralyzed. Guillain-Barre might stabilize there, stay that way for months, or you might get better. Or it might go further. Your paralysis might get worse. Your respiratory center of the brain might become inactive. You can't breathe. That's where the deaths occur. If you don't die, and paralysis becomes progressively worse, then the diagnosis changes. You now have multiple sclerosis. The only difference between multiple sclerosis and Guillain-Barre is, with multiple sclerosis you get progressively worse. In Guillain-Barre it stabilizes. You may stay that way for years. Or you might get progressively better. You might recover fully with only a mild residual paralysis. That's Guillain-Barre."

One day, at Atlanta, Texas, I visited with Dr. Joe Nichols, the author of *Please Doctor, Do Something.* Dr. Nichols was then the president of Natural Foods Associates, and he spent two decades telling the story that health was seated in soil fertility management, and not in hot shot medicine from the AMA establishment. Twinkies and Dingdongs, Cokes and junk food, he said, simply did not add up to good health and mental acuity. Dr. Joe detailed the strange origins of the strange conceits offered by Charles Edwards in the opening lines of this chapter, and recited them from the podium in virtually every big city in this nation.

One often wondered what drove men like Joe Nichols, and successor leaders of Natural Foods Associates—people like apple grower A.P. Thomson, fertilizer specialist Hugh Paddock and airport owner, Irma Hooks.

"I had a dream one night," Nichols told me. "In that dream I saw my unborn grandchild beset by the perils our food system is foisting on all of us. That child had a right to be born without a scrambled brainpan, physical infirmities, and without being an early candidate for degenerative metabolic disease. I heard that child cry out, *please, doctor, do something!*"

15

BATHHOUSE OF ENERGY

If anything, the exercise called editing and publishing *Acres U.S.A.*
meant being in the right place at the right time. I have a feeling that
I've always been in the right place at the right time. This penchant
usually conspired to turn basic stories into a continuum. For instance,
one of my first interviews—a staple in *Acres U.S.A.**—was with Harold
Pratt, the self-taught nutritionist who developed many concentrated
food supplements and biological testing techniques. Pratt mentioned
Galen Hieronymus and his strange energy concepts, which Pratt could
barely tolerate, much less understand.

For half a decade I tended to agree with Pratt. And still there were
all those "interest" people, clubs that assembled everything ever written by Nikola Tesla, and backgrounding them were those French scientists Chris Bird and Peter Tompkins wrote about in *The Secret Life
of Plants*. Finally Phil Callahan uncorked his famous *Tuning In To
Nature*, and the articles in *Acres U.S.A.* that told of Irish round towers
as antennas that somehow concentrated a special energy and defined
knowledge archeologists barely suspected the ancients capable of having. Much as a hammer can chip away at a granite column, the news
in the field chipped away at me. I recalled Bill Albrecht telling me to
study nature, to watch what was going on in the field, more than in
the texts. "You'll find a lot more new there than you will in hard
chemistry and molecular biology. Watch the lowly field mouse," he
said. "And watch what sharp cookies like Gene Poirot are doing." He

---

*This book could easily have been extended another 149 chapters, that being the
number of interviews carried in these many years.

might as well have said, watch the bat and the talapia, the torpedo fish and the lemming.

The lemming is a field mouse in the Scandinavian regions. This little animal has been a handy literary device for writers who never tire of comparing mindless human action to lemming marching to the sea to drown—the presumption being that some instinct drives lemming to self-destruct in order to achieve population control.

The problem with that insight is that it appears to be hopelessly wrong. More likely, lemming are guided by Phil Callahan's coherent wavelengths transmitted by fish in the sea. Albrecht also cautioned, "You have to have a vision." Without some informed speculation on how things work, he said, there can be no progress. Thus, from my chair, it was not out of line to point out that glowworms, and certain microorganisms in decomposing meat, emit luminous radiations. Certain species in the sea put out so much radiation they make the water literally light up. A French scientist, namely Jacques Arsene d'Arsonval of the Paris *Academie des Sciences*, wrote voluminously about these wave connections, and a Russian engineer named Georges Lakhovsky set down many of the principles Phil Callahan was later to refine as proof of insect and plant communication in the infrared. Lakhovsky spelled it out in a little work entitled, *The Secret of Life*. What Lakhovsky said was transparently clear in its implications. He compared the nucleus of a living cell to an electrical oscillating circuit. The nucleus of that cell was made up of tubular filaments, chromosomes and the mitochondria. It had insulating material and was filled with a fluid containing all the mineral salts in sea water. This fluid conducted electricity. He compared the filaments in that cell to oscillating circuits capable of oscillating according to a specific frequency.

In covering this story, Callahan's insight meshed with what some of the fringe science people were saying. On the deck of a Nile River boat—with plenty of tape as a backup—I gathered in hours of interviews, all of which were later transcribed and made part of the *Acres U.S.A.* record. Phil Callahan was matchless in explaining the subtle low-level energies that, so far, didn't move a needle, but were there! Peter Tompkins may have missed one secret of the Great Pyramid in his book of the same name, a secret Callahan understood. At ancient Thebes (now Luxor), in the great Karnak temple, Callahan measured the character of the stone, not only in the columns and walls, but in the soaring obelisks as well. Callahan did not scoff at tales of levitation. He realized that the ancients who built the Great Pyramid knew

187

the dimensions of this planet as they were not known again until the seventeenth century. By observing the stars, these builders could and did measure the day, the year, the hour and the minute. They linked time with distance because they knew the circle had 360 degrees, and accordingly they computed latitude and longitude with great accuracy. Phil could explain that the record these ancients left in deathless stone reveals that Eratosthenes was not the first to measure the circumference of the earth. Hipparchus was not the first to develop trigonometry. Pythagoras did not originate his theorem. And Mercator did not invent his projection.

The Founding Fathers of the U.S. wrote into the Constitution language that said, *Congress shall coin the money, and regulate the value thereof . . . and establish standards for weights and measures.* It is all too obvious that whatever else money is supposed to be, it must be a measure of value. Obviously, the value of money cannot be regulated unless there is a standard. I have thought about this standard or lack thereof for a long time, and it was this consideration that finally led me to the Great Pyramid.

In fact, that special clause appears in the Constitution for a very special reason. It was included to prepare the ground for the adoption of a new decimal system of measures which was then being advocated by all enlightened people. It was reasoned by Jefferson that a truly desirable system of measures should coordinate time, length, volume, weight, and that nature's God should preserve the accuracy of these measures by aligning them with the vault of the heavens. After the French Revolution, Congress considered adopting the French metric system. But Thomas Jefferson, whom Congress respected as the authority on such matters, opposed the plan on the ground that the French system was inadequate since it did not coordinate time and length, volume and weight. And this opposition from the camp of the progressives doomed the adoption of the decimal system in the United States. It remained for a modern and more ignorant era to adopt the faulty metric system to accommodate the equal error of free international trade based on exploitation rather than equity.

The question for contemporary agriculture became at once apparent as I listened to Callahan. Should a paper like *Acres U.S.A.* dare be interested in what Callahan said was the key to life, namely low level energy systems? A few agronomists had written about energy from the cosmos, notably Rudolf Steiner and Ehrenfried Pfeiffer, but their insightful suggestions had been consigned to "intellectual underworld" status.

The rationale for some parts of this low level energy was stated in *Acres U.S.A.* as follows:

"Our bodies contain approximately 200 quintillion cells. In this fabulous number there are hardly two cells vibrating with the same frequency, this being partly due to the incessant activity taking place within the cells, and partly to the specific characteristics of different tissues, plus other factors. Moreover, from a biological point of view, it would be impossible to find at any given time two individual cells exactly alike in every respect. Every cell of every individual tissue of any particular species—plant, animal or man—is characterized by its own oscillatory shock. In disequilibriated cells, it would be necessary to generate as many wavelengths as there are different cells in any given body. The problem would thus seem to be insoluble. With remarkable imaginative insight Lakhovsky finally evolved a solution. He designed a new type of radio-electrical apparatus, the multiple wave oscillator, generating a field in which every cell could find its own frequency and vibrate in resonance. The practical results he obtained in various hospitals soon confirmed the validity of his theory. His agricultural experiments were equally impressive."

This was the key a number of hard knocks inventors relied upon to rediscover Tesla's multiple-wave oscillator, and harness it to field situations. Galen Hieronymus was pursuing the low-level energy principle decades before *Acres U.S.A.* came on the scene. More recently, Jerry Fridenstine entered the farm market with his Towers of Power. Hieronymus has called his farm approach Cosmic Pipelines.

By the time I ran several interviews and background reports on low level energy, hundreds of towers had already appeared on the farm landscape. Of the nation's three hundred farm magazines, I alone decided not to ignore the story—right or wrong! Moreover, there were afloat in the nation thousands of radionic units.

Radionics is simply a low level energy system that can be directed. Dr. Pat Flanagan explained the concept in an *Acres U.S.A.* interview.

"When an operator's mind and emanations from the tuner are on the same wavelength, a type of resonance is established, and the detector indicates this mode. The Hieronymus detector is simply a sheet of bakelite or plexiglass under which is placed a flat spirally wound coil, connected to the output of the amplifier and the ground. When resonance is established, there is a change of tactile characteristic in the top of the detector. The change of characteristic is detected by lightly running the fingertips on the surface of the detector plate while tuning the vernier dial of the prism. Hieronymus established numbers which correlate with the known chemical elements and combinations . . . Although the Hieronymus machine cannot be explained by modern physics, it does have merit by the fact that the results can be duplicated."

Flanagan came by his insight quite naturally. At age fifteen he invented a neurophone for the deaf because he realized that the human brain was not hard wired, as neurologists and anatomists had believed. This concept suggested direct nerve connections, say, from ear to certain brain areas associated with hearing, from eyes to visual areas, and so on. Flanagan believed the brain to be holographic, meaning that many areas of the brain are capable of performing multiple functions. The neurophone relied on this concept, and used the skin to set up a new hearing organ. These things fascinated *Acres U.S.A.* readers, and instead of balking when I presented topics other farm papers would not touch, they asked for more. At *Acres U.S.A.* meetings, speakers could emote with impunity about ideas that would have earned them a stoning half a century before. Radionics frequently led the field. And the consensus prevailed that scientists who hadn't done a few hundred hours of work on the subject really weren't worth talking to. Jerry Fridenstine put it this way. "Radionics enables you to work with and direct a minute amount of energy. Everything in the universe emanates an energy. It is radiating that energy and that energy is on a specific frequency. If you had ten radios on a Nile riverboat, you could have each one of those radios tuned to a different station. In other words you could be listening to Bach over here, Beethoven over there, a ball game over here, rock-n-roll over there and the news elsewhere, each one of them tuned to a different frequency. That is what we are working with in the towers of power, and that is what you work with in radionics. You work with specific frequencies to produce a specific effect. So, let's say you have a milk cow with mastitis. Mastitis resonates at a specific frequency. So the modulation of that energy has a specific sign wave. By using a radionic instrument, you can turn that resonance 180 degrees. In other words, you can take the exact modulation of the resonance of that disease and reverse it 180 degrees. If, say, the modulation is a + 10, and you have a - 10, everyone who's gone through the fifth grade knows that + 10 and - 10 equals 0. By putting that resonance back into that specific animal, you can actually eliminate that disease."

Some radionics people claim they can zap insects and cure everything from shingles to the heartbreak of psoriasis. I don't know whether these claims are true or not. The scientific establishment so far has succeeded only in driving to an early grave men with credentials and standing who even entertained investigating low-level energies. In *Acres U.S.A.* I expressed the view that zapping insects—even if it worked—did not repair the problem, because insects are simply a symptom of something wrong in plant metabolism, and killing the little critters, by poisons or energy streams and blasts, was back to dealing with effect, not cause.

Nutritionist Harold Pratt did not fully appreciate what his friend Hieronymus was saying way back *when*, because he knew little history and none of the language of the subject. The idea of a plant swimming in a bathhouse of energy eluded him, as did the strange terminology that still hasn't resolved itself—Wilhelm Reich's orgone energy, Baron von Reichenbach's odic force, or the *X*-force by the Britisher Eemon, and of course eloptic energy, by Galen Hieronymus, all terms describing vibrations or energies not part of the electromagnetic spectrum.

"If they could come up with a needle to show the energy flow," Callahan said, "the low level energy people would be taken seriously."

Callahan may be right, and he may be wrong about that.

But there is no needle. Farmers, however, say they can measure the results, and farmers have become alienated from their intellectual advisers because over a thirty year period too many have been engineered into bankruptcy with faulty technological and economic counsel. In the field I have been shown crops that picked up new life, loafing barns full of cattle with regained health, and across the kitchen tables farm wives have related how certain health problems have become resolved within a short period after the black box or the tower or the cosmic pipeline has arrived. "When you're aborting 75% of your calves, and some guy shows up with a tower and a system for correcting the problem in your aluminum barn, and the abortions stop, you don't give a diddly what the professors think," one, two and three Pennsylvania farmers told me in words almost exactly alike. Others now see their modern metal sheds and barns as veritable Faraday cages, and the only correction possible as black boxes and towers that invoke the principles of the multiwave oscillator.

My own interest in the radionics machines was heightened when I had the occasion to feed tests to several operators for which I already had the answers. In ten minutes—using their little black boxes—these several operators handed back the same answers that had cost me the swelling in my wallet when I sought them the conventional way. Most radionics people remain closet operators. They recall the uneasy days when government Neanderthalers romped all over the Constitution, entering meeting halls, smashing machines, putting out of business people who simply wanted to unravel nature's mysteries. Thus, there are today hundreds of operators who obtain soil readouts via radionics machines, saving themselves between $30 and $60 a sample, all without the *university* even being aware of it.

It may be that there is nothing to all this, that the real cause of recorded results is a planet in a new sweep, the dust of a comet, or a revised swing of the stars, or hyperactive imaginations collectively aligned. But the news is out there with or without ratification by officialdom. Many officials, in the early 1980s, had other things on their minds.

16

BLOCKBUSTER STORIES

From the chair of official science, the highest form of animal medicine continued to be annihilation of the flock or herd as the 1980s got underway. The case reports that paraded through *Acres U.S.A.* over fifteen years would fill the pages of a book the size of this one. During the summer of 1984, my family and I drove to Pennsylvania to visit Jim McHale, the commonwealth's former Secretary of Agriculture. McHale had been a keynoter at the earliest *Acres U.S.A.* meeting in 1975. After leaving office, he joined ex-Governor John Shapp in an eco-farming business enterprise. After a few false starts the idea of biological nitrogen fixation caught hold. Even the universities were testing the concept and often inventing new nomenclature.

One of McHale's distant neighbors in the state was enduring a top secret operation, but word leaked out and the press arrived. Frederick L. Wright and his son Rick raised rare birds, keeping alive a diversity of species seldom seen on farms or in zoos. Wright had some 10,000 customers in fifty states and all continents except Australia. He worked with Third World countries and with self-help programs. Through the years he and his family developed a number of varieties of birds from old-fashioned breeds ideal for homesteading. No antibiotics were used on his unique flock. Most ranged freely as the wildlife of which they were a part.

Wright's birds were condemned by a task force because of USDA's extermination policy, the highest form of animal medicine being to kill the patient. Because of unscientific growing conditions, improper handling of bedding, poor feeds and chemical stress on poultry, epizootics had become commonplace in Pennsylvania. A run of avian flu had already resulted in 14.2 million birds—chiefly broilers and laying chickens—being killed in the Pennsylvania heartland. USDA reasoned that the exotic birds might have been in contact with avian flu. The experts did not elaborate on how this was possible, although they might have noted that wild birds also lived in the quarantined counties.

I consider myself a tough newsman, but frankly Wright's story moved me to near tears. He related how a portable gas chamber—Nazi style—was pulled into the yard, how the birds were seized by a crew big enough to take a fortress. And then he told how his children cringed, had nightmares, and lived in the kind of fear a WWII Jew on the run might have experienced. The final indignity to this gentle Amishman's home and farm came after the killing crews had departed. An independent contractor came and sprayed the farm, the remaining animals and near the feed supplies with permethron under the Ectiban formulation. The Neanderthaler handling the chore said he didn't know what the chemical was.

I have tried not to make *Acres U.S.A.* a "horror story" sheet. Most of the reports over the years, filling thousands of pages, have had an upbeat theme—*Biological Nematode Control, Understand Micronutrients, Reclaiming Pedigree Cows,* and so on. Sometimes a special report throws sparks and sends ripe tinder up in flames. Our running reports on weather modification activities—many of which have telescoped two centuries worth of floods into a single decade—often exhausted our print overrun.

During the 1970s, weather modification became one of the most enduring stories in *Acres U.S.A.* My own introduction reached back to my days in Denver, when Roscoe Fleming on *The Denver Post* was ghosting a book for Irving Krick. Krick had taken up weather modification where Irving Langmuir—the father of weather modification—left off. Krick later stood accused of bringing a seven year drought to Chad and Ethopia in order to accommodate the Kenya tea trade. During WWII, Dr. Irving Langmuir developed a smoke-screen device which could cover extremely large areas of ocean in a very short time, thus hiding ships at sea from enemy aircraft. Out of these experiments came nucleation, finally weather modification.

The technology for weather modification now has library shelves straining, so extensive have scientific entries become since Dr. Irving

Langmuir's early ventures into the field. But as is the case with the life of Christ, little new is added by thousands of volumes. Equally little is being supplied by the science politicians who rationalize their weather making tragedies. For sheer purity of thought and expression, what Langmuir wrote still stands out. Even now what the great Nobel Prize winning scientist proved and set down in the literature of science points to the giant Hitler-sized lies National Weather Service bureau people palmed off in the wake of two Kansas City floods.

By 1950 and 1951, science-business people had discovered the money potential of cloud seeding. Generators were set up from New Mexico to Wyoming, and mischief was headed east. Dr. Langmuir warned at that time that the rainmakers could turn on the rain, but couldn't turn it off. In the summary of his life's work, he commented briefly on what happened.

"From May until July 1951, there were floods in the Missouri Valley, mostly in Kansas and Nebraska. [Kansas City's industrial bottoms were under water.] This was during the time when periodic seedings were being carried on. These rainfalls had an exceptionally high seven day periodicity. When the seeding stopped, the periodicity in the rainfall stopped abruptly and there was an end to the heavy rain."

On October 12, 1950 the National Academy of Sciences met at Schenectady, New York. At that time the following findings were presented to the most prestigious science forum in the nation, if not the world. A record of that presentation was published in *Science* magazine that same year. Here is an abstracted passage from that presentation.

"Preliminary studies indicated that the known seedings in Arizona and New Mexico may have led to unusually heavy rains in eastern Kansas a few days later at distances 700 to 900 miles from the points of seeding."

I had taken to keeping the baseball scores on floods early in the 1970s. Several entries stood out.

August 1969, James River Basin, Virginia.—153 dead and millions of dollars in property damage as treated Hurricane Camille dumped almost 30 inches of rain in less than eight hours.

February 1972, Buffalo Creek, West Virginia.—118 killed and hundreds of homes washed away as a dam made of coal mine waste gave way after heavy rains.

June 1972, Rapid City, South Dakota.—236 dead and $100 million in property damage after a large, slow-moving thunderstorm unleashed torrents of rain on the slopes of the Black Hills.

June 1972, Northeastern U.S.—120 killed and more than $2 billion in property damage as the remnants of Hurricane Agnes produced widespread and destructive flooding and flash flooding in Virginia, West Virginia, Maryland, Pennsylvania, and New York.

July 1976, Big Thompson Canyon, Colorado.—139 drowned and millions in property damage after a thunderstorm deluged the western third of the canyon with 12 inches of rain in less than 6 hours.

July 1977, Johnstown, Pennsylvania.—76 dead and more than $200 million in property damage when up to 11 inches of rain fell on a seven-county area in nine hours during violent thunderstorms.

And then came the Kansas City flood of September 1977. As if in anticipation, I called into my office a retired Navy weatherman named Gerald Admires, who was growing apples near Holt, Missouri. The recorded conversation became an interview in *Acres U.S.A.* one month before a sizeable section of Kansas City took its weather modification bath. In the issue after that, I had my headline and also ample satellite photos illustrating exactly what Admires and one of his associates had warned would happen.

The facts I reported were simple enough. After several weeks of steady rain, soil systems in the greater Kansas City area had become super-saturated. Then, on September 12, the really heavy rains arrived. In one twenty-four hour period, rainfall measured twelve to sixteen inches, according to scattered local reports. Water piled up on the Kansas side of State Line, spilled over the banks of Brush Creek, and in a matter of hours extinguished the lives of twenty-five people. Property damage has never been calculated fully.

National Weather Service bureau people promptly declared the flood an Act of God, a once in a century affair—nay, a once in a thousand years probability. Relief agencies brought hot coffee and cold promises to the black people who had been made "Red Cross poor" by the raging waters. Business folk were offered low cost loans, money which many could lay off at higher interest rates. In days, the tennis courts on the Plaza were cleared. Black people areas didn't return to normal for years.

The Kansas City flood ushered in the longest zip exchange in the history of *Acres U.S.A.* Kansas City Mayor Charles Wheeler responded to one of my missives by saying there had been consultation with the National Weather Service, and that the delay in answering my letter was necessary because an in-depth study was made. I then asked for the study. No answer! I filed for a copy of the study under the Freedom of Information Act. Within the required time, the National Weather

Service responded saying that there had been no such study. I did not say the Mayor lied. I merely left it to the readers to characterize the nature of his response.

In reporting this story, I engaged experienced meteorological help to read available satellite photos of what had happened. In the November 1977 issue of *Acres U.S.A.*, a translation of those photos furnished a conclusion: "Storm systems from three directions moiled over Kansas City, heavy with silver iodide nuclei seeded earlier over Colorado, California, Oregon and Illinois. Cloud seeding in the west sent moisture needed there aloft as ice crystals until they met a midcontinent area of high humidity." In the Kansas City area, the man-directed rain came down as though a giant tank in the sky had been turned bottom up.

Through correspondence, research and investigative reporting, my staffers and I found that the Kansas City Police and the Army Corp of Engineers, and several government officials had prior knowledge of the impending floods, but decided not to warn the public. This warning came from Colorado weatherman, F. Neil Bosco. Among data submitted to the Kansas City Police Department were notations on how storms which originate in Colorado, California and the southwest cause storms in the Kansas City area.

A key to the weather modification story surfaced when Edward Teller, the atomic scientist, faced an audience in North Kansas City and said that we had to experiment with weather modification, *even if it hurt a little*. I continued to log in the floods through all of 1977 and 1978.

Eventually the story slowed and faded from the paper. There were more accidents, and they hurt more than a little, but the modifiers improved their skills and became a little less reckless—for the moment!

Another blockbuster story kept the phone lines ringing, and demand for reprints alive. It came styled *A New Payment in Kind Comes to Nebraska.*

A New Payment was not what I would call a continuing story. It arrived on the front page, and promptly fell out of the paper, but its impact was more than the trace of a first magnitude star.

I trailed that story myself and found the key in a piece of evidence all other investigators had missed—a dead kitten. Arthur L. Kirk, age forty-nine, was deeply in debt simply because—like many other farmers—he tried to substitute debt for earnings. The day arrived when the sheriff's deputies came with a piece of paper and drawn guns. Kirk, angry and insulted, ran them off his place. Officials later complained to the local prosecutor how they had endured this humiliation.

Armed with a license to kill, they returned, this time with a SWAT team. When they left, they had farmer Kirk ready for a body bag. Empty shells and certain household articles had been removed. Remaining on the killing ground was a dead kitten, its ears cut off and its hide laid back to expose countless outraged nerves. Mourners at the funeral suggested that the cat had been tortured to bring Kirk out of his house, where he could be gunned down. Inspection of the dog kennel where he died, and reports of his wounds suggest that the farmer received two non-fatal wounds and was allowed to bleed to death.

New farm groups were becoming a fixture in the countryside as the countdown for annihilation of the family farm continued. In any county one could encounter the passionate state of mind. American Ag Movement came on in the late 1970s. Much like the National Farmers Organization, it too set unrealistic goals and nurtured unreal expectations. Some farmers listened to a fellow named Jim Wickstrom, who was trying to organize a Posse Comitatus, which the public prints liked to turn into an ogre, even though it never got off the ground. Pressured beyond endurance, some farmers determined that paper money was a hoax, that the income tax was illegal, that a few good hangings of judges might freshen the air a bit. Most of this was talk, and *Acres U.S.A.* was always on the scene with a reminder that the headbreakers had more new equipment and riot gear than common sense.

The killing of Arthur L. Kirk was nothing more than a Nazi knee-jerk reaction. The paper the deputies served could have been mailed to him. His often quoted remark that he "would take some of them with me" has been made by thousands of besieged farmers, and even became a line in the movie *Country*, and if SWAT teams were to take them all out, the blood bath would rival Mao tse Tung's death machine when the Kuomintang fell.

One at a time the folk heroes arrived. There was Gordon Kahl, for instance. Gordon Kahl fled federal marshals who tried to gun him down and hid out in Arkansas. He was finally killed in a manner that suggested total war rather than police activity. Kahl had become identified with the tax protest movement, and was selected to serve as an example. He was in Medina, North Dakota, where he could have been arrested. Instead, federal officials elected to set up a roadblock on a lonely stretch that Kahl had to travel to reach home.

The details have been reported in the public prints and have also been made a matter of record in trial testimony. The Kahl party was composed of two vehicles. One transported Gordon Kahl and his friend Dave Broer. Another transported Kahl's wife, his son Yorie and his wife, plus two friends. The two-car convoy saw two unmarked cars forming a roadblock dead ahead. They had no way of knowing the road had been blocked by officers.

A moving roadblock came up behind Kahl and his party, preventing retreat. Men jumped from the second set of police vehicles amid screams of, "Take your positions." One of the marshals allegedly yelled, "You're going to die." At that moment, two men pointed their guns at Gordon Kahl. With that, Kahl and friend reached for their own guns. Yorie did the same. Someone fired, and Yorie went down. A second shot was fired, and Yorie was hit again.

According to published reports on the incident, no one identified the blockade as lawmen. Testimony is also in agreement with the fact that Kahl fired at an agent who was then aiming at his son Yorie for a third shot. Kahl missed. Then Kahl fired at a second agent and hit him. Gunfire erupted in earnest as Kahl fled the scene, hoping to draw the danger away from his wife and son and the others.

In a few hours, more than one hundred men and twelve vehicles—including an armored personnel carrier—were in the field, hard on the hunt for Kahl. Agents surrounded Kahl's house and reduced it to shambles, much like a house near Anzio Beach after the invasion of Italy in WWII. After twenty four hours, a SWAT team stormed the house. It was empty.

Yorie was taken to a hospital where he lingered between life and death for days. Mrs. Kahl, sitting up with her son, was cuffed and taken to the sheriff's department for the usual handling and incarceration, pending bail. Yorie and his mother were tried for the murder of two federal marshals. Mrs. Kahl was found innocent.

One of the lawmen testified that Yorie had gotten off the shots that killed two marshals, this after he had been near mortally wounded twice. Apparently the jury and the judge believed that incredible yarn, as did an appeals court. Yorie is now serving a life sentence.

Gordon Kahl admitted he shot the lawmen in letters that were received by a number of newspapers, associates and even the court. He was tracked to Arkansas, where an informant "Y" saw him in May of 1983. Informant "Y" turned the information over to Agent "X."

An assault party was formed, and Kahl was firebombed to death. The people who gave him shelter were charged with murder, even though they were in handcuffs at the time of the assault in which a sheriff was gunned down, possibly by part of the assault team, according to some of the people who have investigated the case.

A footnote of sorts belongs to the Gordon Kahl affair. Two weeks after the firebombing of Kahl, a man named Ray Wade and a *New York Times* reporter sifted through the ruins of the burned-out house. They found a human foot chopped off above the ankle. Andy Lenarcic, a writer for *Freedom*, one of the newspapers that covered the killing, insists the foot was willfully dismembered, and claims to have hard physiological evidence to that effect. This is not difficult to believe, since hand and foot amputation of Anna May Aquash for identification was in fact an FBI *modus operandi* after the confrontation with Indians at Wounded Knee a few years earlier.

"Uncivilized activity is uncivilized activity," I editorialized, "whether a dead human or a live cat is involved, and this realization has some few farmers near Grand Island, Nebraska wondering about what manner of people now staff the ranks of policemen."

Even when *Acres U.S.A.* was reporting the debauchery of the nation's lifeline, I tried to keep in focus a balance. During the 1930s, only 25% of the people were unemployed, even though national income fell by 50%. Fully 75% had jobs and income, and enjoyed the fine standard of living powerful dollars could purchase. In our own era not all farmers are going broke. Some have survived without debt. Some never fell for the chemical gambit in the first place. Across the nation, fine operations continued to function in harmony with nature, always enjoying any update on nature's stern requirements.

The updates come from all over the world, so much so, in fact, that I initiated an *Hectares International* section. One correspondent has even shared his insight from behind the Iron Curtain, both with articles and via letters to the editor. Jurgins Reckin from East Germany is one of our few Iron Curtain subscribers. One day he sent in the diagram that appears on the facing page.

I used it to illustrate a front page story, and to tell readers about Lee Fryer's then new book, *The Bio-Gardener's Bible*. Looking back over the years of publication, it seems that the publication of Phil Callahan's *Tuning Into Nature* was blockbuster stuff. It explained how insects communicate, and in due time it prompted me to observe—in *An Acres U.S.A. Primer*—that "It is well within reason to suggest that a subclinically sick plant will have an altered wavelength. Is this why insects attack the undernourished plant, the one with missing trace nutrients? If so, then the questions have been answered by the eco-farmer who has discovered the biochemistry of immunity not only in genetic engineering, but also in fertility management." I suggested that the publication of Lee Fryer's *Bio-Gardener's Bible* would be equally blockbuster stuff. For Fryer explained in most understandable terms what others have only hinted at. According to word I received at *Acres U.S.A.*, the editors of *Crops & Soils* became infuriated at the thesis in Fryer's book. It challenged the most cherished ideas of the fossil fuel crowd, and if implemented in American agriculture the ideas contained in the *Bio-Gardener's Bible* would recast the mode of main-line agriculture.

Reckin's diagram said it all. I now doubt that I've ever published an article on agronomy that couldn't plug into this one drawing that is surely worth a million words.

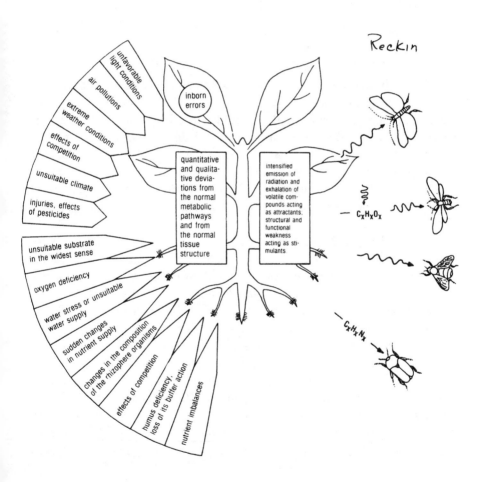

17

LAND PATENTS

The mail has always run heavy at *Acres U.S.A.* The most trouble-some area has never been answering questions about soil systems, crop management or animal health. Such questions were easily answered, always without recourse to coal tar derivatives or toxic genetic chemicals. The mail was always lead heavy with questions about law, human rights, and how come judges have powers that occupy hardly a syllable in the Constitution? "Is the Constitution the supreme law of the land or not," one reader wanted to know, "or do treaties supercede the Constitution?"

"How is it that I can't get a jury trial on controversies involving more than $20.00 as stated in the Constitution," and "How come the Congress doesn't obey the Constitutional requirement of making nothing other than gold or silver legal tender in payment of debts?"

Most people would say, "See a lawyer," this on the laughable assumption that an attorney could answer. Either-or questions are often beside the point. It might have been better to ask, "Are we under law or are we under an admiralty form of equity." Over two dozen issues, I stayed on to answer these things. For a time the bottom line became an in-depth story entitled, *Land Patents*. Its influence spread several times beyond the total subscription list and reprints are likely to circulate for years to come. Within two months after *Land Patents* appeared, the Virginia office of Bureau of Land Management unofficially reported that over twenty-five thousand individuals had filed for their land patents.

The *Land Patents* story was not a case of a newspaper making the news. A young fellow named Marvin Porter of Kidder, Missouri, walked into the office one day. He was under the hammer, and in weeks would be sold out. In the meantime he and some of his associates had read and digested the works of Thomas Hart Benton, and in the process they had learned the kind of history most economists are totally ignorant about. They turned up an Act of Congress dated April 24, 1820, which had the effect of creating allodial titles to land that, before the Revolutionary War, were feudal in nature. The law itself simply set a price of $1.25 on public land, but demanded payment in specie, meaning gold or silver, and forbade payment in the fiat bills that banks had created.

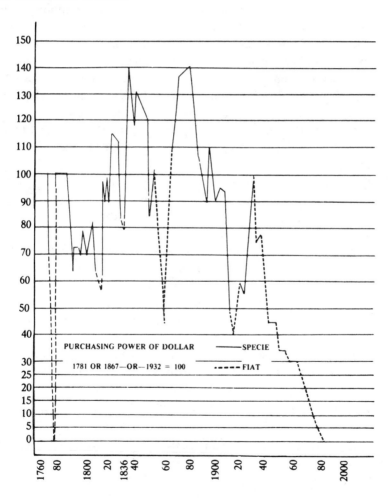

PURCHASING POWER OF DOLLAR ————SPECIE

1781 OR 1867—OR—1932 = 100   ∙----∙ FIAT

A good chart talks, and for this reason I drew up the above graph to explain the meaning of the land patent. Base period 100 marked the beginning of the nation as a going concern. By walking *Acres U.S.A.* readers through American history in terms of money, I hoped to make clear the fact that fiat money under the Federal Reserve was not all that different from the fiat money that touched off each of the farm liquidations and revolts in history.

When the Founding Fathers launched a new government, they did so with an educated understanding of common law, specie money, banking, fractional reserves, and the character of man. It was understood by Jefferson and his political allies that for most people with an understanding of financial matters, the main objective in life was to structure some way to achieve perpetual revenue independent of any further expenditure of energy, all at the expense of the common man.

At the time of the American Revolution, money and banking had already become fairly sophisticated. Still commerce rested ultimately on specie—that is, hard cash, or gold and silver bullion, or coins that were in effect a commodity themselves, or bills of exchange that could be converted into specie because they were as "good as gold." The base line of 100, and the dates that designate the foundation of the nation, reveal that the dollar was worth 100 cents in terms of specie when the revolution started.

In the late 1700s, the common specie coin in circulation was the Spanish mill dollar, a coin commonly called a piece of eight. The piece of eight continued to be the standard money unit throughout the entire colonial period. The Spanish dollar was minted in Mexico. Mexico had a lot of silver, and Spain had control of Mexico. The Spanish dollar and its fractional parts circulated with the official quarter of the dollar in the U.S. A quarter was *two bits* and a dollar was *eight bits*. The term is still used today. It, of course, goes back to the Spanish coin called the *reo*. One reo equalled 12.5 cents—a bit. Eight reos converted to a dollar in specie—all hard money.

The continental dollar changed all that. There was the issue of continental currency during the Revolutionary War, and there was that Hamilton Bank, and an outcropping of shyster banks that issued fiat money. We know exactly what happened in the first instance because Thomas Jefferson and Thomas Paine both left superb records. Until the issue of continental currency reached $9 billion, these units of currency circulated at nominal value. But depreciation after that point was great. The rate of exchange in Philadelphia, from January 1777 to May 1781 climbed from 1.25 to 1 to 500 to 1. On May 31, 1781 continental bills ceased to circulate as money. They were afterwards bought on speculation at various prices, from 400 to 1 up to 1,000 to 1. When this happened, there was nothing to do except to return the purchasing power of the nation's bond to the people. Congress recognized this in 1780 and anchored the value of American money to specie.

When Hamilton's bank came on-scene, the fractional reserve principle permitted banks to again flood the nation with fiat money. This enabled the money creators to engineer swings between inflation and depression. Farmers usually purchased land at inflated values, then found themselves unable to pay when commodities touched deflation bottoms. On April 24, 1820, Congress provided for relief of agriculture by allowing bankrupted farmers to get recapitalized on cheap frontier lands. In so doing, Congress tampered with the contract, with equity, in short. It was this measure that gave birth to the land patent because it decreed transfer of government land by law as well as by quit claim deed. It carried with it a caveat that this land could not be attached for debt based on inflation and taxes generated by fiat money.

In the opening land patent article I quoted Thomas Jefferson. "If the American people ever allow the banks to control issuance of their currency, first by inflation and then by inflation, the banks and corporations that grow up around them will deprive the people of all property until their children will wake up homeless on the continent their fathers occupied."

The late Bill Avery came to the *Acres U.S.A.* office during parts of the 1970s. The Liberty Amendment was front burner stuff at the time, and Bill was an adamant enemy of its "cynical" intent. "The reason I call it cynical," said Avery, "is that it promotes the very thing it pretends to denounce—enforced collectivism." Avery went on to inform *Acres U.S.A.* readers, via editorials and other inserts into our pages, that the problem was not so much to get government out of business as to get business out of government. "The government," he said, "is the Constitution. The bureaucracy is private enterprise."

The Liberty Amendment went down in flames soon after that encounter. Later Avery told me he had a signed letter from Willis Stone saying that a reversal of his Liberty Amendment position was tantamount to repudiation of a lifetime's work. Soon after the Avery challenges, Stone turned the promotion of the Liberty Amendment over to ultra-right wing activist Cleon Skousen of the John Birch element.

The land patent, the money system, and the use of contract law to annihilate the Constitution became story lines that grew with comprehension, and they both explained the land patent and undercut the idea that Pollyanna would somehow keep America out of slavery.

What the farmers were saying as they paraded through my office was that two hundred years ago, America was a nation of free men. Today it is possible to count the free men in a community on one hand. The rest are beholden to the government and rules of bureaucracy, and are prisoners in equity law, not because they understand the system, but because they are ignorant of how it functions.

When the colonies were under English rule, all title to land was vested in the Crown. There was no such thing as absolute ownership. Technically, lands in the new country were held in free and common socage under grants from the Crown.

The law of April 24, 1820 restated the proposition that title to land transferred from the English Crown to the United States, and to the states, by the treaty of Paris, which ended the Revolutionary War. That sovereign power, in turn, now elected to divest itself of such title and transfer the same to individuals for payment in specie. Allodial lands, the principle had it, were to be held in absolute ownership, the same as an individual's personality.

Legal concepts are difficult for most readers, and they must be no different for lawyers. Otherwise Chief Justice Warren Berger would hardly have pronounced 80% of the nation's lawyers incompetent.

Lord Mansfield became Lord Chief Justice of the King's Bench in 1756. It was under his sway that profound changes were made affecting the rights of Englishmen. Then as now, these changes were used to create the legal grounds needed for corporations to plunder the earth. In Mansfield's era, the law was structured to give immunity to the East India Company for all it would do to enrich the firm and the King. In order to do this, Mansfield incorporated into the ancient common law of England the body of international law called the Law Merchant—a law above all other law, a type of law called *equity*. Laws made on the basis of Mansfield's decisions brought the American colonies to revolution. They permitted search and seizure, denied jury trial, and imposed taxes that were repugnant then, and were ruled repugnant later on when the revolting colonies declared their independence. And it is the very same concept of law the power barons of commerce continue to impose on all of us in the name of one world.

And what was the origin of this Law Merchant? It was the law of the high seas, the law of the international market—the law of no nation in particular, but the law only of the traders and the corporations. It was enforced by its own courts called *piepowder* at fairs and markets, but in the domestic law courts of no nation, because it was based on summary judgment carried out upon the writs of assistance, and without jury trials. The theory was that conditions on the high seas were so rough, they required dictatorial control—summary executions, flogging, and so on.

This Law Merchant came from the rigid and hated Roman Civil Law, and it embodied the "guilty until proven innocent" concept. Thomas Jefferson, a gentleman almost all judges need to study, wrote to John B. Cutting in 1788: "I hold it essential in America to forbid that any English decisions which have happened since the accession of Lord Mansfield to the bench should ever be cited in a court . . ."

American common law, through the Seventh Amendment, derives chiefly from the law of allodial titles to real property. It is these private rights in real property which the courts of equity have been cultivated to destroy in favor of "land in a few strong hands." Under the Constitution, no corporation can lay claim to privacy of papers or search without warrant. All have contracted with the state for the right to do business—the franchise.

The Constitution also provided for free men, individuals not beholden to the state for the right to do business, grow crops or sell the same. Indeed, two hundred years ago, most men were free. Most farmed, and the Congress went to great lengths to see to it that the land was not taken away from the farmers by shysters, speculators and money creators. In administering the Act of Congress, April 24, 1820, government agents quit claimed title to land and set up rules of procedure so that patented land could not be taken as collateral for loans calculated in terms of flim-flam money. It was intended as an insurance policy against exactly what was happening to 240,000 FmHA, Land Bank and PCA borrowers in the 1980s. Lincoln extended the same concept to western lands with the Homestead Act. With the homestead unavailable for bank and lending agency takeover, and with personal bankruptcy available every seven years, free men could hold off the tentacles of tyranny forever, or so the reasoning had it.

Over the past forty-five years, Americans have slept soundly. The courts of equity have been used to regiment men, resources and commerce based on the maxim that "to trade with a merchant is to become a merchant," and this makes every individual liable to trial by judge (not jury) on the mere fact that each individual gets and spends, possesses and consumes, and this has been translated to include everything, even eating and giving birth, making them all franchisable

207

activities. Under this perverted interpretation of law, there is never a controversy that needs to be tried by jury, except rape, robbery and murder.

But the law is the law—and the land patent is conveyance of title by law. A judge who is given the proper citations can hardly rule otherwise. At least that is the theory. In reality, land patents collided with debt, and debt won by taking over the courts.

First, the holders of allodial land—no overlord being evident—could not even be taxed without their consent. Unfortunately, the allodial holders of land elected to tax themselves so that education could be socialized, roads built, and the cutting edge of a bureaucracy set up. There is an oft-repeated statement that ignorance of the law is no excuse. With millions of laws on the books across the country, such an adage has to be nonsense. And it is. The aphorism orginally said, "Ignorance of your rights is no excuse." And so it seems that farmers abandoned a measure of their rights through ignorance. The judges do not bother to tell them why they lose in court on grounds that servants (the court) do not tell masters (the citizens) their rights. Masters are presumed to know their rights.

As reports on land patents continued to fill the pages of *Acres U.S.A.*, a few stray lawyers and lots of attorney generals were contacted by the public prints. It was all insanity, they said. Someone was taking people for a ride, they said. The law of the contract prevailed, they said. When the newsmen contacted me, I simply said, "Unless the attorney general has done a hundred hours of work on the land patent, he simply isn't worth talking to." I was often quoted exactly that way. In California the recorders in the court houses got together and decided not to register redeclarations of land patents because they were "frivolous." In Wisconsin the legislature made it illegal to cloud a title. The lawmakers went so far as to declare the common law lien null and void.

The sneers and hisses didn't bother me. They were offset by a parade of attorneys coming by the *Acres U.S.A.* office telling me about the new bargaining power knowledge of the land patent had bestowed. Farmers are generally made to believe that courts will rule against them, and often this is true. Every state in the union has a law that requires buyers of farm products to pay creditors when the farmer's finished commodity is sold. No other industry is so burdened. A judge cannot rule differently. Still the fact is that when the court isn't wired, mortgage holders are terrorized at the prospect that a judge may go against them.

The world has turned over several times since the wisdom of the Founding Fathers lit up the sky. Today the federal government is the prince of land grabbers. Using every device available—programs to control floods, projects to preserve wildlife, monuments to rescue history, and a predatory expansion of government itself—the federal government has taken title to fully one-third of the American land mass. All the agencies of government now active could not be housed in all the office space of the nation's ten largest cities. The government lending agencies, FmHA, PCA, Land Bank, and others, grant something like $750 billion credit per annum—more than the nation's seventy largest lenders. These same agencies are now front-runners in making people homeless, just as Jefferson warned. And still the laws and decisions supporting land patents remain on the books.

A long inventory of cases supporting the land patent prompted me to publish *Land Patents, Memorandum of Law, History, Force and Effect of the Land Patent*, by S. Jay Stewart, which was promptly infringed in its entirety by a man in Iowa City, Iowa. S. Jay Stewart and I filed suit to stop the infringement in its tracks, but neither of us figured we needed to serve papers with a SWAT team that had a body bag in tow, as was the case with farmer Kirk.

I added a codicil of sorts to the *Land Patents* book under the title, *A Learning Tree*. I noted that the Founding Fathers understood that ownership of land was the fountainhead of freedom because it made the individual the sovereign. With an absolute title, he was beholden to no lord or master. This sovereign in fact created the United States. The first words of the Constitution are simply, "We the people . . ." Even high school students know that the original thirteen colonies were slow to accept the new Constitution until a Bill of Rights had been promised—the first ten amendments.

Why wasn't the matter of absolute land ownership made part of the Bill of Rights? The question is difficult to answer, so many years having intervened. But careful reading of history provides a probable answer. The idea of patented land—that is, land passed to individuals by law—was so secure at the time of the Founding Fathers that no one believed it to be in danger. The Constitution contained the mechanisms a freeholder could use if he wanted to claim allodial rights. Patented lands were passed from states to individuals even before the Constitution was written, especially during the term of history when the new nation was governed by The Articles of Confederation. It simply did not occur to the Founding Fathers that the several states would entirely turn their backs on the public policy that underwrote the

American Revolution. When Andrew Jackson drove the money changers from the national temple, the United States were still frontier in character. Superbanks did not have their talon hands at the nation's jugular, and the judiciary did not entirely agree with the idea that protection for the money lender was more important than protection for the rank-and-file citizen.

But slowly, by degrees, legislatures at the state level came to believe that a run on a bank was more lethal than the sacrifice of an individual farmer. After all, hundreds of citizens depended on the solvency of the bank. And judges, even today, see it as their first duty to protect the creditors. The mortgage—handled in a court of equity—is always given highest standing, and the issue of absolute ownership is shunted aside as something archaic in a world of computers, fiat money and bankers lending their credit.

In fact, it can be asserted with superb logic that state legislatures have repealed some parts of the Bill of Rights, sometimes with the blessing of the Supreme Court. The right to bear arms has been abridged because the Supreme Court, in a Michigan case, said the restriction was on the federal government, not the state government. Trial by jury is almost a thing of the past, except for rapists and murderers. Almost all courtroom activity has to do with equity, that is with contracts and business dealings under maritime law, meaning the law of the merchant. This is a realm into which almost all citizens have been delivered via the cleverness of lawyers.

This much stated, I was not slow in advising all land holders to get a land patent covering the acres or town lots in their possession. I published an appropriate document to be filed in the local courthouse. The cost for taking such a step was nominal.

What a land patent title holder could expect after redeclaring such a title remained sheer speculation. The naked law dictated one thing, present public policy and equity law another—and declared public policy dictated still something else. As an example, one farmer—whose case was reported in *Acres U.S.A.*—went to court with a superb presentation based on solid law. The court sidestepped the issue by refusing to address it, and by ruling on the usual claptrap that mortgage companies bring before a court of equity. It was apparent that the judge saw the land patent as an issue too hot to handle. Another farmer redeclared the land patent in his own name. His lender would not loan him any more funds until he took the patent off his land. An influx of requests for land patents at the several land management offices was bound to reverberate in Washington.

As letters and telephone calls inundated my office, it became obvious that many farmers saw the land patent as a crucifix that could be held up over Dracula. Display it in court, and every other argument drops dead, those who jumped to simple conclusions had it.

It hasn't proved that simple. But the fact remains that when S. Jay Stewart, the author of *Land Patents, Memorandum of Law, History, Force and Effect of the Land Patent*, clouded a title under foreclosure siege, the insurance folks took notice. Under rules of discovery he found a letter in which Chicago Title Company questioned whether title insurance would be available to cover deeds when a land patent had been filed. This translates to mean that no marketable title could emerge after foreclosure if a land patent was securely in place. But could the land patent really be in place under the Law Merchant?

The land patent story finally dropped out of *Acres U.S.A.* Even its strongest proponents came to the conclusion that it had been undone by events, cunningly constructed, they virtually erased the U.S. Constitution.

On the curve of history, Jefferson's self-evident truths seemed destined to collide with a scheme Lorenzo Tonti put into effect in France in 1689. Tonti had developed a scam that would deliver wealth beyond the dreams of avarice to an informed few. The tontine started out as an insurance program in which the investment was made on the basis of profits expected from forfeitures. As early as 1872, in an Illinois case styled *Rawson* vs. *Fox*, it was pointed out that it would be bad public policy to transfer to banks the then emerging plans for tontine speculation. The lenders saw it differently. Charging interest on money created out of thin air wasn't profitable enough. The super-rich needed a system that would transfer the wealth of the nation into the hands of a few by creating "the most gigantic trust on earth," Congressman Charles A. Lindberg Sr. said. This trust ultimately emerged as The Federal Reserve System. S. Jay Stewart, and all those involved with the land patent idea finally concluded that no judge in the United States would or could undo the Fed, the modern counterpart of the fiat money creators the land patent law sought to negate in 1820. It would take a veritable revolution to recapture the American dream. And a revolution was forming in the countryside.

18

THE REVOLUTIONARIES

Revolution starts between the ears, and by the mid-1980s there was definitely revolution in the countryside. It was not a militant revolution, although the pundits and uniformed headbreakers hard on the hunt for more gadgets and equipment liked to portray it as such. Barbara Walters and Hugh Downs—on their then popular 20/20 TV show—swallowed the militant farmers bit and assigned large memberships to the mythical Posse Comitatus, all this while the real revolution consisted simply of a few farmers asking the right questions.

The basic questions had been asked before.

"How has this process been contrived of stripping threadbare most of the populace, which once at least owned small patches of virgin land?" This was one of the opening questions in Ferdinand Lundberg's *The Rich and the Super-Rich*, yet not a hint of an answer emerged from the eight hundred pages that followed. Small wonder, since schools fail to teach very much about the Constitution and how it has been usurped, and *The Federalist Papers*—once cited as a complete commentary on our Constitution by the Supreme Court—is now out of print in all of its editions. *Acres U.S.A.* might not have fared better than Lundberg in answering his question had not Bill Avery provided counsel.

Avery was a paralegal, a writer with flair and a researcher so thorough that when he nailed down a principle, it held its own against all comers. *Acres U.S.A.* readers had to learn a new vocabulary when they encountered Avery's treatise, *The Law Merchant*. Words like *subject*, *prize, tontine, irrecusable obligation, private law* and *negative constitution* all figured in the nation's freedoms being undone.

I explained the word *tontine* in the chapter on land patents, but I didn't detail how the principle actually backgrounded something, repugnant to the Constitution, being made quite acceptable. Before the Wilson administration, the Supreme Court routinely declared a general income tax law unconstitutional for want of apportionment. Corporations had their incomes taxed as early as 1909, quite legally, because the artificial person known as the corporation was a *subject* of the state under the franchise clause, much as a person in Europe might be a subject of a king. The name of the game was to extend the income tax to individuals, which was alien to the Constitution, and therefore repugnant. People, after all, were sovereign. They did not owe their existence to the state. Quite the contrary, the state owed its existence to "we the people." The only way individuals could have their incomes taxed legally was to agree to it. Clever lawyers figured that there were two ways this could be accomplished. The people could allow their incomes to be taxed under contract, or they could vote the tax on themselves via constitutional amendment. The manipulators did not want to wait for a constitutional amendment, so they turned to the use of the irrecusable obligation, and to some extent to the recusable obligation. According to *Bouvier's Law Dictionary* of 1914, the first is a term used to indicate "a certain class or contractual obligation recognized by the law which are imposed upon a person without his consent and without regard to any act of his own." The recusable obligation is based on some voluntary act that triggers an obligation imposed by law. The line between irrecusable and recusable is as sharp as a razor's edge. All the clever people had to do to expand the income tax from corporations, partnerships and other businesses to individuals was to define those who bought and sold anything as merchants, and subject to the law of the merchant. No wonder that later courts would say the income tax amendment conferred no power or authority not already available. Before the 16th Amendment was pronounced ratified (which ratification has since been proved a fraud), the income tax had become *fait accompli*.

The income tax became the first major target of the new revolutionaries in the countryside almost a decade ago. Most of the first wave fought with ignorance, and were trundled off to prison, or had their resources looted. They took their stand on the basis of the money issue, or clauses in the Constitution that promised jury trial and freedom from self incrimination. They believed the income tax law illegal.

213

Hardly any of them understood how they had been volunteered to their feet for the purpose of paying that tax. Some of them simply saw their substance whistled away, and they fought back without using the right weapons on the right battlefield at the right time.

It took people like Bill Avery to define the name of the game. First, he said, the U.S. Constitution is a negative constitution. It allows illegal laws to exist as long as no one makes timely objection. It also allows the Congress to pass laws that are *private*. A private law has to do with particular individuals, associations and corporations. Laws that set up corporations are private, meaning they do not pertain to the public at large. The income tax law is a private law within the meaning of the term.

After the nation was engineered into the Great Depression of the 1930s, moves to make secure the income tax came on fast and furious. There was HJR-192, for instance. It declared payment of debt to be against public policy and substituted language—"discharge of an obligation"—in its stead. The date was June 5, 1933. People standing in soup lines and hunting employment didn't comprehend the meaning of this semantic flim-flam.

They didn't even know why it was necessary, except that governments always seek to preserve legitimacy, and the nostrums of the 1930s were terribly close to being illegitimate in terms of the Declaration of Independence and the U.S. Constitution. True, there was still a bit of legal money, silver coins, U.S. Notes, copper cents and the like. But there were those Federal Reserve Notes, private money. When HJR-192 made private bank credit (namely Federal Reserve Notes) legal tender, and changed "payment of debt" into "discharge of an obligation," this Congressional sleight of hand wiped away Article I, Section 10, Clause 1 of the U.S. Constitution and its prohibition against anything but gold and silver coin being a tender *in payment of debt*. And with that Resolution, trial by jury went out the window in cases involving even a small debt, as did any defense based on the money issue. That is why the Jerome Daly types lost and were taken off to jail in irons.

A couple of years after HJR-192, the Social Security Act came into being, and the high court promptly upheld it as a valid income tax device. It immediately became an *adhesion contract* that put the citizen under control of private law. For the few who wanted to fight, there seemed to be no weapon as long as the courts used their clout to help the absconders rather than pronounce their devices subterfuges. To the masses, quite oblivious to what was going on, it made little difference. They would endure any abuse of power, any loss of freedom, any indignity, as long as the Social Security program remained in place.

The small confederation of Cassandras that objected and objected some more might as well have talked to a fence post as the undoing of the U.S. Constitution continued.

There was the 17th Amendment, the one that took from the state legislatures the right to name Senators and thereby control of a part of the national government. For a government that took pride in its legitimacy, there was the most illegitimate act of all, for *The Federalist Papers* amply document that Article I, Section 3 of the U.S. Constitution was the "exception" to the general amendment process. Any change in suffrage of the state legislatures required the consent of *all* states, and not the three-fourths majority counted for ratification by then Secretary of State William Jennings Bryan.

All the above walked hand in hand with the establishment of the Federal Reserve, the ultimate in the debauchery of the nation. Circa 1980s, it was a more mature understanding of the Fed that created revolution between the ears.

The details of the Fed formation were fairly well known when *Acres U.S.A.* unloaded its brand of historical reporting. Not realized at first was how this banking act became the open sesame for emptying the countryside, wiping away parity for agriculture, annihilating allodial acres, and the freedoms assured one and all by the American Constitution.

Ever since the days of the goldsmiths, bankers have created money out of thin air via the fractional reserve. The anatomy of this creation is simple enough. The banker creates a non-interest bearing debt and exchanges it with the bank's customer's for a similar debt plus interest. This is deposit money, a currency created with a transaction and extinguished with another transaction. Presumably administered by men of great wisdom, this system is used to create inflation within the constraints and ambitions of the borrowers.

The Fed became something quite different. It became the tontine in its ultimate refinement. For a time it was possible for an individual citizen to operate outside the rules of the Law Merchant, but as the turnbuckles were tightened—a notch at a time—it became almost impossible to escape entrapment by the principle of the irrecusable and/or recusable obligation. For the courts ruled that use of bank credit, credit cards and other instruments of debt imposed a merchant's status, and therefore an obligation to file a tax return, all under the dictatorial rules of the Law Merchant.

No judge has ever bothered to tell protestors in the dock that the IRS Code is not a public law, but a private contract law. Had it been written as a substantive public law, it would have been repugnant to the Constitution because it forces a citizen to bear witness against his own person. Again the revolutionaries found their ground cut out from under them. The income tax, it turns out, is quite constitutional simply because the code is a private law and lives outside the Constitution by contract, chiefly to accommodate the needs of the Federal Reserve.

The birth and life of the Federal Reserve could never have been invented by a novelist. A scribbler of stories could not possibly be that imaginative. The Fed in fact became a necessity for the J. P. Morgan types because between 1813 and 1913—in spite of wars and depressions—a market basket of goods sold for as much at the end of the period as at the beginning. A commercial banking system evolved in these markets because the gold exchange values of things produced coming into the markets were briefly monetized as though they were so much gold by the commercial lending process. The crop coming to market became money which was extinguished as it was consumed. Debt existed, but it came and went. Because of this economic scenario, there was out-migration from agriculture only as mandated by the state of the arts.

On December 23, 1913, Congress chose to hand over the power to create money, "and regulate the value thereof" to a gigantic trust. Composed of member banks, this trust was nevertheless controlled by a secret club of preferred stockholders. R. E. McMaster of *The Reaper Newsletter* furnished *Acres U.S.A.* the identities of the latter, having obtained the list from Swiss and Saudi Arabian contacts. I do not know whether this list is correct or not, but then neither does Congress or the President of the United States. Apparently controlling stock in the Federal Reserve is held by:

1. Rothschild Banks of London and Berlin.
2. Lazard Brothers Bank of Paris.
3. Israel Moses Seif Banks of Italy.
4. Warburg Bank of Hamburg and Amsterdam.
5. Lehman Brothers Bank of New York.
6. Kuhn, Loeb Bank of New York.
7. Chase Manhattan Bank of New York.
8. Goldman, Sachs Bank of New York.

There are approximately three hundred people, known to each other and/or relatives of the owners, who hold stock or shares in the Federal Reserve System. They comprise an interlocking, international banking cartel of wealth beyond comprehension. Member banks in the Federal Reserve own token amounts of stock, but never enough to gain control or enjoy dividends.

Once established, this gigantic trust set about the business of contriving the process of "stripping threadbare most of the populace which once at least owned small patches of virgin land."

I mentioned the term *prize* in the opening lines of this chapter. A prize is a euphemism for enjoying the fruits of another's labors. When the Fed opened shop, it had no assets to speak of. But the prize beckoned. The economic killing grounds had simply to be identified, and the real owners of the United States had to be maneuvered into place for the slaughter. This meant a depression had to be created so that the Congress could discern needs and create programs that needed funding. Bonds had to be sold, not so much to the savers, but to the Federal Reserve. The government created a debt and gave it to the Fed. And the Fed created a debt and gave it to the government. The books balanced, except that the government's debt bore interest, and the Fed's didn't. Sometimes the government turned around and paid for its bonds by printing currency and giving it to the Fed on the basis of the bond. Congressman Wright Patman often complained that bonds already paid for were still in the hands of the Fed, and interest was still being collected.

S. W. Adams, the author of *The Federal Reserve System*, has computed that the Fed—with no productive capacity whatsoever—parlayed $52 billion assets at the start of World War II into $1,250 trillion by the end of the war. The debt wasn't necessary because there was enough earned income—a consequence of the WW II stabilization measure—to pay for the war. Debt creates inflation, the reason for being of the Fed. All the citizens of the United States have been maneuvered into servicing this debt with their income taxes and liens on their property via hypothecation.

It thus becomes clear why parity for agriculture during the decade of the 1940s became such anathema to the Fed. With the real wealth of the nation monetized at par, there was little reason for debt, not even to fight the war. Interest on the public debt fell to 1%, and government programs requiring loans—from an organization that simply created money out of thin air—were almost faded from the scene. After the war, Truman was even able to balance several budgets. Parity had to be struck down so the nation could be plunged into debt, and all its resources transferred by hypothecation to the biggest trust ever created on the face of the globe.

In leagalese, hypothecation is a right a creditor has over what ostensibly belongs to another. In the U.S., the treasury has a perpetual lien on all the property of the nation. Under this lien it collects tribute to pay the Fed its interest, the several government instrumentalities merely acting as conduits. The ultimate aim of debt expansion is to create inflation, mergers, foreclosures. That is why the taxes on a home cost more per annum than the original equity payments. That is also why farmers are being removed from the land as tontine speculation comes to fruitation.

A recent summary in my *View from the Country* column in *Acres U.S.A.* is a proper recap of the hidden agenda . . .

Everywhere the American economy is being deinvested. Industry is being moved out. Every privately owned bank and lending institution is technically insolvent and will go into bankruptcy. All will go under, not en masse, but one and clusters at a time. The plan of the internationalists is to take the U.S. economy down that way, a notch at a time, to annihilate the banks until approximately eight conglomerates own them all, the big winners being the owners of the Federal Reserve System. At that point most industry will be off-shore. When they have taken the economy down as far as they wish it to go, and have taken over most of the farmland of the U.S., and all of the banks, and have de-industrialized America, they will bring the American economy back totally under their control a little at a time. Such a scenario will likely require a war for purposes of power consolidation.

At the time of the American revolution, we are told, sales for books such as *Blackstone's Commentaries* were twice as brisk in the colonies as in England. The same is true in the countryside today. The modern revolutionaries do not collect guns—as the hack newspaper writers would have the public believe. Instead they buy doorstopper books like *Documents Illustrative of the Formation of the Union of the American States, Bouvier's Dictionary*, and they study common law via tapes and short courses.

This revolution—much like the revolt against hard chemistry—is not likely to yield results in the near future. But a shadow of dissent, no bigger than the palm of a hand, is clouding the brilliance of the absconders.

Once, when I took my sons with me to see Dr. William A. Albrecht at the University of Missouri, he gave each of them ancient books on chemistry while we visited. Later he turned to the boys and said,

"There's news in those books, isn't there?" One of my sons responded by nodding in amazement.

Sometimes we have a hard time understanding real news as opposed to happenings. The gospel in church is often referred to as the "good news." Those papers that tell about the forming of the American union are also good news, sans dateline. From my chair the news stories that informed and instructed were the best news of all.

19

A BETTER COUNTRY

Charles Kuralt, the roving TV correspondent, once said, "It is a better country now." He had traveled through more rural counties than any major newsman in America for over twenty years, and he had vivid recall of indignities to blacks in the South. Even the conviction of Leonard Peltier on a conspiracy charge in connection with the confrontation at Wounded Knee was now a decade old. Few people remained alive who either remembered or had heard of the infamous sedition cases in Nebraska during World War I. Jewish people in America may have endured a few catcalls in the distant past, but pogroms simply have not existed in this nation. The Henry Ford slanders of the 1920s were no longer a memory circa 1980s. It was, indeed, a better country.

The Hugh Downs and Barbara Walters 20/20 TV show held out a different view. With Geraldo Rivera asking the questions, and a prime time camera grinding, the nation's viewers were given a long close up view of some real live Jew baiters. The troubles of agriculture were a consequence of Jewish control of the media, banking, the government and the education machine, the subject of that interview said. Hugh Downs and Barbara Walters added their woeful comments and in effect warned the nation to gird for action.

At Jewish synagogues across the midlands, the 20/20 tape was replayed, and long discussions worried the people about how to head off this aborning holocaust. Backed by alarmed elders in the East, younger people moved to head off the inevitable. One young man—a Jew and an editor—found himself in Iowa as a research director for *Prairiefire*, a newly formed watchdog operation dedicated to smoking out those who thought black thoughts and uttered dark rhetoric.

"Historically, the activities of far-right and anti-Semitic individuals and organizations in the farm-belt are well documented," opined one Daniel Levitas of *Prairiefire*. "From the early days of Populism many influential activists and orators found they were able to motivate farm and rural people by employing anti-Semitic rhetoric. Mary Elizabeth Lease, a leading populist from Kansas who achieved notoriety in the 1890s, spoke often about the British bankers and the influence of the Rothschilds. William Jennings Bryan, perhaps one of the most well known populists of that era, also espoused right-wing beliefs."

What have we here, I said to myself as I looked for the source of the newsletter in hand, and marveled at William Jennings Bryan being turned into a right-wing politico. It had been sent to me by a subscriber, Dan Schmitt of Marshalltown, Iowa. Schmitt had been active in the Iowa Farm Coalition, and *Prairiefire* was a member. He was concerned, and for this reason he was sending me a copy of a memorandum being circulated. At first I recalled the gold and silver days of William Jennings Bryan, when the British silver market dictated the price of wheat in Kansas. Drop the silver price a penny in London, and wheat would drop a penny a bushel in Kansas. By selling silver down on the speculative markets, the British bankers indeed brought ruin to the high plains. Mary Elizabeth Lease abjured Kansans to raise less corn and more hell. But why this ancient woolgathering?

The answer emerged on page three of the Levitas newsletter. Page two was devoted to Lyndon LaRouche. Of late, LaRouche had taken on the role once held by Harold Stassen in running for President every four years. LaRouche people had been sharing the airports with the Moonies, cabbaging on to a few donations and pushing nuclear power as a pronouncement from on high. Since *Acres U.S.A.* had made the connection between nuclear contamination and ionized chemicals at least a dozen years earlier, and since the man had all the earmarks of fascist, we dismissed LaRouche by awarding him our Flat Earth Society certificate, suitable for framing.

The Levitas letter went on, and soon the pattern became clear. Tommy Kersey was named. He was the young fellow who had stood rifle at ready between bank agents with foreclosure papers and a black farmer named Oscar Lorick in Georgia. Lorick later said he wished the SWAT team had killed him. To settle the confrontation, some good Samaritans purchased the mortgage. Then they took all the farm earnings, leaving Lorick with hardly enough money to eat. We had carried the story in *Acres U.S.A.*, and over the months we had mentioned Larry Humphreys and his Oklahoma-based Heritage Library because of its many entries on land patents. Humphreys was a rich boy with right-of-John-Birch ideas, and as director of the Lorick affair he tied farming to militancy, but no more than did the Grange or the Alliance for Progress. The Lorick incident was that—an incident, and not a movement. Rick Elliott of the National Agricultural Press Association was mentioned by Levitas. I had encountered Elliott when he and a dozen of his friends came to our St. Joseph, Missouri-based conference. At first I fell for the "press" gag and allowed several of them free entry. Then it came to me that this group had nothing to do with the press, except that they were friends of Elliott who published *The Primrose and Cattleman's Gazette* out of a Denver suburb.

Elliott was a big bluster of a man, fast talking, hyperactive and seemingly dedicated to seeing justice done for the farmer. He had it in his mind that individuals could be turned into lawyers, and that they could clog the machinery of the courts with racketeering suits and the like. Elliott finally made the news in journalism trade papers, not so much because he wrote anti-Semitic articles, but because he was being required to face down a number of indictments for the racketeering he said he abhorred. Elliott's paper, ran anti-Jewish articles, the more slanderous the better being the policy. Through the years I came to know some of Elliott's operatives. Anti-Semitism did not figure in the thinking of most of them. They were attracted to the fast-talking Colorado man because they wanted to peel the hide off the farm credit system and the Federal Reserve.

Obviously, *Acres U.S.A.* knew what was going on. In taping perhaps two hundred major and minor interviews, many of which were printed word for word, we had touched base with everything from left to right. At our conferences the many splinters in agriculture became a whole piece of furniture. Socialists and far-right-of-John-Birchers, Jews and Catholics, Mormons and Reorganized Latter Day Saints, Farm Bureau and NFOers, Grange and Union—all assembled under one roof in peace because we had identified a higher issue, a higher purpose. Not one thought in terms of guilt-by-association, the McCarthyism of the era when I was a student and there was a communist under every rock.

It remained for the Hugh Downs-Barbara Walters inspired witch hunt of the 1980s to breathe new life into the Joe McCarthy modus operandi. An important succubus that drew nourishment from *20/20*s sensationalism was styled *Update on Anti-Semitic and Racist Intervention in the Farm Protest Movement,* issued by the Center for Democratic Renewal in January 1986. It was this report that Daniel Levitas quoted to the Iowa Farm Coalition, and the charge was that *Acres U.S.A.* promotes "far-right publications." Cited was a book by Richard Kelley Hoskins, *War Cycles, Peace Cycles.* I had in fact conducted a telephone interview with Hoskins, and had read his book. The two or three passages that offended Levitas were historical passages such as one might find in the writings of Jewish historian Arthur Koestler, especially in *The Thirteenth Tribe.* Ah, but I had committed the crime of carrying the *War Cycles, Peace Cycles* text in our bookshelf offerings, and Levitas did not approve. Further, he had proof that I ran the writings of a racist, and was therefore one myself. He quoted an earlier tract by the *War Cycles Peace Cycles* writer that was both out of print and out of circulation. My first response was, *So what!* I didn't know about these things and I certainly wasn't responsible for another's sins.

A half dozen years ago an organization called Rural America established a regional office in Des Moines. Rural America was a liberal advocacy group, meaning that it both fabricated and endorsed all the Band-Aid measures ever thought of to help farmers, just as long as prices were kept low. Rural America's Des Moines office was essentially a two man operation, with a Church of Christ minister named David Ostendorf director, and Daniel Levitas research director. In the mid 1980s, Ostendorf and Levitas separated—peacefully, we are told—from Rural America and replaced that Washington-based do-goodery with their own vest pocket group called Prairiefire.

In the early 1980s, Rural America had put together the Iowa Farm Unity Coalition, namely about ten groups dedicated to seeing justice done at the farm. In due time Prairiefire became the chief staffing agency, did the organization's *Clergy Newsletter,* maintained a hotline, and handle Coalition clerical work. Levitas named himself a one-man constabulary hard on the hunt for right wing groups.

Getting tagged by this new brand of McCarthyism was no laughing matter. Over the years I have put the editorial pencil to approximately a thousand articles a year. In that time I have never allowed anyone to use *Acres U.S.A.* as a sounding board for racist hate, anti-Semitism, not even anti-Arab diatribes during the oil crisis. In truth, I cannot recall even one person being interviewed who sounded off in this vein. I have been told about malfeasance of Jesuits in Central America, about the errant policies of the Pope, about the illegal political parties called Council on Foreign Relations, Trilateral Commission, Committee for Economic Development, about the role of the Federal Reserve, but the anti-Jewish billingsgate that has washed back over our editorial office has been no more offensive than Jesse Jackson calling New Yorkers Hymies. And Jackson might well have responded, *Those who have never used the word nigger, throw the first stone!*

In my type of news game, I've talked to people from a spectrum so wide it defies real description—movie stars and motor cycle thugs, ward healers and Senators, pimps and Presidents—in the last case Harry S Truman and Dwight D. Eisenhower. I've gritted my teeth trying to make parity come clear for Missouri Governor Joe Teasdale, and almost caused the enamel to flake off doing the same thing with farm leaders. I have never felt that there were people I wouldn't talk to, or news stories that I wouldn't track. So getting a line on American Nazis—closet and open—and fringe lunatics such as members of The Order, Posse Comitatus and The Covenant, the Sword and the Arm of the Lord (CSA) wasn't all that difficult. In many cases their newsletters and newspapers simply arrived at *Acres U.S.A.*, because everyone from Jehovah's Witnesses to inventors of perpetual motion machines were always trying to influence the editorial content of the paper.

When the Levitas *ja accuse* arrive, I promptly ran up a phone bill that looked like the national debt. In a world of clashing ideas, there were many who were always at war between the ears, and most of these battles were so classic they made Eric Hoffer's thirty-five year old *True Believer* principles reassert themselves in flashing neon. "For the hopeful can draw strength from the most ridiculous sources of power—a slogan, a word, a button," wrote Hoffer.

Even while I was an editor at *Veterinary Medicine*, I was well on the way toward trailing the news stories of true believers. One day I marked up ad copy for the owner of a small biologic house who soon arrived in the public prints as Bob DePugh, proprietor of the Minutemen. DePugh had swallowed hook, line and sinker the official news that there was a communist under every rock, and so he organized a private army to do battle in the war that to him seemed imminent. The name for his organization was an alias. It should have been True Believers, a staple in history. As Eric Hoffer was to point out a year or two later, this true believer was really a guilt-ridden hitchhiker who thumbed a ride on every cause from Christianity to communism. He was a fanatic who required a Hitler, a Stalin, a Christ (or at least a St. Paul), or a Bob DePugh to worship and die for. This true believer was the mortal enemy of public policy in any nation, and he insisted on sacrificing his person, his family and his children for the dream of "bearing unbearable sorrows," and "beating unbeatable foes," Don Quixote style. He was a Cyrano de Bergerac, John Brown, Ireland's Ian Paisley and Menachem Begin rolled into one.

In following this story I called in due bills and hustled introductions. I simply had to talk to some of the crazies involved. I wanted to test their hatreds and feel the scorch marks from each passionate state of mind. I cabbaged onto small facts and leads the way a bum picks up spent snipes and fallen wallets. In a few days appropriate conclusions flowed from a pad full of note—and one, two and three hours of taped interviews.

No, indeed, there was no Posse Comitatus. There was no plot to hate or demean Jews.

Actually, the Posse Comitatus was an ill-fated attempt to pick up on private army creation where George Lincoln Rockwell and the American Nazi Party left off. Rockwell loomed large in the early 1960s because he achieved maximum newspaper coverage. He did this by switching from being a constitutional conservative to an armband-wearing Nazi. With street confrontations between blacks, anti-Vietnam peace forces, and Jews, the unknown Rockwell made international headlines. His followers backed down the Black Panthers—and build an army of street brawlers who would fight without flinching. Before he was assassinated on August 25, 1967, Rockwell was interviewed for *Playboy* by a black writer named Alex Haley, who later became famous for writing *Roots*.

Rockwell's bodyguard told me that the American Nazi Party could put five hundred people in the street at the time *Another Mother for Peace* and other peace forces were forming up. "Rockwell had a type of charisma, he had the ability to attract people like a magnet, and I freely admit I was one of them," George Lincoln Rockwell's bodyguard said, speaking into my tape recorder. He hoped to be ready when history's inevitable turn arrived. He knew that no leader could conjure up the conditions that made social revolution possible. But it was his duty to be ready, to wait.

The master image that comes shining through behind them all—the Army of God, which dynamited abortion clinics, the Klan, the CSA, the Nazis—is the press and its insatiable demand to sell papers, if not door to door, then at least at the grocery counter. With newspaper reports paper-thin on the Joseph Mengele types, the need for flamboyant headlines even forced recognition on motorcycle hoodlums who obligingly took on the swastika insignia because it was suitably re-

225

volting. They would just as easily have worn the fangs of Dracula if that would have earned them press recognition.

An exception, please! The Black Muslims under Malcolm X rated media attention for a time, but that same organization, disciplined and dangerous under Louis Farakkhan, and numbering in the thousands, has all but been blacked out, almost as if true believers didn't count once there got to be too many of them.

The Order was started by a man named Robert Matthews, who earlier attended a church in Hayden Lake, Idaho called Aryan Nations. Aryan Nations was the child of one William Butler, who preached with a big swastika flag in back of him, his mute declaration that he was a true Hitler Nazi. Butler's brand of evangelism proved to be too tame for Matthews, who in any case had turned up a book by William Pierce styled *The Turner Diaries*. Matthews based his organization, The Order, on this text because he got it into his head that nothing had a peaceful solution, that there had to be blood in the streets, period! He developed a theory that if he followed the outline in *The Turner Diaries*, The Order could get rid of what they called the Zionist Occupation Government (ZOG), or the Democrats, or the Republicans, whatever. The Order first robbed a Brinks truck, then executed Allen Burg, a Jewish radio announcer in Denver, to set the tone of activity for the future.

There were twenty-six of them when the federals gathered them in, "probably the most dangerous individuals in the United States," because they would kill without hesitation, and because they would "stand up." In prison language, standing up means refusing to name associates, and in some circles members of The Order earned a certain respect by taking their forty and sixty year sentences without betraying those who had escaped the government net.

But The Order wasn't made up of farmers, and it didn't recruit farmers. It was made up of misfits, failures willing to rid themselves of irksome freedoms. And so they followed an irresistible leader so they could hand off to him their individual responsibilities. In another era they would have become communists, or Hitler Nazis—it mattered little which—and they would have concentrated their hatreds on a single foe, the capitalist, or the Jew, or the foreigner, because fanatical faith is required to rationalize cowardice in the soul.

There has been no connection whatsoever between The Order, CSA, the original Posse Comitatus and agriculture except guilt by association. The fringe people like to operate from among the trees, thus their presence in rural areas—and this to people like Prairiefire meant they

226

must be farmers. Levitas and his Prairiefire associates seemed to live in a world straight out of the cowboy movies of the 1930s. Bad people wore black hats. Good people wore white hats. Transported into the 1980s, this meant that those who talked about the Committee for Economic Development, the Council on Foreign Relations, the Trilateral Commission, the Federal Reserve, about injustice in the courtroom, about distortion of legal principles and constitutional rights were all bad people because these things in themselves were black hats—or right wing. Black hats for the bottom line of the Levitas syllogism means anti-Semitism. Just about any farmer who has friends and neighbors in for a visit *ipso facto* becomes a Posse Comitatus leader, and those who run afoul lawmen took on Posse Comitatus status, at least in the releases Prairiefire issued, and news media from one end of the country to the other—*Farm Journal* included—printed without question.

In the 1960s, National Farmers Organization (NFO) was constantly characterized as militant, and a sentence or a paragraph later came the word *violent*. In the public prints these entries in the lexicon went together, just like *devout* and *Catholic*, *ham* and *eggs*, *anti* and *Semitic*. Had Prairiefire been on hand, NFO would no doubt have been characterized as anti-Semitic because the organization often ran articles of exposition and analysis on black hat items.

No doubt about it, reports that a mythical Posse Comitatus "is known to be active in twenty western Kansas counties" sold newspapers. "If there were no Nazis, the news media would have to create them," a retired true believer told me. "There is no Posse Comitatus, but there will be. Sooner or later someone will see all that press coverage going to waste, and simply assume the name—and so the news, like prophesy, embodies its own fulfillment. But for every person who is really dangerous, there has got to be fifty to one hundred others that the media is treating exactly the same." In formal English, a figure of speech that is grammatically incorrect, yet makes an excellent point, is called an *enallage*. "Has got to be" is equally dramatic and correct. In rural America, many people are waking up to the diatribes of the guilt by association watchdogs and saying to themselves, "Last week I didn't know what a Posse Comitatus was, now I *are* one."

Not all people who organize are true believers. There are those who are of a different stripe, practical men, all of them. Unlike those with a passionate state of mind, practical men look not for self-sacrifice and blind obedience, but for advancement and reward. They follow the road mapped out by self-interest. The modern church, more than its early Christian counterpart, is more practical than zealous. The institutionalized farm organizations have become staffed by so many practical men, they are done for. Vest pocket operations such as Prairiefire, and Jewish researchers such as Dan Levitas are more practical than fanatic, and those who seek to defend Jewish people from the danger of another holocaust are not stupid. They are the cousins of people like Jonas E. Salk and Albert Einstein, no fools, any of them. They know the condition of Jewish people in America, that fully one-third marry with gentiles, that according to economic station they are fully integrated, so much so that Arthur Koestler was forced to observe that the ghetto was dead. Or as Chaim Weizmann put it, "The Jews are like other people, only more so." Moreover, they know that anti-Semitism in the countryside is less than a whisper, and the influence of militants and private armies on legitimate farm organizations is nonexistent.

It is nevertheless a practical thing to raise money, to collect dues. If any group can be made to believe that salvation is at risk, that ruin and perdition are forthcoming if funds are not provided, those who *have* and even those who *have not* will dig deep into their pockets. The best thing to happen for the fund raisers of certain organizations was the Barbara Walters-Hugh Downs program, and its warning about dark clouds building in the countryside. "The people who are running Prairiefire are not farmers," an expert on strange organizations summarized. "But they are interested in keeping a holocaust image alive." Much as priests and other ministers, some four or five decades ago, sermonized about Christians being boiled in oil as though it had happened the night before, the tales of woe that have been used to torment Jewish people have been dishonest in their intent, if not in substance. Successes of these Ian Paisleys are measured by the flow of funds and the invitations to black tie dinners in what Theodore White called New York's perfumed stockade. If this amounts to preying on people who have suffered enough, it is at least no worse than the preying a whole nation has been doing to those who feed them. The slander of a small paper like *Acres U.S.A.*, likely as not, was simply a business decision, for if there is to be a formidable adversary in the countryside, it has to be created.

I called the *Prairiefire* office and told the secretary to have the research director return the call because "we'd better talk." The call arrived in due time. At that time I stood accused of having a Levitas unapproved speaker at a recent conference, and when I rejected this by saying the man in question had never been on the program, and that I did not recall seeing him at the conference, Levitas in effect said,

228

Oops! The telephone conversation was unsatisfactory, and for this reason I followed with a letter, and after that with a second letter, always answering point for point the guilt-by-association charges levied against me personally and against *Acres U.S.A.* in general. I was particularly stung by the anti-Semitism implication because I had been in a minor business venture with a Jewish lady for the past twenty-nine years.

"Your orientation is terribly close to the one that prevailed during the McCarthy era," I wrote. "At that time anyone who associated with, gave comfort to, or even listened to the defense of anyone accused of being associated with a communist was considered a communist." I recalled a young lady in Denver who, once upon a time, was good enough to share classroom chores with me. Later, after graduation, she lost her job in the Denver school system because of a faceless accusation. The person who said she was a communist was never identified, and she was not allowed to defend herself. Privately she confided that she had given over a few dollars to attend a beer party, and the group sponsoring the party was later identified as a college communist front organization. That's all she knew about it. The world has turned over several times since then, and now the resident ogre is the right wing. Right wing, ipso facto, is clearly linked with anti-Semitism in the view of the new witch hunters. Some would go so far as to make Hillsdale College in Michigan (a very conservative school) and Barry Goldwater in Arizona anti-Semitic.

"People have a right to conservative views, and all conservative views are not the same," I wrote to *Prairiefire*. "Some people are conservative in economics, and quite liberal in social affairs."

More to the point, I said, is the fact that there have been no significant efforts by unholy groups to exert influence over progressive and legitimate farm protest movements. When I was associated with NFO there was small talk about organized labor trying to exert influence over that bargaining organization, but no one in the wildest fantasy could have assigned influence to the miniscule amount of racism left in the countryside. There has been nothing beyond that, not in the past fifteen years, and I believe I have as good a reporting system in rural America as anyone else, with hundreds feeding information to me.

I knew about Robert Miles, a stern looking fellow who liked to pose for pictures in klan-type robes. He'd spent six years in the slammer for sending Michigan school busses up in splinters and flames. But measured as a threat to either the government or any class of citizens, he and his counterparts have had about as much clout as the killers Isaacs brothers and George Dungee, who wasted six members of the Alday family in Georgia, and now, thirteen years later, gained a new trial. The counterparts to Miles fill a few pages in any roster of misfits. Sometimes perfectly innocent people are named. And the public prints, guided by a lexicon conceived in ignorance, have their rules for inclusion.

Anyone who objects to the Trilateral Commission is automatically considered a right winger, ergo anti-Semitic. There are people who have discerned that the 17th Amendment to the U.S. Constitution was fraudulently ratified. Ditto for the income tax amendment. They are automatically anti-Semitic, according to this convoluted logic. And any discussion of international bankers—that is strictly a no-no. Much the same is true of the international wheat traders, who—as lyricist Bertholt Brecht of *Three-Penney Opera* fame aptly put it—"organize famines." As mentioned in the early chapters of this book, lazy minds find comfort in formula, and the formula being used by *Prairiefire* surely refined laziness to an absolute degree.

I was definitely on a roll when I wrote to Daniel Levitas the second time, angered as I was that the name of *Acres U.S.A.* was being sullied. "In a free society, people have to be free to say what they will up to shouting *fire* in a crowded theater. We are not in a crowded theater by any stretch of the imagination. Many of the people you detest are merely marching to a different drummer. Their hunt for a common law, for the roots of the American Revolution, and their battles in the court, even with IRS, have no link to racism and pose no danger whatsoever to the establishment, certainly not to the purity of the farm organizations. . . In other words, you are outside your role in trying to impose the kind of Hitleresque controls you seem to propose."

In one of his letters, the *Prairiefire* research director had castigated *Acres U.S.A.* for its reports on the Arthur Kirk killing and the Gordon Kahl affair (see pages 197-200). "Your comment about Arthur Kirk is the most frightening of all," I wrote, "and smacks of fascism. If Kirk had anti-Semitic tendencies, it did not come to my attention when I trailed the story. None of the wire stories recited this either. The story had to do with police action and the matter of how a court paper—that could have been mailed—figured in the slaying of the man. You seem to suggest that since he slandered the Jewish people, execution was appropriate. Policemen who I have been close to freely admit that there isn't one policeman in ten who will not perjure himself to protect a fellow officer or deliver vengeance for one. That was the point. I suggest you broaden your outlook and sidetrack your inherent paranoia.

"Much the same is true of the Gordon Kahl case. He could have been arrested in town an hour earlier, but instead an ambush was set up. His crime was that he gave comfort to, agreed with and finally joined some tax protest people . . . The suggestion that Kahl's son took two slugs in the spleen and belly, and then was able to get off the shots that killed two officers is too ludicrous for even a New Yorker turned ruralist to swallow. That was the point of my story. It was a legitimate report . . ."

I do not usually write a long letter if I have the time to write a short one. But I turned to the long letter because I did not want to use the pages of *Acres U.S.A.* for charges and counter charges that could serve little useful purpose. I realize that the Jewish people endured a great deal during World War II, and I realize that the Volga Germans—many of them relatives—who lived in some one hundred and two colonies below Saratov, U.S.S.R., endured equally as much. They were loaded in boxcars during thirty degree below zero weather and sent to Siberia. Some boxcars, we are told, were unloaded like cordwood, the passengers having been frozen to death. People with dark episodes in their recent history are sensitive and have a strong antenna. They feel threats and hear voices that simply are not there. As for the small organizations of wild people, "they cannot even find a forum except for the one you give them," I wrote *Prairiefire*. "Lumping conservatives and writers and publishers who merely report in with a few crazies under some guilt-by-association norm is wrong, and goes beyond denunciation. I am surprised that Catholic Rural Life, Farmers Union, NFO and the rest of the Iowa Coalition allow you to inject your nonissue into the farm crisis this way."

This much said, *Acres U.S.A.* returned to the chore of reporting as usual. After all, America was a better country than the one I had known as a youth.

20

THE STING OF THE WASP

An editor cannot live by hard nosed copy alone. He needs compassion and gentleness, which in my case a fine family has provided. There also comes a time when the world of manuscripts and print must be set aside for more important things, such as the *Acres U.S.A.* girls' softball team and local politics.

Girls' softball commanded some attention because my daughter Jennifer pitched and played second base and several other positions while I sponsored and coached the team. Jenny first made the *Acres U.S.A.* columns in July 1973, at which time I announced her arrival as a new staffer. She was pictured at one week of age. The report said that "Jennifer will undergo a period of training before assuming duties as an *Acres U.S.A.* staffer." The next time Jenny made the paper was May 1985. She was now twelve years old. She and a classmate named Erika Gomez had captured a first prize at her school's science fair. The report, *Music to My Leaves*, detailed the influence of music on the growth of plants. The overall project at termination suggested that a certain sound has a positive effect on plant growth, and that sound combined with foliar nutrition has a positive influence on plant health.

The idea, of course, emerged from a report in *Acres U.S.A.* styled *Sound and Nutrients in Agriculture*. A geneticist named Dan Carlson had been experimenting with sound waves in the 4 to 6 kilohertz range on coffee groves in Kealakekua, Hawaii, and on jojoba plants in Arizona.

To treat with sound, Carlson developed an oscillating, bird-like music and embedded it in East Indian or classical music acceptable to most listeners. A solar or battery powered sound unit mounted on a tractor moved through the fields, its pulsator alive and audible over thirty five acres. A spray rig administered a fine mist of foliar nutrients.

Dan Carlson believes he has developed a unique, high-frequency sound pattern overlaid by pleasant music that somehow functions by opening the leaf stomata to better absorb nutrients, moisture and other dynamic influences present in the environment. The nutrient solution is sprayed on the plants while stomata are still opened by the sound.

It may be that nature assigned birds the sound and nutrient function. As dawn breaks, birds present a veritable concerto just as nutrient-laden morning mists are about to dissolve. Could it be that the robins and warblers are politicizing on behalf of their friends, the plants?

I have always been interested in local politics, but a heavy travel schedule combined with constant study of the materials affecting a life in the day of an editor kept my participation to a minimum for many years. This changed when a lady from the photographic studio I used came to see me. Her nephew had been beaten half to death in a cell at the Raytown police station. The ambulance report she showed me related how he had been picked up unconscious, his legs and wrists shackled, and tied with thongs. Why it was necessary to use that much force on a boy who weighed less than one hundred pounds eluded me. For the moment I declined to help. My excuses were the ones people give when they say something they are ashamed of. Raytown, Missouri had a reputation as a redneck town. It was run by "The Man," one Marion P. Beeler, with the advise and consent of an old-line political coterie. Most people looked the other way when cops pulled blacks from their cars simply because they dared drive through town. In broad daylight young men of all races were slammed in the kidneys with heavy flashlights or swagger clubs. I had seen such abuses myself and reported them to my alderman—but nothing happened.

Raytown became incorporated too suddenly—in fact, only an hour or two before it was to be annexed to Kansas City, Missouri. Without a proper tax base, the business community developed bad habits, such as paying cops under the table, and allowing them to "handle things," a euphemism for procedures that were less than legal. Business people believed they needed a tough ex-M.P. as police chief, and paid him off with raw power, and excused just about everything because he kept the troublemakers in line. His greatest credentials were two verbal tributes: "He kept the niggers out of Raytown," and "The Man will handle it."

In time he had more short courses and certificates than Aunt Mamie's prize Chihuahua tucked under the belt. The Man did handle things. At one time a policeman arrested a diabetic, jackknifed him into a jail cell, and allowed him to die. The police investigated themselves and concluded it was an excusable mistake because the arresting officer thought the victim was drunk. Hassling high school kids and writing lots and lots of tickets were simply workaday fare for what The Man called the police force, the "backbone of the community." I think it was the strip search that jolted me most. With a string of decisions strong enough to bowl over an ox, the U.S. Supreme Court made it almost impossible for police departments to continue some of the old ways—the off-hour knock on the door, the bright light interrogation without counsel, the fall downstairs, and several other forms of terror. Then out of international meetings came the strip search. It had been used successfully in Nazi Germany, in Spain, with Brazilian police—even when the *Esquadras de la Muerte* were called in for an execution—and in other police states. Here, no one laid a hand on the prisoner—hardly! The Man was having housewives strip searched. In the local paper I called it visual rape. And in the same local paper, the Man denied my charge. He didn't like my bland statement that the only place things are easy for policemen is in a police state, and that things were too easy for policemen in Raytown.

Finally I determined I had to do something. I told my wife I was unwilling to go to my grave knowing what I knew without lifting a knuckle to do something about it. My decision made, I filed for alderman of Ward 2, and I won. At the first meeting after being sworn in, I dropped the second shoe. I started introducing ordinances. My first was designed to defrock the Chief of Police. It proposed to change his position from being "elective" to being "appointive." Sometimes I caused others to bring ordinances, such as one taking the collection of fines out of police hands and putting them with other city functionaries. The battle lines were drawn that quickly. My name and quotes seldom missed being in the local prints. This gave me a high profile, and a certain immunity from being waylaid and beaten up by parties unknown. It also filled the council chamber week after week with howling supporters of The Man.

After a straw vote or two, it became established that the Board was hopelessly deadlocked. This meant the Mayor would have to break the tie. My problem was that I didn't entirely trust the Mayor. He had promised to vote with me, so I checked him out. I had a voiceprint made at a demonstration table during a business meeting. The expert said he'd stake his career on the proposition that when the speaker on the tape had his feet held to the fire, there would be a change of heart. Clearly, I needed something fortuitous to arrive. Fortuitous indeed was a happening at the regular Board meeting in the summer of 1981. One of the aldermen fell asleep at the switch. I had the floor and was explaining a resolution I intended to bring. I even read some of the language, and for some reason the chair failed to slam down the gavel. When I was certain the alderman from Ward 1 didn't know what was being discussed, I called for the question. The vote went as expected. And the "lost" alderman did as expected. He abstained, and under then prevailing rules, the abstention went with the majority. This meant that there would be two elections—one to determine whether the Board could take control over its police force, a second one to determine whether the local tyrant could retain his colonel's wings.

One fortuitous happening deserves another, and it arrived on schedule. A young black woman sued the city, the police department, and the Board of Aldermen. She had been accused of stealing a large bill from a local bank, and was promptly fired. The bill in question turned up a day or two later, a case of cling to a paper clip. Nevertheless the police had arrested the young lady at her home several days after the incident, cuffed her, strapped her in a police vehicle, and—at the station—subjected her to a strip search in a show up room replete with its one-way mirror.

It was the kind of political fodder we never managed to get in the '72 NFO election, and I decided to make the most of it. The "most" meant a political flyer that got a little too clinical for some people, but it was dynamite. It was furbished and refurbished by every case on strip searches the John Marshall Law School could send me. Using over forty college educated women my wife helped recruit, we hung that flyer on every door in town the weekend before election number 1. Political observers have since informed me that it was "too much too late." The Man survived having his position made appointive, but election number 2 was just around the corner. All the excitement had prompted an ex-Kansas City policeman to throw his hat into the ring. The full effect of that strip search flyer was now to be felt.

The Man struck back.

First he issued a "white paper" which the local prints felt impelled to publish, even though they denied me equal space. The Man felt this was necessary because the phone at police headquarters simply wouldn't stop ringing.

Next he sued me for libel asking for actual and punitive damages of nearly a quarter of a million dollars. The Man had often sued opponents. His objective, always, was to teach upstarts how to spend money. His own costs were met by "donations" from local businessmen.

Both of The Man's moves misfired badly. Each sentence defending strip searches was more damaging than total silence. Then the business of suing a town alderman had an effect not expected. I am not certain to this day whether the lawsuit or the white paper was most damaging to "The Man." Certainly I did my best to keep both in the headlines. When the *Kansas City Star* reporter and the local prints asked me about the lawsuit, I responded—"Well, I've given it to an attorney. As soon as he quits laughing, we'll file an answer." One of them printed it that way. I carried libel insurance. It was really the business of the insurance company to handle the matter. The Man may have intended to bleed me, I said, but chances were better than even that his role would change from bleedor to bleedee as soon as the election was over. In the meantime it meant answering legal papers and sparring my way through a deposition. I always like to schedule depositions late in the day—after 5:00 p.m. if possible. By then most attorneys are half alive, having assaulted themselves for eight hours with coffee as thick as crankcase oil. Most are ready to suffer a sugar crash. A two glass protein drink at any afternoon hour could make my responses sharp as a tack. When I feel particularly cruel, I like to give one-word answers. This keeps the opposing attorney off balance most of the time. I felt quite relaxed answering that deposition. A few weeks later, I voted then drove to Omaha to attend a gasohol meeting.

I had a telephone call at that meeting. It informed me that Marion P. Beeler, The Man, had been defeated, and his twenty-five year reign of terror was over. My first thought was that Dad wasn't alive to share the victory.

A few years earlier, Dad, age ninety-one, had announced to those who were in the living room with him that he no longer needed his wallet. He threw it on a table and repaired to the bedroom. In a few minutes he was gone.

He had grown up with horse power, then steam threshing machines, and he had lived until a man could walk on the moon. And without benefit of credentials or ceremonial clap-trap, he had come to understand that agriculture was really subservient to a shadow economic plan—in the U.S. no less than in the tsar's Russia—and that the usurpers had captured the American dream without firing a shot. The people would stand still for military defense expenses, but wouldn't lift a knuckle to defend the American economy. The little Hitlers survived at every level—almost! Dad always said the man would fall.

At home, there was more—an audit, a several count indictment, guilty pleas and there were slap-on-the-wrist fines. No matter, The Man was through. No police force would have him, not even to harvest nickels out of parking meters. I did not refile for the alderman's post when my term expired.

One day, just before I released the manuscript for this book to the publisher, I accomplished the return of a native bit. The old farm house, built half underground—with raw dust between laths and siding as insulation to protect against those high plains winds in Ness County, Kansas—was gone. It had been torn down many years ago, not to make way for anything—probably because it was falling apart. The pond that I, as a child, figured was approximately the size of Lake Huron—its dam pushed aside—was no more, and the creek was bone dry. The old shelterbelt had vanished before bulldozer blades, as had the farm homes within a short pony ride.

Grandpa's home, a palace of a place as I remember it, could only be traced by its foundation. It had shrunk back from the dimensions of my memory to where it was now a miniature house, hardly big enough to store baled hay or the dried cow dung we picked up and kept for fuel. The old buffalo wallows, left over from frontier days, had been blended by dust and snow and rain into the prairie, and some had been turned under when greedy men broke too much steppe, and were now exposed to erosion by wind and water. The great cottonwood that shaded the edge of the pond had vanished. It had been broken almost beyond repair when a tornado hurled a round metal grain bin—folks called it by its Volga German name, *ambar*—across the house, shaving away a few shingles and deposited it in the cottonwood tree. Dad had cut away the damaged limbs, and with ample pond water furnishing drink to its meandering roots, it soon repaired itself. The last time I saw it the dust storms had sanded its bark almost raw.

As I stood there, a dust devil danced across the very yard where my brothers and sisters and I had played softball and Annie-Annie-over. And the world of yesteryear came alive again. My next older brother Joe was coming around the house, softball in hand. It was a game of honor, stealth and duplicity. The game called for a softball to be

237

thrown over the roof of the house without touching on the first side. If the ball was caught it could be run around the house and hurled at any member of the opposing team. If anyone was hit, that was a point. Side passes and quick end runs had to be made within seconds, otherwise the opposing team was entitled to the warning cry, *Annie-Annie-over.*

My brother Joe was a master at the game, and opinions in the family had it that he would one day make his mark for sheer cunning. For a time, Joe disappeared into the meat grinder called World War II, and then the locals read about him as a lead scout in the 163rd Regiment, 41st Infantry Division, "The Bloody Butchers." "On numerous occasions," one citation read, "he volunteered for dangerous missions of reconnaissance with combat patrols." For much of the war, his comrades in arms considered him a one-man army. However, on Jolo Island in the Sulu Archipelago, he was wounded while attacking an enemy position, grenade fragments taking out an eye and inflicting six other serious wounds. Still he continued to fight. Finally with blindness overtaking him to a point where he had to hold open his remaining eye, he withdrew from the field, aiding and guiding three badly wounded soldiers to a battalion aid station over a mile from the action before he collapsed. The last of the shrapnel was removed as late as 1977. He was awarded a Bronze Star, but I think being made a Knight of Malta meant more to him. The last happened at the Yacht Club in New York, with an old underground fighter in WWII—His Excellency, Archbishop Lorenzo Michel de Valitch—presiding.

I drafted most of the "remarks" Congressman Alan Wheat dropped in to the *Congressional Record*, adding a line that said Chevalier de Malte Joseph Anton Walters was invited into the order because he rejected wealth without work, pleasure without conscience, knowledge without character, commerce without morality, science without humanity, worship without sacrifice and politics without principle—Ghandian principles, all of them.

A second dust devil danced across the yard as I stood there, and was swallowed by the stone walls of chicken house ruins.

We often played knight and infidel, cowboy and Indian, soldier and enemy, G-men and Dillinger, learning skills the army could never teach many of the city boys, and that old farm was a perfect place to grow up.

Dad was sweeping the yard with a straw broom just as his forebears had done in Katherinenstadt on the lower Volga, and for a moment the good times returned with harvest, with laughter, with pies brought to

238

the wheat field, with a swing in the buff from a rope out over that prized pond. Brenny, that fine old pony, was there, standing gentle as a lamb, yet as alert as a wounded sparrow. She was no plug, or mustang—or even a quarterhorse. She was a thoroughbred. During the hard times Grandpa had led a small group to Mexico to buy cheap land. The language was too tough for the Volga Germans. In one instance, an uncle had to communicate his wish for eggs by assuming the stance of a chicken and crowing in a Mexican restaurant. He got the eggs—fried hard as paving stone. Brenny was the legacy of that trip, bargained away from a Mexican with a gold coin.

One day, hard on the hunt for jackrabbits with my brother Bob on the horse, we sidled up to a big old sandpit on the property, and sure enough a couple of big jacks gave us a target. I shot and missed, but Bob nailed the critter on the run, a feat of marksmanship I marvel at to this day. Bob earned a Bronze Star in General Patton's army, but something happened to him during the war, and he sickened and died a few years later, still a young man.

The man who ended up with a deed to the place, it was reported, turned that old sand pit into a veritable gold mine. He supplied enough sand to county paving crews to pay for the farm in one year.

One day my brother Fred and I went hunting without permission. He was too little to carry a rifle, and I was barely able to handle the .22 myself. I shot a prized cottontail and caught several kinds of hell when I returned home, but the rabbit ended up on the dinner table just the same, the best I ever tasted. Fred, many years later, was standing with several friends in a Korean compound when a mortar shell arrived. He was killed instantly, and with that I lost my best friend.

Fred and I used to work as a team when we were posted as lookouts. Our job was to watch for strangers when Dad was involved in his strange alchemy. Once in a while we would watch the clear liquid drip from a copper coil, and stare in amazement when the grownups poured some in a dish. When it flamed, that was proof, I heard one of the grownups say.

Later, after the dust storms and hard times had driven us away from those wonderful western Kansas steppes, we dropped our German idiom and added an "s" to our surname in an effort to disappear into the melting pot. But Hitler was on the rampage, and a syllable or an accent was enough to earn the sting of the WASPs—the White Anglo-Saxon Protestants. True to form, Fred and a still younger brother Albert and I devised a strategy. When we biked down the streets of Iola,

Kansas, we seldom went together. One would trail the other. When an attack came from the WASP bullies, the second and third rider would arrive. I think I ended up with the most scars, but we always rendered a good account of ourselves, much as if we were among Joe's beloved Knights of Malta on the Isle of Rhodes besieged by the overwhelming forces of Sultan Suleiman II.

Those were the wonderful days, and like most people I may have sought unconsciously to recapture them. I think perhaps Mother helped.

The family, Mother said, had a written record, once upon a time. It covered the period from when the forebears of both grandparents left the Bavarian Alps in 1763 to settle in Russia on the lower Volga. It told wondrous stories about villages being sacked by Kirghiz tribesmen, about adventures and murders and Russian wolves. Someone made entries until well after both grandparents arrived in Ellis County, Kansas. That longhand history vanished one night when Mother was still a young girl and her home went up in flames. Years later, when my brother George started writing *Wir Wollen Deutsche Bleiben, The Story of the Volga Germans*, it would have been priceless, but it was gone. An old Russian proverb had it, "What is written with a pen cannot be removed with a hatchet."

"Nonsense," said Mother. "A fire can wipe out every word." The printed page duplicated many times and scattered to the winds, that was something else!

The nearest thing to swinging from a tree in the buff at age six— before cares and worries and ambitions took hold—has been editing and publishing *Acres U.S.A. Acres U.S.A.* circulates in some twenty countries. Its readers have used its news at committee hearings and before high councils of government, but—more important—also to govern their lives. Farmers around the world have come to rely on reports in *Acres U.S.A.* to make a transition to environmentally sound agriculture.

I have expected no great rush in this enterprise. For it is certain that men take leave of their senses as a group. They come to their senses individually, one at a time.

INDEX

Bird, Chris, 186
Bishop's Pastoral, 127, 128
black candle ritual, 3
Black mountain (in Texas), 36
Black Muslims, 226
Black Panthers, 225
Blackstone's Commentaries, 218
Blaser, Richard, 168
Bleem, John, xii
Bliss, Russell, 142
Blomeke, Steve, 67
Born (of Bunge Grain), 69
Bosco, F. Neil, 197
Bouvier's Law Dictionary, 213, 218
Brannon Plan, 29, 116
Brannon, Charles F., 26
Brecht, Bertolt, 71, 230
Brenny (the horse), 1, 239
Bromfield, Louis, 50, 51
Brookside Dairy Farms, 51
Brookside Laboratories, 51
Brown, Herb, 36
Brown, Mike, 147
Bryan, William Jennings, 215, 221
Buffalo Creek, Virginia flood, 195
Bunge (grain), 69
Burg, Allen, 226
Burgstahler, Albert W., 174
Burk, Dean, 174, 176
Butler, William, 226
Butz, Earl, 65

calcium peroxide, 104
Caldwell, Gladys, 174
Callahan, Phil, 135, 137-140, 151,
  186-188, 191, 200
Campanella, Tomasso (poem), 33
Campbell, Mo., 168
cancer, 177-181
Cargill (grain), 69
Carlson, Dan, 232
carrageenon, 103
Carson, Rachel, 39, 41, 43, 143
Carter [Jimmie], Panama Canal
  giveaway, 15
Carver, George Washington, 163
Catch 22, 70
Catholic Rural Life, 231

cell, 20
cellular farm, 152
Cervi, Gene, xii
Chamberlain, Neville, 82
Chicago Title Company, 211
chicken cancer, 35
China, People's Republic, x, xi
Christensen, Leo M., 160, 162
chromosome, 20
CIA, 70
Clay, General Lucius, 157
Clergy Newsletter, 223
Cocannouer, Joseph, 135
*Coming Revolution in Agriculture,
  The,* 152
Committee for Economic Develop-
  ment, 29, 224, 227
commodity values, 9, 10
Common Sense, 107
composting, 36
Constitution, U.S. (and measure-
  ments), 188, 202
Continental (grain), 69, 70
continental currency, 204-205
Coolidge, Calvin, 24
Cooper, Gordon, 168
Corning, Iowa, 23
Cosmic Pipelines, 189
Coulter, John Lee, 27
Council of Economic Advisers, 74, 75
Council on Foreign Relations, 224,
  227
Covenant, the Sword and the Arm of
  the Lord, The, 224
Creighton University, 8, 158
Crisis Papers, 107
Crops and Soils, 86, 201
Crouse, Earl F., 24
Cryts, Wayne, 152

d'Arsonval, Jacques Arsene, 187
Dahners, Greg, 75
Daly, Jerome, 214
Darkness at Noon, 82
Davis, John H., 24
DDT, 41, 60, 61
de Chardonnet, Hilaire, 160

de Valitch, Archbishop Lorenzo Michel, 238
Deaf Smith County, Texas (refluoridation), 172
debt, 215
debt, public and private, 9
Degenerative Disease Center, 129
Denton, Charles F., 36
DePugh, Bob, 224
Despain, Donald, 159
devil at Yocemento, 4, 5
dioctyl sodium, 103
discharge of an obligation, 214
Distilled Feeds Institute, 163
DNA, 139
Doane Agricultural Services, 87
Documents Illustrative of the Formations of the Union of the United States, 218
Dole, Bob, 126, 127
Dollar wheat bulletins, 25
Dow Chemical, 147
Dow, Herbert Henry, 161
Downs, Hugh, 212, 220, 222, 228
Dreyfus (grain), 69
Duggar, Benjamin M., 46
Dungee, George, 230
dyes, food, 104
Dykeman, Ray, 69, 124

Earth Foods, 134
East India Company, 206
eco-agriculture, birth of, 74
ecology principles, 38
Economic Report of the President, 112-114
Edwards, Charles C., 169, 170
Eemon (author of X-force), 191
Egypt, 187, 188
Eichman, Adolf, 84
Einstein, Albert, 228
Eisenhower, Dwight D., 26, 224
electromagnetic spectrum, 136
Elliott, Rick, 222
eloptic energy, 191
Engelken, Ralph, 152-154
Engelken, Rita 152-154

Environmental Protection Agency, 59
epsom salts report, 52, 53
Equality for Agriculture, 109
erosion measured, 59
ethics, 82, 86
Everitt, J.A., 25
Exploding the Chemical Myths, 86, 91

Farakkahn, Louis, 226
Farm Bill of 1948, 10
Farm Bureau, 86
Farm Holiday Movement, 24
Farm Journal, 227
Farmers Union, 231
Farrar, Walt, 75
fats and oils, 154-158
FDA, 169
Federal Reserve, 211, 215-219, 224, 227
Federalist Papers, The, 212, 215
Fenzau, C.J., 86, 87, 91-93, 95, 135
Flanagan, Pat, 189, 190
Flannagan, John W., 14
Fleming, Roscoe, 194
flim-flam money, 207
floods, 195-196
Fluoridation of Public Drinking Water, 171
fluoridation, 171-17
Fluoridation, The Great Dilemma, 174
Fluoride, The Aging Factor, 176
Fluorides, 174
FmHA, 207, 208
Food and Drug (*see FDA*)
Food Committee of the United States, 156
Food Power from the Sea, 141
Forbes, John, 71
Ford, Henry, 220
franchise clause, 213
Franklin, Ben, 103
Freeman, Orville, 132
Fribourg (of Continental Grain), 69
Fridenstine, Jerry, 189, 190
From My Experience, 50

243

245